WE ARE ONE

stories of work, life and love

Elizabeth R. Gottlieb with a foreword by Danny Glover

Published by Hard Ball Press.
ISBN: 978-0-9862400-2-7

Cover art by Edith Williams
Exterior and interior book design by Edith Williams, Elizabeth Gottlieb and D. Bass

Information available at: www.hardballpress.com

Library of Congress Cataloging-in-Publication Data
Gottlieb, Elizabeth
We Are One – Stories of American Workers

1. Labor Union—Nonfiction. 2. Work—Nonfiction. 3. American oral history.

DEDICATION

This book is lovingly dedicated to the thirty-four people who graciously shared their stories for this collection, and for all the men, women and youths who build our homes, cook our food, sew our clothes, heal our ills, fly our planes, play our music, and teach us well.

Contents

Foreword

For thirty-three years, my father, James Glover, worked for the United States Postal Service. And, for that entire period and for the remaining twenty years of his life, he was an active member of the National Alliance of Postal Employees (now renamed the National Alliance of Postal and Federal Employees). As one of five children, I grew up attending the union's celebrations of significant historical events and moments, the annual picnics at Alum Rock Park, near San Jose, California, and I was around the usual surreptitious gossip surrounding the union. I can remember especially the collective joy and jubilation of these moments through the employee's union, during a unique and transformational period within America's historical landscape. Even as an adult, I had the privilege of attending a national convention with my father before his passing in 2001. While in his presence, fellow members honored him and looked up to him because of the person he was, and the contributions he had made to the legacy of his union, not because his son was Danny Glover.

For me, the union represented a strong and everlasting sense of community. It was at the heart of the relationship between people, through commonality and purpose, building bonds that last a lifetime. We Are One: Stories of Work, Life, and Love is a book that reveals a great deal. It explores the idea of the self as part of a community and how individual success is tied to a connection with others.

This portrayal of so many different life occupations offers a window of insight into the wide variety of social worlds out there. What's it like to be an airline pilot, a race-car driver, or, a coal miner in West Virginia coming from generations of miners? What's it like for a Native American ironworker in Montana during his first time up on the iron bar and how does it compare to taking his first step off the reservation? What does a boilermaker do? How nerve-wracking is it for a professional violinist to audition for a regional symphony? What's it like to be a stage actor before, during, and after a performance? How does it feel to be a professional baseball player trying to make it in the major leagues?

These folks and many others talk about the daily details of their work and the ups and downs of life, opening their hearts in a way as to make it impossible to not relate to them. The idea that they are all in unions is symbolic. We are all united in some way if you dig down deep enough.

People's ideas of success and their sense of who they are in this world are big questions and inspire reflection in our own lives. We are given the gift of meeting individuals from a wide and rich variety of places and positions in society. It's great to know their stories not only because they show us that each and every one of us is important, but also that our individual well-being does not evolve in isolation. Knowing these people, hearing their stories, learning from their wisdom, through their suffering from tragedies or their winning of awards, or both; their definitions of success reveal an underlying theme that unites us all. We can all relate to success's many variations.

These assorted, distinct, union members expose the common thread running through their lives about family, community, and success. The people in the book have union membership in common, but more important, they share in the reality and dreams of living a life where they have the freedom to be safe and healthy, to be supportive of others, to be heard, respected, and fulfilled. In their cases, it's the union that helps facilitate and nurture these needs and enables people to work toward the dreams we all aspire to achieve.

While at an event several years ago I was speaking to the daughter of a friend of my father. His name was Big Jack. My father and he were lifelong friends from the National Association of Postal Employees. Big Jack was at least a foot taller than my dad, who was about 5'3" or 5'4". It was long after they had each passed on. His daughter told me, "My dad had a lot of friends, a lot of friends, but there was only one or two that he would invite around his family, and your dad was one of them." Those are the kinds of things I remember as I read through this book: the experiences of their lives, friendships, love, and meaningful work. These are the things that make life worth living, and this book tells that story.

Danny Glover

Introduction

In these pages we have the honor of getting to know a group of very interesting individuals who also happen to be union members. Diverse in age, gender, race, socioeconomic status, and occupation, people talk about their work and why they are in a union. If you are unfamiliar with unions or the word 'union' has a negative association for you, this collection of personal stories will offer you a refreshingly accessible and extraordinary perspective.

From a ballet dancer to a baseball player, garment worker to teachers, nurses, a coal miner, boilermaker, filmmaker, musicians, and an Oreo Cookie maker, to name a few, people were asked through open-ended interviews to describe themselves, their work, their feelings about their work, their ideas about success, why they are in a union, and how the union has had an impact on their lives.

We are privy to inside information professionally but also to personality and dreams. People are amazing. So many of us have gone through challenging experiences in our own lives, facing adversity and sometimes failing, but usually surviving and, at times, turning these into moments of great success, and in each case, learning something new. The people in this book teach us about the true value of relationships and connection with others. The manifestation of "union" within the lives of these people goes deeper than one can imagine. You'll be surprised.

In today's world and throughout the history of organized labor, the propaganda and misinformation, and emotional stakes of employees and employers are often quite intense. Workers simply trying to have a voice or improve working conditions are often met with threats of losing their jobs. Rumors of corruption run rampant, feeding peoples' fears of strikes and huge dues payments, often giving way to an extreme lack of understanding about the true nature of unions. The result can lead to a hopeless situation in the fight for dignity and justice on the job.

Why does the right to organize typically devolve into such an emotional struggle? It is personal to defend your rights to safety, decent healthcare, your well-being, and even more so for that of your family. Fighting for your rights is about being heard or taking care of your basic needs, from how much food you can afford to how much autonomy or respect you receive while working. On the employer's side, it's personal to feel you must share your power, and perhaps your profits, and, to relinquish even a small bit of decision-making control. Politics and philosophical differences can be personal, too.

In the late 1980s, I initiated a union organizing campaign at the nursery school where I worked. The administrators started making unilateral changes that we teachers felt were bad for the children and for the morale of the staff. When I mentioned the idea of "union" to my supervisor, I was literally laughed at, which is really perfectly symbolic: She confirmed that what we thought and needed didn't matter at all to her. When people are voiceless, when their needs and opinions don't count, no matter the situation, the result could be, should be, a push toward fairness.

Workers across a wide spectrum of trades, careers, and occupations bring a uniquely enlightened perspective to their work that administrators often cannot see. Coal miners notice crucial safety concerns in the mines, flight attendants know how emergency procedures can run more smoothly, teachers know what works for their students...The list goes on, revealing the essential perspective of workers.

When people come together in a union, they can improve not only the quality of their workplace, but they can also curb corporate greed, aid a flailing economy, and bring about wider cultural change. Seeing these changes can be enormously inspiring. In today's society, it is crucial to maintain a healthy, accurate and broadminded perspective on the reality of the workplace, the balance of power, and how people are currently feeling, living and surviving. For this reason and to plainly address many myths and fears, this book reflects the personal and very diverse nature of how unions have affected the inside and outside lives of various workers. Depicted through photographs and words of real people are the raw, honest, firsthand portrayals of what "union" has meant to them in their work, their families, their lives, hearts and souls.

Elizabeth Gottlieb

The strongest bond of human sympathy outside the family relation should be one uniting working people, people of all nations and tongues and kindreds.

Abraham Lincoln

Interviews

Dorothy Baca

Costume Designer & Costumer, Albuquerque, New Mexico
Full Professor, University of New Mexico
Costume Design and Costume History
International Alliance of Theatrical Stage Employees (IATSE)
Costume Designers Guild of America Costumers Union IATSE 705 (LA)

I see myself as an anthropologist, using clothing and costuming to help the audience in understanding that people have different lives, and yet, in the end, we're all the same throughout history. I consider myself the keeper of my family's history, and of the importance of what clothing is to a society. Of course my role in my own family as a mother, grandmother, wife, sister, and cousin comes into that. The importance of what I do is being connected to people.

I grew up in northern New Mexico, which is very old. I realized as I got older that I really grew up in Europe, because it has a strong sense of history and connection to the earth. So, I think that's kind of the root of where I started to think about clothing and costuming and how people made decisions about what they wore and when they wore it and all the rules of society that have to do with clothing, and how it connects to celebrations, particularly Spanish Catholic. New Mexico has a lot of celebrations and a lot of specific clothing rules. I think those are getting lost, particularly in America. We're losing all of the rules that apply to clothing and understanding of the society by what people wore.

New Mexico was one of the original Spanish colonies, coming from Mexico up into New Mexico. Roots here are from the late 1500's to early 1600's, and both my paternal and maternal side of the family have old Spanish names. Some you don't hear anywhere else except here in New Mexico or South America. For example, "Baca" is an old Spanish name that doesn't even exist in Spain anymore, but it's very common here. I've always grown up with a sense of history and the role of celebrations and the rules of society and clothing.

Northern New Mexico didn't have a lot of connection to Mexico, and it wasn't connected to America for a long time until the Western expansion, and even that didn't touch a lot of New Mexico. I think the isolation made a difference. I think growing up like that is actually what rooted me in costume design. I'm like a great storyteller. I love to tell stories, and costuming is really a way to communicate storytelling. You say a lot about somebody by the choices you make for that character. Spanish people have a strong tradition of storytelling. And being isolated, storytelling was a way of entertaining people in the isolation — not having a lot of access to books and entertainment that came through the towns and more highly populated cities. I think it's rooted in the Spanish rural traditions and also the sort of isolation of Northern New Mexico. The language here, until very recently, is a Northern New Mexico dialect of Spanish.

Where I come from is what roots me, for sure. I was in California for 30 years, in L.A., but I always was New Mexican. If you see me, I look like any number of… You know, people think I'm Jewish. People think I'm Iranian; people think I'm Turkish; they think I'm Greek or Italian; I'm kind of like a universal ethnic person, and in L.A., Baca isn't a common Spanish name, so people wouldn't just presume I was Spanish. In New Mexico everybody knows that's a Spanish name. In L.A. I didn't have a specific identity as I do here. I think my aesthetic is very Latino. My sense of color proportion. I did a lot of shows that were sort of ethnic or young people kind of craziness because I don't come from the East Coast, sort of upper class, tasteful social structure, or a Southern sort of aesthetic.

You know, I think every part of the United States has its own aesthetic and sense of itself that reflects in its clothing: how you use color, how you deal with proportion and all those things. Coming from New Mexico, I was better at shows that were about ethnic people or about colorful, wacky things, as opposed to, like, very tasteful, East Coast society, or whatever. I think that decided my career in a lot of ways because I tend to be better at that fantasy, magical stuff than street clothes or classic office-wear. Some of these movies are modern society, and I'm not as interested in that as with historical origin.

In L.A., I was a costume designer or costumer, depending on what show I was on. My brother also was a costume designer. He and I put a company together and we designed the clothes for Bette Midler, the

mermaid costume, where she's in a wheelchair. That kind of weird, quirky, mixture of reality/lack of reality, bigger than reality stuff, is my signature.

How do I dress? I always try to keep what I'm wearing somewhat neutral. I wear a lot of black. I wear a lot of jewelry — big, clunky jewelry. But my clothing is all usually dark colored and with very simple lines because I don't like to compete with what I'm looking at when designing. I think that's really kind of common for designers to sort of find a neutral uniform for yourself. You have to come across as artistic and knowledgeable about clothing, but you don't want to compete with your clothing or your design. I wear things that are pretty classical, usually dark, solid colors. For me, getting dressed is earrings, necklace, bracelet, rings. I collect a lot of jewelry. I have a lot of Native American turquoise and silver, I have a lot of Spanish and Mexican silver from the 40's, all kinds of eclectic costume jewelry. I think that kind of defines me.

I'm really short - 4' 10". So when people describe me they say, "Oh, you'd know her…She's really short and she has all this big jewelry on," which, as a designer, you're not supposed to wear big jewelry when you're small. But it doesn't matter. I think the only rule is to break rules.

Most of costuming, unfortunately, isn't creative. A lot of it is organizational. A lot of it is dealing with people and personality. A film crew working on the set could be a hundred and fifty people that you're dealing with, and what the director likes, what the actor likes, what everybody thinks that character's about. It's very collaborative. So it's more about organization than anything else. You have a lot of money but you don't have a lot of time.

I did a lot of television: half hour sitcoms, and episodic. The most famous episodic stuff I did was "Murder, She Wrote." It was on an eight-day shoot per episode. Sometimes you're juggling four shows at a time; you're in prep for one; you're shooting one; you're in post for another, and you've picked up another. The last T.V. series that I did any designing on was "Dr. Quinn, Medicine Woman," which I loved because it was historical and a lot of fun to film all these different levels of the people that lived in Colorado Springs at the time. That was interesting because it was a woman executive producer-creator and the star was a woman. It was a different environment from a very male dominated industry.

Theatre is different. Now that I'm teaching in academia, I think it's more creative and it's more focused on the creative. But again, it's very collaborative. Time and money are still important, so you have to really focus on how to get your vision without compromising. You have to work with the lights and the tech and the author and all these other things. It has to all come together on stage. With film, unfortunately, you don't see it until it is all together. The advantage of theatre is that you have rehearsals and you can tweak things as you go, like add something to it to make it work better. In film it's kind of like you gotta make it work right then. The time pressure is different on film: it's harder, more strenuous.

With theatre, you get to be more creative; you have a little more time to think about the props and stuff. They both have advantages and disadvantages. Film has a lot of money, a lot of resources, and you're connected all over the world. You can always find an expert in anything who can give you technical advice. But with theatre you don't have to worry about the weather. You don't have to worry about all the reality that you don't see in film, but it's really there. How do you make them look naked when they're not really naked? How do you keep them warm when it's actually cold outside? I shot something in St. Louis in July. They were supposed to be in a snowstorm in 1902. The wool, the layers, and, you know, it was really 100 degrees and humid. How do you keep that reality from infringing on the world that you're trying to create? Theatre, you don't have to worry about temperature, wind, how the microphone is working for the sound people or how much noise did that make or how do we keep them from sweating through everything?

Reality is the hard part of filmmaking, the part that doesn't show. The process is a little bit different; the process of getting it to look like it's all perfect and clean when the reality of how it was shot is so different. In theatre it's kind of the opposite. You have this very controlled world that allows you the freedom to do stuff that's really magical and mystical because you have so much control of the elements.

A lot of filmmaking is modern dress clothes, so you're not really designing, but you're trying to establish a look for each character; something that says something about their character — who they are in society, what their job is and what their relationship is to the other characters.

But you know, it's different when you're talking about a period show. Historical periods have a structure to them. Like, what did people wear to tea? What's formal? What did people do when they'd go to dinner? Things like that. In modern dress, it's a little more subtle, and a little less specific and the choices are infinite. So, design is kind of a vague word because if you're doing modern dress and you're not constructing everything, you're still designing the world that they live in and what the characters are in that world. Even in the modern dress world, you're still making the choices that

create the story for the characters.

I design myself and I also mentor kids that are designing. We do about eight shows a year and five dance pieces that students design. So, even when I'm not myself designing I'm always in the process of getting students to understand how you design, how you think about design, how you problem solve, how you get from your idea to something on stage that actually works, how to encourage creativity but also getting them to understand that there are parameters. How the body moves; what distance does; what the eye can see from a distance, all those technical things. To me it's a dream job because I spend 90% of my time in a creative environment, and 10% in the administrative crap that I have to do because it's academia. But, the teaching and being with the students and being in the theatre is absolutely energizing.

L.A. is a really creative world, but it's also a stressful world because you work really long hours. When you're on a show you have no other life; you're focused on that show. It's demanding, and your job is going to end when the show ends, so you're always looking for another job, and that's stressful. The beauty of academia is that, once you're an academic and tenured, you have so much creative freedom because you've stopped having to worry about getting another job. It could make you lazy or it could make you much more creative and flexible. It's like, you don't have to worry about the money, you're just worried about having the time to do what you love to do.

Film is very political. Like most industries that make a lot of money, it's a full time job just keeping the connections. The politics of it is strenuous. I'm not making nearly the kind of money I made, but I'm not under the same amount of stress that I was when I was working in film. I worked

in film until three years ago. I've been teaching for nineteen years, but during the school year sometimes I'd work on a film. In the last three years I haven't worked in film at all. I haven't had to keep up with who's doing what and who's where and what's happening in the industry in New Mexico — all that stuff that becomes time consuming and takes a lot of energy away from your creativity.

When I first got to L.A. in 1975 it was very hard to get into the unions, and there was little nonunion work. I did a few nonunion jobs and it was abusive. You did a lot of work for not much money and your crew didn't get taken care of very well. For the film industry the unions have been really protective of people. Once you got in the union, you were pretty much guaranteed a good career, unless you imploded in some way. But they kept control of how many people were in the union. The old system was the head of wardrobe would assign you to shows. I worked at Universal for a while, and the head of the department always assigned me the show; movies and pilots and this kind of stuff, so I didn't have to work very much, which was great. My reputation just stayed within Universal for a long time, then things really changed and the unions really changed. Particularly for film, you really need the protection of the union. It's protection for the workers. There's a lot of safety rules. When the rules are not abided by, then it's pretty dangerous on a film.

A couple of times when we were filming "The Twilight Zone", they had children that were working at night. They were totally illegal; they used Vietnamese children whose parents didn't speak English, didn't have an agent or a manager. They didn't have the social workers that usually protect children. You probably don't know this story: the helicopters went too low and be-

I think success is leading a good life. **Leaving the earth at least a little bit better off than it was before you.** *Your relationships with people are good, you don't spend a lot of time around negative stuff; I think that's success.*

headed the actor and the children that were in the scene. There's another story where there was a nonunion film where a gun went from insert, where they're doing close-ups of shooting, and then it went back to the production itself and the prop guy, who was handling the weapon, wasn't actually a gun expert. He forgot to check the gun and it killed an actor. There's a lot of stuff like that.

You try to make sure that the actor has a good dressing room and the crew is fed, how much you're paid, that you have health insurance, all that kind of stuff is basic. But then there's even more extended rules that are set by the union that really protect everybody. Something as simple as how much time there is from the time a crew member leaves the set till when they have to be back on the set. Different breaks, stuff like that, to make sure people are getting enough rest and have enough time to bathe and sleep.

With our union here in New Mexico, it's nine hours. If you realize that you might be driving up a half an hour or an hour to your location, with two hours of driving time on your nine hour turnaround, that only leaves you seven to go home, check your mail, bathe, eat, deal with your real life and be back. It's not really very much, but at least it's more than they used to give people. I'm very pro-union, and it's very disappointing that the percentage of nonunion films that are made are huge now. Again, having a nonunion film come into a place,

there's a lot of right-to-work states where films go because they don't have to abide by the union. It's kind of across the board. There are some films that are pretty big that are still non-union. There are commercials, rock videos, it goes across the gamut of entertainment. For example, here in New Mexico, we're really trying to promote filmmaking in our state, but the governor's office commissioned an outside company to produce all the commercials for tourism in New Mexico. Before, the unions were really strong and that wouldn't have happened. It's been a huge change since I joined the union in the late 70's. It's really different now than it was then.

I'm fifty-nine. I have a feeling I'm never going to get to retire. I'm on inactive status with the Designer's Guild and the Costumer's Union. I reached the maximum number of hours to get full benefits when I retire, so I will have that. But, when I went into teaching, the retirement fund that I went to was handled by AIG, and a few years ago I lost most of my retirement with AIG, which has not been recouped yet. I got some of it back, but not a lot of it. Because of that I switched to a retirement fund that is a state controlled plan that doesn't take the kind of risks that AIG did. AIG was that big investment company that lost millions of dollars and my retirement was in that.

If I retired in L.A. from the film industry, there's a lot of support. My medical care and all that stuff is much more

complex and much more out of your own pocket than it is when you're in L.A.. L.A. has their own clinics; health and welfare is kind of controlled by the industry. They even have retirement villages that are supported by the motion picture industry. If an industry member falls on hard times, they have low interest loans that can help people. They're very supported there. But, if you retire somewhere else, you don't have that. So, retiring from the film industry here doesn't allow me to take a lot of benefits.

I'm actually starting on a new retirement program that I'm not even vested in yet. Fortunately, teaching, or academia, is a career that doesn't have the same age-ism that film industries have. I mean there are a lot of academics in their seventies here. It's not an industry that, the minute you're sixty or sixty-two, they expect you to leave. I think some people retire younger, but most people stay on later. My guess is when I retire between the two industries, between academia and film, I'll have a pretty comfortable retirement for Albuquerque. It's not a really expensive place to live. So, I'm sure I'll be fine. And I'm covered for medical. I'm more concerned about the next generation.

I do want to retire someday. I'm not sure when. I'm not looking forward to it right now. I'm not saying, "Oh in four years I'll be retired, or eight years." I don't have any kind of goal. I think I'll retire when I'm feeling like I'm not mentally up for this anymore, losing too many brain cells and I can't remember things off the top of my head. Or, I have to think a lot harder to be able to do this. Right now, it's not physically challenging or mentally challenging, where I just feel like I really have to work hard

all the time. I'm doing exactly what I want to be doing in my life. If I retired, what I would probably do is take a lot of classes and, you know, probably do about the same thing I'm doing now. Do a lot of reading, take classes, maybe write more papers than I write now, present more than I present now. But I have to say this is a world that's totally comfortable for me.

I'm fine. I'm doing great. I love what I do. I love having something to get up to do every morning. I'm a little slower than I used to be. I get cranky if I work 11 or twelve-hour days, which in film a twelve-hour day would be short. This actually is like a retirement job or a second career job for me. I don't feel like there's a lot I haven't done that I still need to do. I guess some people who are retiring feel that way. In that way, the advantage of being in a creative world means that you did get to fulfill a lot of stuff that other people might not have gotten to do. I actually don't have a bucket list. I love what I do. I love being around young people. They're so creative and brilliant and they just energize me every day. There's nothing I'd like to do except maybe go and teach somewhere else. I might take a sabbatical and teach in Wales or somewhere else, but I would still teach and I would still do costumes. It would just be kind of cool to do it somewhere else; to get the hang of somewhere else.

I think success for me is finding what makes you happy, and, what really brings you joy. And I think that's actually hard. I think most people don't know what success is because they don't know what really makes them happy; what really inspires them. You know, some people think it's money or some people think it's things.

Yeah, I made a lot more money and it was a lot easier to have, like, the housekeeper and a gardener, and my life was a lot easier when I could afford to have a lot of people do stuff for me. But I don't know if I was happier. I think success is leading a good life: leaving the earth at least a little bit better off than it was before you; your relationships with people are good; you don't spend a lot of time around negative stuff. I think that's success.

Nathan Banks
Violinist, Worden, Illinois
American Federation of Musicians (AFM)

I'm a freelance violinist. I'm going to be thirty-two in April. I've been doing this for about twelve years, I guess. I got my first orchestra job when I was nineteen. I started playing the violin when I was three, at the Suzuki program at Southern Illinois University at Edwardsville. My dad was a professional french horn player. He never quite managed to make it into a big orchestra, so he left that life and became a band director and moved up to this area where both of my folks' parents lived. And there was a Suzuki violin school at SIUE. You know, I was three, I didn't know what the violin was or what Suzuki meant. But that's how I got started as a violin player. It wasn't until my mid to late teens that I decided to pursue that as my career.

Sometimes playing the violin can be terrifying. Auditions are particularly nerve-wracking. What I really like to do is to play as a member of a violin section with an orchestra. I always feel the most comfortable there. When you're playing in a violin section of an orchestra, that's when you get to play the biggest and best music - the Beethoven symphonies and the Brahms symphonies and Mahler symphonies - and that's my favorite kind of music. You can't really play that sort of music if you're a chamber musician or if you're playing in a string quartet.

When I'm not playing the violin, I enjoy lots of things that are related to information, like in mathematical terms. I'm interested in things like cryptography and computers, and I play chess online and other strategy games. On the surface, they look like they're unrelated, but the way that I'm interested in them all boils down into sort of how information is stored and transmitted, whether it's in a floppy disc or in a book or written down by hand by a monk.

Really, I'm very interested in how people learn things and how knowledge is preserved and lost. Not a whole lot of crossover with being a violinist, but when we're playing music by Beethoven, for example, Beethoven's been dead since the early part of the 19th century, you can't just go and talk to him and ask him what he really meant. We have to go by the information that Beethoven left behind. He wrote letters which give you an insight into his mind and life. And you also have Beethoven's scores. We actually have original autographs of some of his scores. For example, his third symphony, he originally dedicated it to Napoleon because Napoleon was supposed to be this great champion of liberty, and when Beethoven heard that Napoleon had crowned himself emperor, he grabbed his pen and he crossed out the dedication with so much force that he actually slashed through the paper. That actual autographed score is in a museum and you could go look at it.

So, a typical week for me is I go to my private studio where I teach violin lessons on Monday and Tuesday. On Wednesday, I pack up and I go to some city in the Midwest where I play with that city's regional orchestra. A regional orchestra is a symphony orchestra that does not have a big enough budget and a big enough audience base to be a full-time orchestra. So, instead what they do is put on a limited number of symphony orchestra concerts, and when they're in session you go and you have rehearsals: probably Wednesday evening, some rehearsals on Thursday, rehearsal and a concert on Friday and another concert on Saturday. And that's your work for the week. Then you go home and you won't have any more concerts with that orchestra for a few weeks. So as a freelancer, I try to line up as many of those orchestras as possible, so that each week I drive to a different town to play with a different orchestra and then can make something that resembles a living wage.

Sometimes this work can really get you down. There's an awful lot of driving, because the way the regional orchestras work, they can't be too close together - they have to have a large enough audience base that they can sustain themselves as not-for-profits. Most regional orchestras have budgets of one to three million dollars so you can't just have one in every city. That means that I have to usually drive anywhere from three to five hours one-way to get to the orchestra. Sometimes you think, "Wow, I could really be using this time for something better than driving. I could be reading or I could be practicing the violin." And the overall pay is pretty low: it's very steady so it's reliable, but, you know, I only make about eighteen to twenty thousand dollars a year, which you can just kind of squeak by on that. If there's a major car repair or something like that, it can be a little scary sometimes

The American Federation of Musicians is the national organization and I belong to several different locals. I originally wanted to join the St. Louis local for a couple of reasons. One is that the union membership looks good on a resumé. When you send it to a major orchestra, they are unlikely to turn you down. They will almost certainly invite you to audition if you have a union membership on your resumé. And since I joined up, I actually got a lot of work from union contractors.

When I first joined up I was pretty young. I didn't have a really clear idea of what it was all about. I just knew that I needed it so I could do certain jobs in St. Louis that I wanted to do, because, you know, they wouldn't hire non-union labor. Since then, I've actually been involved in an organizing campaign.

When I first began playing with the Illinois symphony back in 1999 it was not a union orchestra. In a non-union orchestra your agreement with the company is whatever the management wants it to be. And if they (musicians) don't like something about it, that's too bad for them. So, that works fine if your management is well educated and benevolent, but in the event that the musicians want or need something, then they don't really have many options.

We went through a situation where we had a music director who was both a bad musician and a bad person. For example, this music director threatened the immigration status of some musicians. We have quite a few musicians who are here from Europe on visas or green cards, and the music director threatened to call I.N.S. and

I feel like I'm on the path. I'm not a student anymore but **I'm still always looking for ways to change and improve my playing** *because I hope to someday play with a major orchestra. So, that's kind of the point - that, in my mind is, that's when I've landed - if I can get a major orchestra job.*

make trouble for some of them if they didn't fall in line. We, as musicians, would like to be safe from abuse, but we had no leverage over our management. We can't tell them that they have to fire a music director just because we don't like what the music director is doing. At one point, the music director actually fired our personnel manager, who was well loved by the whole orchestra. Myself and a few others decided that the orchestra was finally mad enough that maybe we could make some changes.

We looked at the orchestra and we said if it keeps on like it's going, it's going to die. It's either going to go flat out-of-business or it will become a community orchestra, which - a community orchestra is a valid enterprise: it gives people who live in a city and have day jobs, such as doctors and lawyers who play their instruments as a hobby, an outlet where they can play orchestral music together. But that's not what we had in Springfield; we had a really top-notch regional orchestra. We had some of the best freelancers coming from Chicago and St. Louis and Cleveland. We even had people coming from the East Coast and West Coast because we had a really good reputation. People in the orchestra world, they know about the Illinois Symphony Orchestra. And, through the time that the music director I told you about was there, our reputation dropped gradually until finally it got so bad that the word out there was, "If the Illinois Symphony calls, say, 'No!' Don't go play there." So, we decided that it was worth saving and we sort of set off this whole chain of events.

We organized a vote of no-confidence in the music director. Then we contacted some of the representatives of the national American Federation of Musicians office, and got some advice on what we were supposed to do. The AFM office has several people who are on staff whose jobs are to organize non-union orchestras, so there are procedures in place that facilitate that. The first thing that we did is we got a bunch of union cards and we had a card signing campaign. You go around and first you make a list of everybody that you think is for the union, and then you ask them to sign a card that says that they would like for the orchestra to unionize and make the local AFM chapter the bargaining agent. And then, if you have more than half the orchestra right there, then you're good to go. If you don't, then you do a little more campaigning and talk to people that you're not quite so sure of.

Once you have all of your cards signed, you send them off to the National Labor Relations Board. That tells the Board there's an interest in union organizing in your organization. So, the Board will call for a Board election, which is a vote of all the employees on whether or not they want to unionize. So, we did that and we held the vote and I think the vote was 54-5 in favor of unionizing the orchestra. At that point, we are a union orchestra. We have only to negotiate our collective bargaining agreement. This whole process took about three years; from the time that we decided that the orchestra was angry enough to take action to just a few weeks ago when we reached our tentative agreement. The agreement has not yet been ratified, but we should have a ratification meeting this month. It was a lot of work but it was very educational for me. I was on the negotiating committee and the organizing committee. I had never done anything like this before.

The main advantage of having the collective bargaining agreement is that it gives us meaningful input into our workplace. We have some say in what conditions we're going to play under and what kind of musicians are going to be on stage with us, and so we don't just suffer from the whims of management. Sometimes management may do a great job without any agreement, but in the case when there is a problem, then you need that protection.

Actually, a lot of people told me that it couldn't be done. That there would be no way we could unseat someone as powerful as our music director with the backing of, you know, quite wealthy people from the community. The thing was that the people in the community were quite well meaning. Our board of directors are actually really good people. They were just getting their information from a bad source. A big part of this whole thing has just been about educating our board members about how an orchestra should operate. It is a major accomplishment, I think. It's one of the main things that I've ever done and one of the hardest things. I had to work a lot on it. I had phone conversations every night 'till the wee hours with the other committee members. I actually wrote a lot of the agreement. And we had a reporter that we worked with, so the community would know what's going on and would get the straight story. I put all the ballots together and wrote the e-mails to the orchestra and that kind of stuff. It was a big effort but it was worth it. I think the orchestra is really going to grow. It's going to bounce back pretty quickly.

I feel like I'm on the path. I'm not a student anymore but I'm still always looking for ways to change and improve my playing because I hope to someday play with a major orchestra. So, that's kind of the point - that, in my mind is, that's when I've landed - if I can get a major orchestra job. That would be the time when I wouldn't be working towards something anymore. I would have the thing that I was working toward and from that point on, it would just be explo-

ration and maintenance. I could stop driving all the time and I could live in one place and I could make a living playing the violin that would allow me to have a fairly high standard of living. I would be, maybe, very comfortable. There would not be a lot of stress because in a freelance orchestra, you often have to play at night to accommodate musicians who are college professors during the day. In a full-time orchestra, it's just like any other job. You go and you have rehearsal in the morning and you break for lunch and you have a short rehearsal in the afternoon, and then you're done for the day. You have time to go back and practice or read a book or watch a movie or whatever you want, and you usually have at least one full day off every week. Big orchestras are usually very conscientious about making sure their musicians have enough time to rest, because playing an instrument is very physically demanding.

So, you would have enough leisure time that you could, you know, sort of stay sane, and you would get to perform concerts on the weekend in some of the greatest performance venues. You know, you get to be an artist. You have enough money that you don't have to worry about doing something else. You could just play the violin and there will be enough money there so that you can eat - and insurance, medical care, a pension.

Ben Bielski

Retired Postal Clerk, Kansas City, Kansas

American Postal Workers Union (APWU)

I retired two years ago last month. I have a picture on my last day of work. I had a crudely drawn shirt, done with a magic marker, where I had written something about the great postal strike of 1970, and I mentioned the name of Moe Biller, who was the President of our union and led that strike. I was giving tribute to the union, and Moe Biller in particular, for my entire career when I retired. That's the photo that popped up in my head. I was paying tribute to the only reason we have a decent retirement - basically because of this strike that the union had.

There was a massive strike that originated in New York City by the head of the postal workers union. His name was Moe Biller. He was in charge of the entire New York Local. He was one of the last of the great fiery labor leaders of the last century. He took the entire local of New York and the surrounding areas out on strike. This was in 1970. It was technically illegal. We did not have the right to strike. We're considered federal workers, sort of like the air traffic controllers around 1980, when Reagan fired everyone. You couldn't do that to the U.S. Postal Service at the time, it was too critical, too vital.

At that time, they probably employed around 900,000 people nationwide. And what they did by closing down the entire New York Metro area in 1970 - this is pre-internet or anything like that - is they locked up the entire system. Most of the international mail was coming out of there, too. So, you basically closed down communications for a big part of the country - all international mail and a lot of revenue. This was before bills were being paid on the Internet. They depended upon checks coming out of the mail every day; it was millions of dollars each day. So, for every day it was quite an expensive proposition and President Nixon at the time ordered the National Guard into the post office, but they had no idea how anything worked. It was almost hilarious.

After so many days, in order to settle the thing, they revamped the entire postal service. They made it into a governmental corporation, and put a board of governors over it, and gave the postal workers' union quite a decent upgrade in their wages and benefits. It helped to get the rights to negotiate. Instead of what everybody called "collective begging" they went to "collective bargaining" when they got that right at that time. Ever since then, it became a pretty decent job.

The whole time I was there, from the beginning, I instinctively knew that the only possibility of being treated humanely was if we were all organized, and we collectively demanded such a thing. Without it there would have been no protections whatsoever. The wages would not have been decent, the treatment would not have been....There would have been no recourse without the union. I knew that instinctively.

Actually, we did better than a lot of federal workers because of that particular strike that happened. We got to negotiate our own contract, and it turned out pretty good. It was the massive size of the work force and the importance of it that gave it a lot of power. It all worked out for me perfectly because that's about the time I was entering the service. My old man - actually, he retired in 1986 - was already there. He'd been working there since 1950. I was only 19 at the time. I didn't realize how important this particular thing was, in terms of my livelihood and everything else.

As the years went on, I would look back on it. Occasionally, a magazine would have an old picture. Moe Biller continued on very strong for another 20 years or some-

If you could imagine, every day, every address in the United States, somebody trudges to that door, so the vehicle force is the largest in the country, and it's extremely labor intensive, so even with machines that sort the mail, you have to have so many people to haul it back and forth and make it to the doorway. In all these lower class neighborhoods throughout the entire country, and the cities, **the only person many people see every day is their letter carrier. They look forward to that.**

thing like that. He was quite a character. He knew my old man. My father, he was in the Kansas City Local for quite a while. I had sort of radicalized him in the late 60's after many heated discussions. My parents would go to most of the national conventions and he got to know Moe Biller. My father was an outspoken type of person like Moe Biller. Biller would always call my father out, so I think he liked him and he got to be friends with him. I would see Moe on T.V. occasionally. We would always get a kick out of him because he was a charismatic, real outspoken sort of guy, sort of what you thought of as the old time labor guys. They were real outspoken and didn't try to come across as some sophisticated negotiators. It was more like, "Here's what it is and here's what I believe, and I'm in your face with it" sort of thing.

I'm in the American Postal Workers Union (APWU). It encompasses clerks, drivers, and maintenance workers. There's also the International Association of Letter Carriers, and they cover all the carriers. And there's another one called the Mail Handlers Union. They handle the mail and transfer it from place to place. I was a clerk my whole career. I did a dozen different clerical jobs,

like sorting mail. We used to have to learn what they called schemes. Like say you're in Kansas City in a certain zone, you'd have to memorize all these addresses and what carrier they went to. You might have 25 carriers, so if you saw an address you'd have to memorize what carrier that went to. As a clerk it took you a couple of months to learn this thing and you'd get tested on it, and you'd have to get 95 out of 100 correct. This was before all the machinery and high tech stuff. They sort most of them now by reading the barcodes and sort by machine.

In those days, when I started, it was all manual. Imagine, you'd have these long lines of people with these cases just sorting this mail into 20 or 30 slots: and the clerks, they would bundle each load for each carrier. It was a whole different time period. Technology wasn't anything like it is right now, or toward the end of my career. In the late 80's, they started to bring these technological machines that could start to sort this mail. Eventually, they perfected it more and more, although it's still heavily labor intensive. That's why the biggest expense they have is labor. If you could imagine, every day, every address in the United States, somebody trudges to that door, so the vehicle force is the largest in the country, and it's extremely labor intensive, so even with machines that sort the mail, you have to have so many people to haul it back and forth and make it to the doorway. In all these lower class neighborhoods throughout the entire country, and the cities, the only person many people see every day is their letter carrier. They look forward to that. It's a valuable infrastructure to have set up and you could do so many things with that.

I worked on the night shift for a long time. If you were a clerk, you started out on the night shift. You'd have no seniority, so you'd have to work the night shift. It was sort of edgy, sort of an atmosphere where you'd be in a large plant all night long sitting in a case sorting mail, which could drive you crazy. Later on, there were a lot of incidences - it became a cliché to say "he's gone postal" - due to the fact that there were a number of incidences where disgruntled people would go into the post office and shoot the employees, and this happened I guess a half a dozen times. It became so that people started making jokes about it that anyone going crazy or insane, they would say they're "going postal." A lot of that is from those early days: that drudgery that you would sit at a case all night long sorting mail and being observed by supervision. A lot of those places were dusty and it wasn't conducive to any mental stimulation other than rote, mundane stuff, over and over again. That was before machines, so they would push you to sort so many an hour.

I spent most of my career having to be there at five in the morning. Before the carriers got there, we'd have to sort. Then I worked at a window where we sold actual products. You'd stand at the window, you know, weigh the packages, sell stamps, sell certified or register peoples' mail, money orders. I had that job, too. Then, off and on and for the last 10 years of my career, I was a relief person, which is very satisfying. I got to move around and do a variety of jobs. Working on the window, you'd meet people every day, and so that was the most rewarding. That was a really sweet gig.

But anyway, that's why I crudely tried to write a tribute to Moe Biller on my shirt when I retired, because he gave me a good 40 years of sick leave, and vacation leave, good wages, and retirement. I don't know if there's going to be another generation that can say that of working class people: I'm the last generation that might get this. Unfortunately, my kids and people coming after that, they might not have this opportunity. After WWII and FDR, it lasted 50 years, but now I don't think they could ever recapture that. As a working class person, it was decent. I mean it was really nice. Looking back over 38 years I did there, and, now, I'm sixty, and I feel good. I'm in good shape and everything and actually got a retirement out of it. I've talked to people who were management, who worked for various corporations and they're like, "Damn! I wished I'd worked for the post office," because they got nothing right now. Many corporations have folded and changed hands, leaving many people with nothing.

Yeah, it was a mundane job and was not a high status thing or anything like that, but at least as of right now, I'm guaranteed a civil service pension. So, there's a lot of people out there, they just don't have anything. They're going to have to work till they're 80 or 90.

I'm not a very materialistic person. What I just described to you is success. I've lived the "good life". You know - decent wages, vacation - and I was able to get a house, and I define that as success. I'll quote Studs Terkel; he said when he came back as a young guy before he was a big name journalist, that his idea of success or what he called the "good life" was having a civil service job and getting to go see the Cub's games a couple times a week. To him, that was the good life. When I read that I said, "Studs, I hit it, man! I did it! I achieved the good life." I had a civil service job for 38 years. I got to go see, in my case it wasn't necessarily the baseball games, but other things. I got to go to musical events and see plays, whatever. So, it was great.

for many years, I worked overtime. You could hardly pass it up, you know, because it would supplement your income. It was really good money. That basically is what it is. I physically feel much better because I have more time now to exercise. Knock on wood. I feel good right now. This is a great time of my life.

And right now, I actually am living with my mother in Kansas City, Kansas, again. She has her old house. I was the oldest of

That's what I would hope for - that sort of a life like that - to be constantly aware of the political situation, **hopefully retain any kind of passion there is for that right up into old age,** *and also commitment, some sort of commitment to social justice, to not become comfortable so that you don't care about anything like that.*

I'm enjoying every day. Every day I get up and say, "Thank you, Jesus!" Actually, I'm not religious at all but it's just...a lot of people around here talk like that, you know. Actually I'm a secular humanist agnostic, but I was raised Catholic -very strict Catholic. I enjoy every day. I see co-workers occasionally that are still working and I think, "I get up every day whenever I want - nine, ten o'clock. I fix four or five eggs, read the entire paper, drink coffee. If I want to go someplace, I can do that. I went on the Nation cruise. I just have time to do things I never could because of the drudgery of getting up early every day and working eight to ten hours. A lot of time,

seven children, so I'm back here. She's all by herself. She's eighty-seven years old. And right now, I've been divorced for about seven or eight years. My ex-wife is one of the most compassionate people around. She struggled in the minimum wage market for several years, but now has found work she finds greatly rewarding at one of the best hospice centers in the city.

Everything's great in my life. You know, there's no conflict; it's just a really great time period for me. But that's where I'm at. I'm in a real good place. I've got my health, I do what I want, and I can pursue cultural things. I used to play in a band. I was a drummer/percussionist in a cover band. It's been 25 or 30 years, but I do have a friend who's a music critic for the paper and we'll go out. He'll take me to a young band that he sees and raves about so, I'll go see that. That's really inspiring sometimes. That kind of stuff is what I live for; that dimension of the arts. I have time for all that stuff now. I do have a part-time job at the YMCA three times a week. I used to be a personal trainer, but now I just take cards and do security. There are a lot of characters down there. That gives me just enough of a deadline where I have to be somewhere 3 times a week.

I have four children. They're all in the Kansas City area, on the Missouri side. I had a house over there. One of my daughters is in her fourth year in the Education Department at the University of Missouri/Kansas City, so she wants to be a teacher, a profession that is being targeted and scapegoated by those backward forces that have been dominating the nation for the last three decades.

All my kids are cool. Maybe I had too much effect on all of them. They don't care about aspiring to careerist goals so much. They're reading too much obscure stuff. They don't have a way to make a living still, and the current environment is hard, you know. Maybe I screwed up and I didn't teach 'em how to hunt. Like a wolf pack, the little ones, you have to throw 'em out into the cold hard world and make 'em learn how to hunt if they want to stay alive.

Maybe that's how I fell down as a fa-

ther. Other than that, I'm very pleased that they're all artistic, musical, etc., etc., and they can sit around and discuss philosophy, but they don't know how to make a living like I had to do. I had to go to work for, like, 40 years and learn how to do this drudgery to keep them all alive. And also the environment was more suited toward that.

My other daughter right now is a waitress at a pretty decent place in a nice area of town where there are high dollar restaurants. She's got that going on. She is very independent and likes to travel and study. My oldest son is twenty. He is passionate and talented about graphic art, but he won't perform the hustle that could make him an investment grade artist. My youngest son is nineteen with a high IQ in almost anything, especially philosophy and music. My five year old grandson is an absolute joy. I could be on the other side of it where they had the instinct to stay alive to the utmost degree, but if they didn't have any appreciation for the arts or philosophy or anything like that, I would be disappointed in that respect, too. I guess if I had to choose, if they had to pick one or the other, they should pick the arts. I just don't see how they're going to make it. The economic climate that's going on, it's not like it was. When I got out of high school, you didn't even necessarily have to go to college. There were jobs in factories, the post office, where you could make a decent living. They're pretty much gone.

I consider myself fairly lucky that I've actually achieved what I consider success. I have my health, I have enough money so I have all my basic survival needs met and I can appreciate the arts. I have an interest in politics; arts and music sort of tie into the political. Everything's interconnected. Like I say, I'm living the good life according to Studs Terkel, and I couldn't ask for some-body who I admire more, with his values, and the way he lived his life. That's what I would hope for - that sort of a life like that - to be constantly aware of the political situation, hopefully retain any kind of passion there is for that right up into old age, and also commitment, some sort of commitment to social justice, to not become comfortable so that you don't care about anything like that. I want to live my life according to these people that I look up to, like Studs Terkel, Bruce Springsteen, Tony Kushner, you know, figures like this. These are my heroes. Also, all the intelligent and conscious working people who toil away for years in quiet desperation, like my mother and father. They are especially my heroes.

Kimberly Marie Braylock

Dancer, San Francisco Ballet Company, San Francisco, California
American Guild of Musical Artists (AGMA)

I'm twenty-two years old. I would describe myself as a loving person but very assertive, and I have a lot of different personalities. I definitely stand on my faith as a Christian who believes in the Bible, and not so much as religion; more so as an actual relationship with God and on the spiritual level. That's where I find my founding ground, and I develop as a person from there.

I'm a dancer. Although my profession is in ballet, I love dancing in, like, the club, or I can dance salsa. I can dance in a hip-hop class or a modern class. I love flamenco. I don't define myself as a ballet dancer, more just a dancer, someone that loves to dance, in general. I think I was born with it. My mom says that I always used to jump and kick in her stomach. She said someone made a comment, "Oh that girl's gonna be a dancer," because I was always moving around. My mom put me in dance class when I was three, so I was dancing at a young age. I just feel like it's a way of expression for me, as opposed to one talent. I feel like it's just my body language that is naturally formed that way, like it's how I present myself.

I observe everything. I analyze myself very much, and I write in my journal. I love writing. I've carried a journal since I was a very young girl, and I write poetry. I write daily and describe how I feel a lot so, in that sense, I always go back to my past journal entries and I see how I've developed as a person. Knowing myself a lot allows me to understand and know other people better so I can relate to them and connect to them,

because I feel that each person has a basic behavior or emotion or feeling that creates that person, but it also shows why they're acting a certain way. So, I try not to judge a person simply on their actions – probably that came from my dad. Since I've known him, he's always believed in God, and he always instructed me, but he never…I never felt like he was judging me or criticizing me, and he always gave me the freedom of my own choices. I always wanted to be like that. I would describe myself as trying to be someone that's understanding and connecting to other people so, in that sense, it develops me into a more loving person.

I went to school in New Jersey, but I went to my dance classes and my church in New York City. I was in New Jersey until I came to San Francisco in my senior year of high school, in 2007. I went to a summer program in the San Francisco Ballet School. That's real common for a ballet dancer; you audition and you get accepted to a certain amount of summer intensives, and I got accepted to San Francisco. I came here for the summer and they invited me to stay for their school year program. Since it was my last year of high school, it was a little difficult making that choice because I was very involved in school and loved my friends. Making that choice to leave was a big deal, but I'm glad I made it because, you know, it created the career that I have now. And, the transition was nice because I came here and lived on my own, without my parents. I moved into a house that was owned by the ballet school, and there were, like, twenty-three dancers in the house, and we were supervised by two people. I went to school for my senior classes once a week, if even that, and I graduated in January as opposed to June. It was a school called Independent High School, meaning you don't have to be in class, like, every day. You just

I love performances. I think I love performing more than anything else. I love being on stage. I feel like that's where I have freedom. You are being put on the spotlight. I mean, you can be in the background and someone may not see you, *but* **you're putting yourself on a painting.**

go and you see your one instructor and you hand in your school assignments and that's pretty much it. You take the California state tests and pass that, and I got my diploma.

It's very common to be accepted into a professional ballet company at a young age. I was accepted, or hired, at age nineteen. The choice to leave New Jersey was smart because, obviously, you have to have the proper technique and skills. But, yeah, taking the opportunity was very wise because I got invited to their level 8, which is the highest level at the school. After that year, I was a trainee, which is as a representative of the ballet school, and then you also perform as a student with the ballet company in some of their shows, such as Nutcracker. So, my first few years in San Francisco, I was involved a lot in the school and in the company. And then I got hired into the ballet company. So I feel one hundred percent grateful that my friends let me go.

Professionally, I am a ballet dancer, and I have a forty-two week contract that requires me to do rehearsals and performances. In my professional work, we have the Nutcracker in December and performances from January to May. I'm a corps de ballet dancer, which is the lowest rank, besides being an apprentice. For our company, there

are three ranks only. As a corps de ballet dancer, you're required to work with all the other female dancers, and you have to always be together, be in lines, the musicality all has to be the same. You express yourself as a dancer, but it's mostly about dancing as a unit as opposed to as an individual.

I love my work. It's such a blessing to be able to get paid to do what you love. I feel like I'm completely blessed, being able to get paid for this. And, it can be difficult sometimes, because someone is criticizing what you love to do; so you just have to really be strong mentally and know how to take criticism. But it goes both ways. Sometimes, I don't always wanna dance, but I have to because it's a requirement. But, for the most part, I can't complain.

In regards to everyday life, we have ballet class each morning that we work. Ballet class is like a warm-up class. If we're not performing a lot, you can use class as the time to really work more on your technique, or a certain thing that you're struggling with and to continuously improve your ballet. But if we're performing a lot, ballet class in the morning is more just a way to warm up your body to prepare itself in order not to get injured for the performance. It's like a balance between dancing for yourself just

for the fun of it and just making sure your body doesn't start dancing while it's cold, so it doesn't get injured. With ballet, you're definitely going to go through injuries; you're definitely going to go through aches and pains, some less than others. I feel muscle aches and joints that are stiff or achy. It happens.

If I wake up on the wrong side of the bed it can be really hard and I don't feel good. Ballet warm-up class is good, but is probably the most frustrating thing about work. If it is a teacher that you like, class could be good. But if you feel really off, class could be awful, regardless of the circumstances of the teacher or the combinations that are given in a class. With warm-up class, it's always fluctuating with how I feel.

I love it in the general sense because it's a way where you're allowed to just focus on yourself and improve. Sometimes it's hard, because we have visitors come in and watch our class, so instead of it feeling for yourself it feels like a production of proving how good you are. So, in that case it's very nerve-wracking.

After class, we have our rehearsals. If the ballet is something that you love to do - if it's a choreography that you love to learn and perform -I feel awesome, because that's where you feel...that's where the freedom comes in to express yourself. But, for corps de ballet dancers, when it comes to full length ballets like Swan Lake, or Romeo and Juliet—ballets that require all the dancers to be dancing in unison—those can be sometimes frustrating because you have to repeat it and repeat it in order to get it together. You ever see the Rockettes? Like that, as an example.

I love performances. I think I love performing more than anything else. I love being on stage. I feel like that's where I have freedom. You are being put in the spotlight. I mean, you can be in the background and someone may not see you, but you're putting yourself on a painting. You know, you're putting yourself on stage to be seen by a huge audience and you know that you're a part of something. You're a part of a production that is being presented to people that want to either escape, you know, from their day-to-day lives, or they want to see something beautiful. I know I'm serving people because I am giving them something. So, that's why I like being on stage and it's the feeling. It's like you and lights and the costumes, and everything about it just makes me feel great.

I'm in a union because once I was hired into the San Francisco Ballet, every dancer that's employed has to be part of the union. I was so shocked. I did not know much about unions. When I got hired into the Company, they were like, "You have to pay this much money to become a member of the union." I was like, "What? Really?" You know, I guess I wasn't that aware, [but] I understood it after it was explained to me. I'm one to ask questions so...What they told me right from the start was pretty much the union protects us and protects our rights and all those things so, that was good to hear. I was fine with it. Essentially, because I was part of the negotiating committee for the union, because they were renegotiating our contract, I was just an apprentice and I was like, "Yeah! I'll be a part of that" and I learned quickly.

I have friends that are dancers, are part of companies that aren't a part of the union, and those dancers have to go through a lot of hell with their bodies, so I'm completely grateful. I think with our union, they created a contract with a lot of...I mean, a lot of ballet companies have A.G.M.A., but I guess for us, our contracts were really negotiated well. The San Francisco Ballet Company is a well-known company so they have more financial ability to negotiate with the dancers, but we have things in our contract that limits how many hours we can work. Like, if we override those hours we get paid extra. We get breaks every hour. There's a whole list of benefits that we get and [physical] therapy and things that will keep our bodies intact. That's the most important thing for me. I just see it as a huge benefit because our bodies are taken care of, which insures us for our longer dance career. We're putting our bodies at risk and our bodies are our career.

If I get injured, you know, and it takes me out forever, you have to keep retirement in mind. Even though I'm young, your body changes from when you're a teenager to when you're a young adult. Your joints aren't as limber and your muscles have to be warmed up more and all these things, and life, you know, is more than just getting up and doing homework and going to school and work. I know I've seen some female ballet dancers dance till they're forty, and then I also have friends that quit dancing when they're, like, twenty-six. It's one of those things; you have to think of all the possibilities and that's what I'm thinking of right now 'cause I don't know how long my body's going to hold up and it's something you can't predict. I would love to dance as long as I can without being in excruciating pain. If I could dance till I'm thirty, at least, that would be pretty awesome. I think that would be a sufficient amount of time.

Success. That's an interesting question, especially in today's world and society. Success I think is so distorted. Everyone's perception of success to me, it seems like it's mostly about fame and money, and that is not me at all. But, I guess success is, like, I just want to be happy with myself. I want to know that I have reached my fullest potential and I haven't given up on myself or, you know, I don't want to ever sit down one day and be like, "Oh, I could've done that." or "I could've done this."

I used to always want to be a manager, like an agent. I'm always imagining myself booking shows and organizing events, organize parties. I like social events so, I've always thought of myself being a part of something like that, and then, on the other side of me, I love writing. And then, I'm also very interested in counseling, like in a Biblical sense, like a spiritual sense. Whether it be part of a church or a missionary group or working in an impoverished country - that type of counseling. I just feel that a lot of people don't understand themselves, or understand why things work out the way they do, and since I've experimented on myself - a lot of emotions and behaviors - I've come to understand that any problems are derived from the heart. I've talked to a lot of my friends about their issues, or my coworkers. I love listening to people and I love helping them understand themselves better so that's why I'm interested in counseling. So, success for me is always progressing to any ambition that I have, and, you know, with all the circumstances given, like if I could do as much as I can to reach those ambitions.

Joyce Bryant
Home Care Worker, New York City

1199 Service Employees International Union (SEIU)

I live in New York City. I'm 61 years old. I'm a mom: I have 3 children and 4 grandchildren. I think I have a nice personality—I'm a loving person but I'm a strict person. I have morals and values and I have rules and regulations about myself that I know I have to follow, and I want people to give me the same respect that I give them. I like to travel. I like to meet different people. I'm an activist. I'm a delegate. I'm just an average black woman trying to live life to its fullest.

I've been a home care worker for [over] 30 years. I love people and working with people. Those are the jobs I've always had: working with people, taking care of people. I took care of people in their home: I cook for them, I clean for them, I did personal care for them. I did medical care for them, like taking them to the doctor or just taking them out for a day in the sun. I talked to them, comforted and cared for them. Most of my clients are old and they can't care for themselves, and most of all they need somebody to talk to them and show them that they care about them.

That was my goal since I was a little girl. I just have feelings for people, that's all. I don't want to see people suffer. I don't want people to be hurt or taken advantage of. Maybe that's because these are my feelings. I don't want anybody to do that to me, so I definitely wouldn't do it to other people. Taking care of people is the world to me. I really, really like it. I really, really do. If there's something wrong with you, I have to be able to give you some comfort. That's just the person that I am.

The reason why I joined the union, most of all, I knew that it was a union for the people, and to help the people, and because being a home care worker, the bosses didn't pay us fairly. They'd take what's supposed to be ours and give us little or nothing. And being in the union, I have been out there, rallying and fighting for better wages and better benefits - it was the right thing to do for me and my family. It made my life better, and my children's and my grandchildren's lives better, because my children do have a good life. One is a nurse, one is an insurance broker, and my son works in sales. They're alright, but I'm looking out for the grandchildren, so when they're grown up, they can get out there and work and get good jobs with benefits.

The union has helped me to be more outspoken. I go out and talk to other people about how the union works. I tell them about their raises, and, if their boss talks about firing people for joining the union, I tell them they [the bosses] can't do that. I tell people who are doubtful about joining the union, "Try it! You might like it!"

I don't want to retire yet. I'm 61, not far from 65, but I want to work still. Home care work is not easy. You have to do a lot. You have to have a heart, because there's no money in it. You're not going to get rich being a home care worker. But long as I live, I want to be able to get up and do something. I don't want to sit around doing nothing, being retired. I want to continue working until I decide to stop.

Sometimes money is not the only thing: success is knowing how to get things done. Knowing a lot is being successful, and being able to do the things you want to do.

That was my goal since I was a little girl. **I just have feelings for people, that's all. I don't want to see people suffer.** *I don't want people to be hurt or taken advantage of. Maybe that's because these are my feelings. I don't want anybody to do that to me, so I definitely wouldn't do it to other people.*

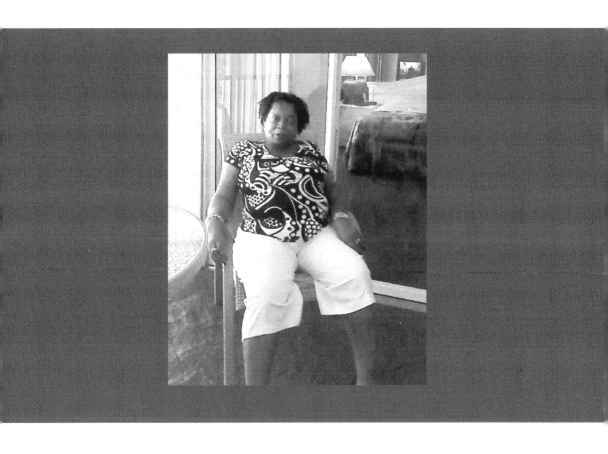

Bob Butler

Freelance Radio Reporter, KCBS San Francisco
Antioch, California
President, National Association of Black Journalists
SAG-AFTRA

I was a Navy brat growing up. We lived in Pennsylvania, Connecticut, California, Massachusetts. In high school I was an athlete, then I joined the Navy and served for about three years during the Vietnam War. After I got out of the Navy I stayed on the East Coast and worked at various jobs, and eventually I came back to California and went to college. What I wanted to become was a disc jockey because I was asked to be a disco DJ when I was on the East Coast, and when I came back, they wouldn't give me an air shift, and so they said, "If you really want to get on the air now, why don't you do the news?" And that's how I got involved in becoming a journalist. It was purely by accident. But, that was many years ago and I'm still there.

I intensely like to help people, that's why being a journalist was so important, because as a journalist you help people. You provide information. You educate, and that's something that was very important to me. It's ironic because in my nonprofit jobs, the volunteer jobs, the boards that I'm on, those organizations are designed to help people. N.A.B.J. (National Association of Black Journalists) is designed to help black journalists find employment, gain promotions. We do training for our members, and we also advocate for fair coverage of communities of color, specifically the African American community. SAG-AFTRA, my labor union, was designed to help workers live a better life. We advocate for fair wages for our members, we advocate for better working conditions, and we provide training. Those two organizations intersect. So, I look at myself as being someone who likes to lend a helping hand to folks and to help them live a better life.

I'm a reporter now, but I didn't start off as a reporter. I started off at KCBS as an intern in 1981, and then became hired as a desk assistant, which is entry level in radio. I went from desk assistant to an editor, which is somebody who is responsible for all the news content we put on the air. I started working [as a reporter] in 1989 after the Loma Prieta earthquake. When we had that big earthquake, it was all hands on deck. It's something I wanted to report, so they sent me out that weekend. I went out to work covering some of the recovery and people trying to get their possessions. So, it took me basically 8 years before I began working as a reporter on a part time basis, filling in for other people. I've always wanted to be a reporter, not an anchor. I didn't want to be sitting in the studio reading copy; I wanted to be out there talking to people. As a reporter you interact with people and you're allowed to tell peoples' stories; you're allowed to speak to people who sometimes can't speak for themselves, so that's very important to me.

There are quite a few stories that stand out. There are two that touch me quite a bit. The first one took place, I want to say, in 1999. This little girl was walking to school and disappeared. This happened in a little town called Vallejo, which is about thirty miles Northeast of San Francisco. She disappeared. Her name was Xiana, and it was a big deal. The public was searching for her. I went out to cover the story one day of the search and I got to meet her family. It was her great aunt and her grandmother and we became kind of close. I got to know the family very well. It was more than a year or so later, they found the little girl's skull down in San Jose. Obviously the family was devastated, and because I got to know them, it had more of an impact on me than it should have. We are not supposed to get involved in our stories, but sometimes, if you're true to them, it's hard not to.

I remember covering the memorial service for her. It was on a Sunday, and sitting there as a member of the media and looking at the family, they were torn up. That hit me emotionally. I broke down and cried just watching them because I got to know them. That's not something you're supposed to get involved in but sometimes you can't help it.

In 2007, one of our colleagues, a journalist named Chauncey Bailey, was shot and killed. When he was killed, it came out he was working on a story about a local bakery. There was all kinds of controversy about this bakery because the guy that started it allegedly had 42 children. Some of the women who had his children had them when they were teenagers; 13, 14 years old. It was really a sordid tale. So when Chauncey was killed, the journalism community got together, because what became apparent was that his death was related to this story.

We started something called the Chauncey Bailey Project, which is a collaboration of all these different organizations and journalists that came together to investigate Chauncey's death. That led to everybody who was involved in planning or killing Chauncey being brought to justice. And it was due to the work that we did, because the person who pulled the trigger was arrested almost immediately, but everybody knew that it was a conspiracy. This guy didn't act alone but, neither the police department nor the DA were investigating the conspiracy. It wasn't until we journalists began really looking into it, and the investigation, that they began looking at these other people. So, because of the work we did, we were able to bring these folks to justice. The current district attorney said, "Yeah, if it hadn't been for you guys we probably wouldn't have done this." We received numerous awards for our Chauncey Bailey story.

One of the people that was involved in the Chauncey Bailey project approached me in 2008 to say that she needed someone to go down to New Orleans and start an investigation, do a story about housing related to Hurricane Katrina. I said I'd be willing to do it. I asked, "What kind of story do you really want?" And she said, "I don't know, but it has to be a story that nobody else has done." We're talking about three years after Katrina. Every story under the sun has been done! How am I going to find a story? But I agreed to do it.

Fast forward to January of 2009 at the inauguration of Barack Obama in Washington D.C. My brother lives outside D.C., so we had a party at his house. There were two ladies there from New Orleans. So, we got to talking with these ladies and I explained, "I'm supposed to do a story down there, something related to housing that people don't know about. What do people outside New Orleans not know about what's happening down there?" The ladies said, "Oh, well the banks started taking people's insurance money. If you have a house, and you have a mortgage, you have to have insurance, and in many cases the banks are taking people's insurance money and using it to pay off the mortgage, which is a double-edged sword. Now you own the house free and clear but you can't afford to fix it. It's putting a lot of people in a really bad position because they can't afford to fix their home, so they're basically being forced to pay rent some place and keep a house they can't fix."

So, I went down there and talked to all these organizations, to everybody under the sun, trying to put this story together. I met this young lady named Kisa, and she said, "Yes, this is what happened to me. The bank took my insurance money." It turned out that by doing that [paying off your mort-

gage with your insurance money] voluntarily, you cut yourself off from some federal disaster aid that you otherwise would have been eligible to receive. In cases like Kisa's, where she agreed voluntarily to pay off the loan, she was eligible to receive some aid. So she got only about $50,000 to fix the house that she had just bought 6 weeks before Katrina. That was not enough money to fix the house. So she had to live with relatives who live 90 miles north of New Orleans. She has five kids. She and her husband had to commute to New Orleans for work and the kids' schools. When I met her in 2009, they had been doing this already for four years.

I began collecting all the documents and trying to figure out what's going on. What became apparent is that the banks didn't do anything illegal. It is in your mortgage document. If you own a house you have to have insurance. So what ended up happening was, the bank, in her case, just took the money and paid out the mortgage and she was left holding a house she couldn't afford to fix.

It took two and a half years to get Kisa's story out. She had been trying everything to get her house fixed and nothing worked. We documented her entire story and it was published in December of 2011. Just days after the story ran, her house was demolished, because it was in danger of falling. She had tried everything: she bought materials to fix the house and people broke into the house and stole all of the materials. They even stole the rusty tub that had been sitting in water for months. It was very tragic. She went to all the organizations: the Red Cross, Salvation Army, everywhere. And, every time she would go to talk to somebody, they would basically shut the door in her face.

So when that story was published, there was an organization in New Orleans called the Saint Bernard Project, a group that helps rebuild homes with volunteer labor. The founder of the Project sent me an email and said, "Man, what a great story this is! There are so many people that are having this problem. Thank you so much for doing the story and can you put me in touch with Kisa? Let me see if I can help her."

In the end, they [Saint Bernard] couldn't help her. But, NABJ had our national convention in New Orleans that year, so I mentioned this fact to the Mayor of New Orleans when I was down there shooting video, and he told us to have Kisa call his office. What they said was because she was a property owner, [she was eligible for] a program called Project Home Again, which was started by the CEO of Barnes & Noble bookstores. He collected a million dollars of his own money into a non-profit with the intention to help people get homes. The Project would buy dilapidated properties and rebuild them on the site. So July 20, 2012, seven years to the day that Kisa moved into her house before Katrina, she did the closing and got the keys to the new house. Again, you're not supposed to get emotionally involved in the story, but I got involved because I wanted to help this lady who had tried so hard to help herself.

That's what being a journalist is: you can speak for people who can't speak for themselves. It's been hard for me to separate the help I provide other people from my life in general because, to me, helping Kisa get a home, that is success. To me, writing stories that prompt the district attorney and the police department to fully investigate Chauncey Bailey's murder to the point where they actually go and arrest all the people who were involved, that's success. When you talk about the important work you've done as a journalist, those two stories were the most important I've done.

On the Union side, when I got out of the service, I was working for ManPower, and they would send me to various jobs. For the most part they were non-union jobs, and I didn't know the difference between union and non-union, but I know that in some of the places I went to work, I didn't like it. I mean, they basically treated people very poorly, and it was like, "If you don't like it, leave."

So when I got the job at KCBS, eventually I became a shop steward for AFTRA, basically by default. I was the new guy, and my colleagues didn't want to do it and they told me I was gonna be shop steward! Slowly, I began to realize the power of somebody who will advocate on your behalf, because, being the shop steward, I sat in on negotiations, I helped to establish policies, I helped establish contracts, and I also sat on the board of our local chapter in San Francisco. I started to get a bigger view of labor and what labor really does, and I'm convinced that unions are a great help to the American people. We have a slogan that we say, sometimes in jest, but it really is true. We say, "Unions, the People Who Brought You the Weekend." You gotta remember, between the 19th and 20th centuries the unions were born because the working conditions were so poor that somebody had to stand up for the workers, and that's what the unions did.

When you said you were doing the book about labor, to me that is very important. AFTRA and SAG-AFTRA are so important. Labor has been under attack in this country for the last thirty years. The number of people working in labor unions has dropped dramatically. I talked to students at California State University, Northridge, and one of the things I asked was, "How many people here know what a labor union is?" And a lot of them didn't know. And, "So how many have you seen what happened in Wisconsin with the unions?" People raised their hands. So I said, "What is it all about?" They didn't really have a good answer except because unions charge so much money that the cities and counties are going bankrupt. O.K., that's what the rhetoric is: that unions charge so much money. But unions were put in place to protect the workers. Unions make sure that you have a livable wage, that you have benefits. Now, do union workers make more than a lot of other folks? Yes, they do. Why is that? Because the unions fight for you. They advocate on your behalf, and they want to make sure that if you are doing this job that you are being paid fairly for it.

You know, labor has been criminalized in the eyes of many Americans - because of work rules, because you're paying too much money, you can't fire them, you have all these protections and stuff. That's not the problem. And that's something that, when I talk to young people, I talk about being in SAG-AFTRA and what it had meant to me, in having affordable benefits. With SAG-AFTRA I have a pension, and my health and my retirement benefits come through the union too. You don't find many companies doing that now. And what I love about AFTRA and SAG- AFTRA, is that my benefits are portable. If I leave my job at KCBS to go across the street and work at another station, with a SAG-AFTRA contract my benefits go with me, my health insurance goes with me, my pension goes with me. And if I have to go work at a place that is not union, because I'm now vested in my pension, I don't lose it. If I don't work another day in my life, I still get my pension, so that's one thing—financial security.

Being at KCBS, when I first started, there I was young and didn't really understand some of the benefits I had, so I didn't even invest in my 401-K 'till I had been at the company nine years. But now, along with my union pension, I get a pension plan, I get a 401-K. So, I'm not going to be rich by any means, but when I retire, because I was in a labor union, and because I got the advice to take advantage of all these things, I'm going to be much better off than somebody who was not in a union.

In my NABJ life, as national president, I'm out there advocating for our members. One of my big goals is to make the media industry more diverse, more reflective of the American scene of the United States. If you look at media companies now, and I do, an annual report that looks at the diversity of television newsrooms' management, it's about twelve percent of managers in media companies are people of color. Thirty-five percent of the country is diverse, but that is not reflected in the media companies. So, for me, success is when I go talk to a news director about lack of diversity and they say, "Well, do you know anybody I can hire?" If I give them a name of somebody that I know, and they hire that person, it gives our members an opportunity that they otherwise would not have had. To me that is success.

I feel successful as an individual through my work life, and I have a hard time separating that from my personal. If you ask my wife, she would say I would be more successful if I did less volunteer work and made more money, and that is something I would like to be able to do. When I was at CBS, that was a six figure job. I was a suit, and I would love to have a job like that again, to have the financial security. Because my wife makes more money than I do, I would like to bring more money home to support us. But, at the same time, she understands how important my volunteer work is; being able to help people. And

truth be told, even when I go work at the radio station - I still work there because our expenses are relatively low - I don't have to work full time.

If I had a full time job that includes things I like to do, helping people, I'd be right there. That's why the job at CBS, when I worked corporate HR, was so important. Here I am, Director of Diversity, my job was to identify candidates for our company - diverse candidates. It was to present people with opportunity. To me that is important. So, I think it's important when you start talking about success.

You know, on the personal front I feel I am very successful. I have a loving wife, I have a son, he has a job, he is working. I am in a position where I can help my family out. I could be more successful if I made more money, but you know, money isn't everything. You have to have a personal life that you feel comfortable with, and there's a lot of people out there making a lot of money who are very unhappy, and I don't want to be like that. I was kind of like that at the radio station. Toward the end of my career, I was working corporate HR, I was making good money but I wasn't very happy. I just wasn't. I am happy now - much happier. Think about it: If I had not been on staff at the radio station all these years, I would not have been part of the Chauncey Bailey project; I would have never met Kisa and done that story. And to me, when you talk about the important work you've done as a journalist, those two stories were the most important I've done.

SAG-AFTRA

w

I intensely like to help people, that's why being a journalist was so important, because as a journalist you help people. You provide information. You educate, and that's something that was very important to me. **You can speak for people who can't speak for themselves.**

Tony Clark

Major League Baseball Player, Retired

Executive Director, Major League Baseball Players Association

I would describe myself as a God-fearing husband and father, who happened to play professional baseball. Sports has been such a huge part of my life. I've truly come to appreciate the life lessons that playing organized team sports teach you. I am married with three kids. I've been married almost twenty years. My wife and I met in college. She was a basketball player. I was in college playing basketball despite having been drafted to play baseball out of high school. So our entire family has been involved in sports, and a whole lot of what we do is not just enjoying sports, but using sports as an opportunity to give back to our community. It's been a blessing.

Discipline, respect, and hard work are three things that have always resonated with me through sports. My Dad was a disciplinarian, and although as a youngster I didn't appreciate it, I came to realize that when you are striving to make the most of whatever talents you have, whether they're athletically inclined or not, the fact is that you will only realize that potential if you are disciplined in your approach and your commitment and if you are willing to work diligently to maximize that potential. Sports has the ability to do all of those things if you are committed to them, in much the same way as any other career would provide that opportunity. But, the realization is that in team sports you have the opportunity to affect positively the team that you are with. I heard it early, but it really didn't settle in

until later, that I realized I had some decisions to make. I needed to be disciplined and I was going to be respectful, and I was going to put in the time and the hard work to get to where I felt like I could get to. And if I didn't, I only had myself to blame. I believe it is the sole reason why I was able to have some level of success with what I did. I was never the most gifted. I was never the fastest. I was never the strongest.

I thought basketball was going to be the sport that I was going to play collegiately and/or professionally. I didn't think it was going to be baseball. I signed a national letter of intent to play basketball at the University of Arizona. Then, in the draft the summer of 1990, I was drafted by the Detroit Tigers to play baseball despite my insistence to them that I was going to school and playing basketball. I was All American in basketball and I was All American in baseball. So I had some opportunities there, but my heart at the time still said basketball. So I was able to go to school, and I worked out an arrangement where I played basketball during the school year. And then, during the summer, I would go play Minor League Baseball. I had a three year window by which to determine exactly what it was I wanted to do.

Unfortunately, my freshman year at basketball, I blew out my back and had surgery. I wasn't able to play baseball that summer as I rehabbed. Rather than going back to school, realizing that I never was

51

the same following my back surgery, I decided to try to play baseball full time. I had some success: moved through the system, my back held up, I was forced to grow up. There were times where I looked at myself in the mirror and realized that I had to step up, or otherwise, I was going to be on the outside looking in. By the end of '95, I got my first in to the Major Leagues.

It was the realization of a dream. Once I realized that [basketball] wasn't going to be in the cards, my focus shifted. You know, for the first few years I used to always joke that I was a basketball player in a baseball uniform because I hadn't spent the amount of time honing my craft the way others had at my age. So, by the time I got to the Big Leagues in '95, it was the realization of a dream. And, I will never forget one of the first things I was told when I got there by Al Trammell, who was the shortstop for the Detroit Tigers at that time. He congratulated me on making it to the Big Leagues, then told me that the easy part was done, the hard part was staying. I didn't quite grasp what he was telling me, at least not until the next year.

So I finished out the year in '95 in the Big Leagues and then the next year, I started the season back out in triple A and I struggled a lot. Now, by this time, I was married and had a daughter. I recall in May of '96 hitting 116 or something at the time, making a thousand dollars a month, realizing that if I didn't improve my situation, this dream that was baseball could come to a halt very quickly. I'll never forget sitting in the kitchen, watching my wife feed our daughter, realizing that this is much bigger than me and I've gotta figure it out. So my commitment changed at that point, and a month later, having done a complete 180 with respect to how I was playing, got called back up to the Big Leagues and never went

down again. I was very fortunate at that point in time to get back on track and call it a career fifteen seasons later.

I think baseball is very unique in the challenges that the game itself presents. Baseball's season is longer than any other sport, and in large part it is the only sport where if you are a position player, if you fail seventy percent of the time, you are still considered elite at what you do and that, in and of itself, suggests a mental grind, a mental challenge that is different than in a lot of other industries. You play every day and the physical and emotional roller coaster you're gonna find yourself on is one that can run you out of the game or is one that, if you learn how to manage it, transcends the game itself. Very few games, very few situations can suggest that if you do everything correct you still may have nothing to show for it. And, the challenge is every day. The best part about our game is that you play every day, and the worst thing about our game is that you play every day. So, if you had an O for 4, you have an opportunity the next day to come back and go 4 for 4. If you're not careful, the emotional and the psychological roller coaster that you can get on, despite doing everything right, can be enormous.

So, I could go 0 for 8 in two games, we lose both games, even though I did everything I could possibly do to help us win. I stop at a gas station to fill up my tank and I get bombarded by baseball fans who aren't happy that we haven't won. So you have a responsibility to your teammates, with the understanding that if you don't perform, you will lose your job, all the while realizing that your family is in the stands hearing the ridicule that you may be getting. As you go out in public, you also may be facing ridicule on any number of levels. All the while you are doing anything you can possibly do to put yourself and your team in the position to be successful. I had a buddy of mine at one point in time offer me this advice: Control the controllables. Most players that are able to control the controllables and keep everything in perspective oftentimes realize that success. But, it becomes a very difficult thing to manage over the long haul. And, it's an emotional roller coaster. You'll see guys throw bats, slam helmets in disgust, trying to control those emotions that come out at any given time. But, the guys that are able to at least stay somewhat even-keeled are the guys that tend to end up exactly where they should at the end of the year with respect to the contributions they're able to make.

So how did I feel when I was done? I knew I was done because my body was falling apart. I knew I physically couldn't do it anymore. So I proceeded to involve myself in a number of different things. I had some coaching opportunities, I had some managing opportunities, I had some offers to do some work with Clubs. I did some radio, I did some TV, so my experiences thereafter really ran the gamut, and I was very, very, very fortunate that I had some opportunities. More often than not, players don't know what's going to happen next and they don't have those opportunities.

Inevitably, after being out of the game for about eight months and having tried my hand at any number of things, I needed to make a decision as to what was going to be next. After speaking with the Player's Association's Executive Director, I realized that taking a position with the Player's Association gave me an opportunity to stay connected with our active, inactive, and retired players, as well as the next grouping of players that come into the game. It gives me an opportunity to try and support, protect, equip, educate, challenge, and be a part of the lives of what is a very special fraternity of guys. I prayed about it for months and woke up one morning and told my wife I think I know what I'm supposed to do. And when I told her it was to take the position with the Player's Association, she laughed and told me that she could have told me that months ago. She knew where my heart was and she knew the challenges that were going to be this job and the realization that if I was going to truly try to have an impact on our guys, this was the best place for me

*....you're excited to be in the position where the game is on the line and if you don't come through, everybody's going to point the finger at you, but if you do come through, the jubilation, the respect that you feel like you've earned is off the charts. So that's the flip side to everything I just articulated with respect to pressure...***the realization that pressure breaks glass but pressure makes diamonds.** *That is the start and the finish. That is the alpha and the omega of a day in the life of a professional athlete.*

Baseball's season is longer than any other sport, and in large part it is the only sport where if you are a position player, if you fail seventy percent of the time, you are still considered elite at what you do and that, in and of itself, suggests a mental grind, a mental challenge that is different than in a lot of other industries. You play every day and the physical and emotional roller coaster you're gonna find yourself on is one that can run you out of the game or is one that, **if you learn how to manage it, transcends the game itself.**

to do it.

It has been an absolute blessing to be able to engage the guys, to support the guys and what I pray is better equip the guys for not just their time as players, but for the time that [they] won't be active players, and can try to have that positive impact on our fraternity for as long as the guys are willing to allow me to have it.

The Players Services Department is responsible for educating and communicating with every player that's in a major league uniform or on a major league forty-man roster. We make sure that their rights, as part of the collective bargaining agreement, are being adhered to. That, in a day-to-day process, is any number of things. Our collective bargaining agreement is a couple hundred pages, and just about every guideline, every rule that is in that collectively bargained agreement, a player has lost money for, has lost their job for, has lost their career for, has sacrificed in order that the group after them had it better than they did. So, when I say protected rights collectively, it could be entitlements, it could be allowances, it could be travel reimbursements. It could be playing game day issues or con-

cerns that need to be addressed. Individually, it means providing support with respect to their contract, with respect to any personal challenges that they may have. End of season, off season, we're simply providing protections for them and making sure that they understand what it means to be a Major League ballplayer and all the inherent rights that come with it.

In 1966 Marvin Miller was our first Executive Director. He began the Players Association in an effort to provide certain rights that any employee should have. His focus and commitment were to developing a pension for players. It was putting forth a structure, a support mechanism, a collectively bargained agreement that showed players how special they were in the grand scheme of things and how that "specialness" meant that they should have certain rights—more rights than they had been led to believe. So Marvin Miller created a union in an effort to have players realize their value and to collectively bargain the guidelines and the rules under which they were going to play, and provide an overarching support in order to protect those rights going forward. Anyway, it was fraught with challenges: work stoppages, strikes. You know, you go from a player in 1966 making six thousand dollars, to having the first increase just because collectively there was a tremendous amount of value in the guys being represented as a union as opposed to an individual.

While I was in the Minor Leagues, I had an opportunity to go to Cooperstown to visit the Baseball Hall of Fame. There, I realized the history that I had an opportunity to be a part of; both the Major League Baseball history and the Negro League history before the leagues were integrated, before Jackie Robinson and Larry Doby. At that time, I knew how fortunate I was to have the opportunity to do what I was doing. After my second year in the Big Leagues, I decided to go to an executive board meeting. I wanted to go to that Executive Board Meeting not because I knew a whole lot about the Union, but because I wanted to learn more about what was happening, what was being negotiated, what was being talked about, whether or not I could offer input into the guidelines and rules by which my career were going to be governed.

I knew, even if I was fortunate, my career was going to be short, and I didn't want to be on the outside looking in. So I got involved, and once I got involved, I started to learn more about the Union itself. And then I began to realize how important my role as a player rep was in representing my team, my club, and that eventually morphed into representing my League, the American League at the time. And then that developed into being someone who was responsible as an active player for players across both leagues. So, my understanding and appreciation for the union grew as I got involved, but initially it wasn't. I just wanted to be involved in having a voice, but, in doing so, I became a true union member.

I have a privilege and an opportunity to be doing what I am doing right now, and I simply pray that that opportunity extends itself for years down the road, because, if it does, that means that I'm doing what I should be doing in support of the guys. The guys appreciate what it is that I am doing, and when the smoke clears, whenever that happens to be, my only prayer is that I did everything I could possibly [do] in support of the guys. If it is five years down the road, then it's five years down the road. If you and I communicate twenty years from now and I'm wrapping up my involvement with the Players' Association, I would color myself tremendously fortunate. My prayer is real simple: that I remain available for whatever the Lord would have me do, and it appears He has me doing what I am doing right now, and I will take that for as long as I can do it.

Success to me isn't monetary. Success to me isn't accolades or fame. Success for me is loving my wife, protecting, equipping and loving my kids, and being the best father, the best husband, the best teammate, the best union official that I could possibly be. If I can say all of that - that I left nothing to chance, I left nothing on the table, that I did everything I could possibly do - I'll be successful. You know, I tell my kids all the time it's not about making the most money or playing at the high level or having the best job. It's about taking whatever gifts and experiences you have and making the most of them: providing support for the person who is coming after you, offering the experiences that you had in an effort to, Lord willing, make better versions of you. I don't' need articles to be written, I don't need anything that would suggest that I need to be in the forefront of anything. But if somebody says, "He made a difference in my life," I'm gold.

Jeryl Davis

Third Grade Teacher, Cooper City, Florida
Broward Teachers Union, American Federation of Teachers (AFT)
National Education Association (NEA)

How do I define myself? If I define myself by thinking about people who I love the most, and who make the biggest difference in my life. I would define myself as a mom, a wife and partner, and friend. Then I would define myself as a daughter and a sister.

As a teacher, I would define myself as having a strong belief in fairness. I try to run my class that way. I think the rules need to be clearly defined and they need to be applied evenly. Kids need to know that the playing field is even. That's what I believe in life, too. I try to live my life in a way that's moral and kind and respectful. We have these values in America where we say people can pull themselves up by their bootstraps and that we all get this equal opportunity, but that's not true, and it's not fair. Some people come to society with a lot more than others, yet we chose to pretend like that doesn't exist. Some people are able buy into great communities, where their kids have a great education, and some people can't. When it's said that everyone has a fair opportunity, I don't believe it. So, I guess the most important thing I believe is in fairness.

Every year the students make up classroom rules, things like, raise your hand when you're talking, push your chairs in, and walk when you're in school. I only have one rule and that's to be respectful and kind. If you follow that one rule, then everything else falls into place. I think that should you look at your life and the things you do and you ask yourself, "Am I being respectful? Am I being kind?" If you do that, then things are going to come out for the best.

Well, we've established that I'm a teacher: I'm a 3rd grade teacher. So, what do I do? Well, I hang out with these little people all day long. I'm constantly aware that I'm supposed to teach them and that they're supposed to master many concepts before they leave me. I'm charged with making sure that the students gain knowledge and that they make progress. In the end, they should walk away a little smarter than when they came to me, and that's important.

I also think it's important that students think about what it means to be good citizens. I try to show the kids what tolerance means. My team and I used to do this big project with the homeless. We started [the project] after some homeless men were beaten up by boys. They beat a man to death. We started doing lunches for the homeless. It was just a small group of people. We read this book called, "Somebody Loves You." It's a book about a man who didn't feel cared for or loved, and somebody sends him a Valentine card, which made a big difference in his life. So we had the kids write notes to some of the homeless. One of the kids wrote, "Somebody cares about you and someone's thinking about you and someone wants you to be safe." And that to me was success, like, they got it; they understood where we were coming from. The person who got the card was really touched. This story somewhat describes who I am as a teacher.

I think it's important to greet every child at the door. I ask about their evening, or games that they played. Then I start by summarizing the day. I talk about what to expect that day. If there's a writing activity that I want them to work on, I will say, "I want you to think about this writing piece." I think it's important that students know what their day is going to look like. I also try to set time limits. I might say, "Okay, this is what we're working on and you need to be done before recess." This helps students begin to understand that deadlines are important and that they need to get the assignment done. It also helps them to begin to manage their time. If you give them deadlines it helps them. They begin to problem solve. I also try to read to them every day. At any given moment there might be some kind of problem that's going on in school or class. Just recently we had to have a class meeting. Two little girls who were used to getting their way were having these huge fights with each other. The other kids started taking sides in the fights and they started being mean to each other. So we had to have a class meeting about how to be part of a family and how to know when to not get involved in other people's arguments. I

thought this was because the girls needed to solve the problem themselves. So that might be part of our day.

I feel good when I'm just working with kids. I can't say, "Oh well, this kid is having trouble reading and his parents are not helping him at home. If they help him at home he would do so much better." That's true, but not all parents can do that. Not all parents can help their kids at home. There are parents who are part of the working poor. There are parents who send their kids to school sick because they can't take off work because they don't have sick leave. So, I try to remember that there are kids who come to us with everything, and there are kids who come to us with a lot of love and maybe nothing else. These children's parents are struggling for the things that they give them. So, that being said, I try to take the kids from where they are and move them as far as I can. I have high expectations for all kids. The parents of my students are great. Most parents want to work with me and talk to me about their kids. I think they feel good about the education that I'm giving their kids.

So, that sounds good, right? But it's not easy. It's not easy at all. Kids come to us in poverty. They do. They come to us with families who are struggling every day, and they come to us hungry and they come to us with lack of sleep and they come to us from parents with bad parenting skills and they come to us unhealthy. We can't just all of a sudden decide that when they step into our door all students are equal and that they're all going to do the same academically. But that's what the government expects. When you talk about education, even our president has decided that teachers should now be held accountable for all the world's woes even though he can't solve the problems himself. And he has the power of the

> *We can't just all of a sudden decide that when they step into our door all students are equal and that they're all going to do the same academically. But that's what the government expects. When you talk about education,* **even our president has decided that teachers should now be held accountable for all the world's woes even though he can't solve the problems himself.** *And he has the power of the Presidency and the money behind him.*

Presidency and the money behind him.

You know there's this Florida state formula that tells how much growth a student needs to have at the end of the academic year. It's based on the state's test scores. If the child doesn't meet the formula's expectation, then it's the teacher's fault. That's extremely difficult to accept. Even though I have high expectations for students and I, too, expect each child to make a year's worth of growth, my formula is not the same as the state's formula. In fact, I don't understand the state's formula at all. I don't know where the bar is. There are a lot of things that make my job harder, particularly in Florida. We're at the bottom of how much we pay for each child's education. We have the class size amendment that our district is consistently and deliberately choosing to ignore. There is lack of funding. There is lack of time. There's this complete lack of sincerity. The Florida state government is in charge of education and should want all kids to succeed. Except during this last term in session, they just left Medicaid on the table, decided not to vote on it. Yet kids come to us needing healthcare. They need to be healthy to learn.

What's horrible about my job, the really bad part, is the lack of thoughtful solutions on how to make education better. There is this idea that somehow, in education, teachers are responsible for fixing complex, deep problems like obesity and poverty. As teachers we really want to do our part and we definitely want to be part of the solution, but again, we can't do it alone.

What bothers me is that my daughter Leah won't go into teaching. She'd be a great teacher. She has a lot to offer students. But she's not going to do it and that worries me. We're not attracting good people to our field because young people see that when you go into education it takes you a lifetime to make a decent living. I worry that at some point we're going to have a shortage of teachers.

I'm a union girl: my husband works for the union, my dad was a union man. My Dad used to say, "If it's this bad with the union, I don't want to see it without it." I know that there are people who say things like, "The union better get me a contract," and, "The union better tell those principals that they can't do this or that." There is this idea that the union is this outside entity that's going to come in and fix all our problems. I never saw it that way and my Dad never did either. He stood with the union and thought that they were doing the best that they could to stop things from getting worse. So in some ways, I came to the union with the same thought. The union does the best that it can. Sometimes it's going to fix problems and sometimes it's not. But, overall, I like this idea that there's collective bargaining, that there are people who are out there who have my interests and that listen to me. I like that we come together and speak in one voice.

But in reality I know that that's not necessarily true all the time. I don't always feel like my voice is heard through my union. I teach in elementary school and I don't always feel like my voice is heard through the voices of middle school and high school teachers. I feel like I'm part of one big collective that's too big at times, and that some of us have different viewpoints. Overall, they know that education is important and that we need to fight to fix the problems. Union staff understand that we must have good quality teachers and good quality pay, [but] my local union is a mess at times. There was a time in the union when there wasn't a sense of welcoming or a sense that it was okay to call if you had a question. I heard our last president tell a woman during a training session to sit down and shut up. He told a member that! Of course the member left training and probably the union too. I would have.

So I didn't always have good feelings about my Local. But there are times when I think my local is doing quite well. I like the union rep that I deal with: he's receptive; he helps me solve problems and comes out and talks to members; he always accepts my calls, and he's there when I need him. The union also started this really good member-training program where members come in and train the teaching staff. It is excellent. They have two great women who came out and talked to our staff about how to understand the evaluation system.

I think that our union is moving into a better place. They're moving towards doing more training and talking about how to be more proactive in getting other members involved. We have a president. So, we are

When I retire I want to visit the five oceans. I've already been to two. I want to hang out with [my husband] Dale. We're going to hang out on the beach. He's going to grow a ponytail and I'm going to wear a funky hat. I'll read a lot. Hopefully my daughter will have some grandbabies for us by then. I could hang out with her and the babies. **I could also tell you that I'd do lots of yoga, but I'd be lying if I said that.**

in a transition stage, but I like what they've done so far.

I do like the FEA: I love going to rallies, I love protests, I love picket lines because it just feels like there are so many people that agree with me. I always like when people see things my way. There's also this sense of unity and this sense of group righteous indignation. When the governor took out 3% of salary for our pensions, the FEA fought it. They filed a lawsuit. They gave my feelings of indignation a voice. They speak for me and I like that. The FEA went to court over the evaluation system as well. Even though we haven't been successful in all of these cases, there's still someone saying this is wrong and we're going to do something about it, as opposed to just feeling like we're helpless and frustrated all the time. I'm also grateful that there is contract language that addresses my job responsibilities. I had a good working relationship with my past principal and so far I have a decent working relationship with my new principal. But it does make a difference when you have contract language. The rules need to be clear and everyone needs to know what they are. That's another thing I think is important about the union.

When I retire I want to visit the five oceans. I've already been to two. I want to hang out with [my husband] Dale. We're going to hang out on the beach. He's going to grow a ponytail and I'm going to wear a funky hat. I'll read a lot. Hopefully my daughter will have some grandbabies for us by then. I could hang out with her and the babies. I could also tell you that I'd do lots of yoga, but I'd be lying if I said that.

Dale and I have a good marriage. Part of it is because we work really hard and we have enough stress in our life professionally that it's really good to be home with no stress and no drama - we can just chill and relax. We value that part of our lives. We do a lot of stuff together. We go to the opera, we go to the orchestra, and we travel. So, to summarize, I hope to hang out with my husband, my daughter and future grandbabies when I retire.

What is success? I have high expectations for kids. As a teacher, I hope to define success as students not only coming away knowing more than when they came to me, but that they also reached their full potential. So, if they know more and if they hopefully take away what it means to be a good citizen, and what it means to be kind and respectful, then I have been successful. I know that kids get a lot of this from their parents but they spend many of their waking hours with me. I feel that I need to play a role in their development and I need to help them become good people who are successful in life. My personal goal in life is to continue to be happy. That's success as well, I think.

Finally, I believe that working in education is hard, but all teachers want to do a good job, and most of us do.

Arturo Delgado

Field Representative Vice President, Oklahoma City, Oklahoma
Laborers International Union of North America, LIUNA Local 107

My name is Arturo Delgado. I'm a father, husband, brother, son. I'm a person that likes to achieve goals. I like challenges. I like to show pride in my work. I like to spend time with my family. Family is very important for me. There are times where work does override family and you just have to stop and say, "It's family time." I describe myself as a person that, if you tell me I can't do something, I'm gonna work harder to prove to you that I can and to prove to myself. I also would describe myself as a good member of society. I try to get involved with family on the community side even though there's not always enough time to do so.

I come from a big family. I'm the youngest of five and I also come from an immigrant family. We came from Mexico at a young age and we've learned to adapt to the American way and keep our roots as well, integrating that with our kids. I would just describe myself as a person that wants to work to the top. I don't want anything given to me. I want to prove to myself that I'm worthy of being at the top when I get there. I am honored to work for and represent blue collar members of our union in the state of Oklahoma. Part of my duty is to represent the members, go out in the field, make sure that they don't need anything, make sure their insurance is up to date, make

sure that superintendents are not in need of any type of certification for our members. Another part of my job is to make sure we screen new members; make sure they have the right skills. A lot of applicants come in and say they know everything but once you put them on the job, they don't have nearly the experience they told you they have. If the worker knows more pertaining to another craft, then I'm not going to spend as much time with that person, but if it's more of what we do then I'm going to dig in and find out, so when a contractor asks for the right person, I have that. I am responsible for presenting quality workers to the job site and when someone comes in with flip-flops, or shorts, or different attire, it already loses my interest in that person, because they're not ready to work. They're just looking for an application. We are very diverse. When I mean diverse I mean in all categories; ages, genders, race. It does not matter. We don't judge people by their age or the color of their skin. What I do is I screen to make sure they have skills.

My job is very diverse in what I do. What I like to do is take care of the paperwork before the laborers get on the job site. So, a lot of the time, normal hours are from 8 to 4:30. I hardly ever leave the office before 6. I don't want people to come all the way to the office to fill out paperwork, especially if I know they live in a certain area of the

neighborhood. I'll just meet them some-where neutral. So they don't have to drive this way and I don't have to wait in the of-fice. Supervisors can be really busy and have a lot of stuff going on. They want someone they can depend on. "Take care of that for me" and it's done. No questions asked, no hesitation, no "I'll do it in a minute."

I'm the person that sits at a desk and helps my members; I work for them. They are the union. They are the organization and I am a part of the organization. They are what makes us a whole. Sometimes union members don't understand that. You sit 'em down and you kind of grab their shoulders

and shake them and say, "If you're not here, I'm not here. You make us who we are to-day."

We are the guy next door, the lady that lives down the street, the single mother that's working her butt off. A lot of people don't realize that. They say, "The union; the big bosses." The big bosses are not the guys that sit behind the desk. The people who are in the field, physically working, are the people we work for so they are the union.

I feel really good about what I do. I'm honored. I help people that sometimes don't have that guidance. I didn't have that guidance. I'm a part of this organization. I like to guide the people that come in here. I like to empower them with knowledge. I like to explain to them why they should take advantage of the classes. Some people don't like to get involved in the political stages, but we have to. I can look back two years ago and say, "Wow. I didn't know anything about this!" and I didn't know any of this and now I'm preaching it to my members. "You've got to take advantage of this. The union is here. We're gonna do this education. We're gonna do this training so you can better work on the job. This is your driver's license to be on the job sites. This is what's gonna make you more valuable" and I'm just happy to be a part of it because I'm helping the guy who needs the help. I'm helping the guy who doesn't know where to go, where to turn. I know that now and that's why I love what I do.

Every now and then we all get our little bumps along the road of life. You need somebody there to help you and sometimes a lot of people don't have no one there to help them. When I was young I came across a couple of those times in my life and someone was there to help me. It's not just, shake your hand, let's take your dues and join the meeting and I'll talk to you later. We get involved with them on a personal level. We just recently had a member that was a green card holder and he registered to become a citizen. He did his test, he went through the process, he filed with the state and he asked us to accompany him and his family. That was actually one of the privileged ones; I got to attend the ceremony. He thought of us as family.

We want our union members to be a part of what we do on a daily basis. We go to these political functions and we team up with lots of organizations like the United Way or other nonprofit organizations that help people.

I'm 31 years old. Honestly, I never thought about retirement. I'm still wanting to achieve a lot of things in life and in my job and I never thought about it. I know the pension is there and growing, but I never actually thought about it. My parents always taught me to go out there and do the best you can and work your butt off. Be proud of what you do. I just never thought about retiring to be honest. I know maybe something will come to me one day, but maybe it won't. I'll be so involved in helping people at this union, that the day I retire is the day you spiritually do die. I don't see myself pulling out at sixty-five or sixty-two and saying, "OK. It's time to go do this."

I want to take my kids and show them places that I've gone to since I've become a part of this union. Being a part of this union has taken me to different parts of the United States that I've never been to and I don't think I would've gone. We go through different trainings and different functions and I've been blessed where I can be traveling, so I want to be able to take my kids too.

I am the father of three girls. They are two years apart. They are 9, 11, and 13. I'm married to a wonderful, wonderful, wonderful lady; Carolina. She's on the same page with me as far as the value of unions.

My father and my brothers are all construction oriented workers so that's where I always thought I needed to be. As soon as I turned eighteen, I went into construction and hit the first union job site. When this union representative job was offered to me, I was scared of it, I didn't think I could do it. I didn't feel I had the drive and I was talked into it. Then, I'd seen the value. I'd seen I needed to help the community. I'd seen where I could do good work and I took it. I learned. Hell, when I first started I even lost some weight. I was so stressed out, making sure I got everything right. It's four and a

When this union representative job was offered to me, I was scared of it. *I didn't think I could do it. I didn't feel I had the drive and I was talked into it. Then, I'd seen the value. I'd seen I needed to help the community. I'd seen where I could do good work and I took it. I learned. Hell, when I first started I even lost some weight, I was so stressed out, making sure I got everything right. It's four and a half years later and currently I'm the vice president of this Local, very involved with the community and with our members.*

half years later and currently I'm the vice president of this Local, very involved with the community and with our members.

Everyday I wake up and I'm ready to hit the streets and when I say streets I mean my job site, I always look at it like, "How would I like to be treated?". You'd be surprised how many members call me late at night with various questions like "Does our insurance do this? My kid just fell out of a tree! What hospital do I go to?" It's kind of a 24/7 job in a way. It could be very easy for me to get to the house on Friday and turn off the phone, and pick it up Monday morning, but it's not me. It's not who I am. I feel like I owe our membership something. It's hard to describe. I feel like I work for them and I gotta do everything in my power to help them.

We're just average Joe's...showing the world who we are. We're people that live down the street. We do work for a living. We have families. We have kids. We have bills. We're just part of the community. We do volunteer work in the community. We're not the union bosses that people portray us as.

I got involved more in politics. When I realized politics is a big part of unions, we don't necessarily help elect democrats or republicans, we look at politicians that will help the working man tomorrow. They are mostly democrats. I have actually got involved at the precinct level. I am a precinct officer and I am currently running for Oklahoma County Vice Chair position. It's not a big campaign thing. My goal is to get more involved in highlighting the laborer's union and what we're doing to help candidates. So, possibly in the future, they can look out for the working man. And possibly we can get more work done in the future once we educate them about what the unions are doing, how we do a training, how we put people of the community back to work in their own community after they've been trained and certified and so on.

I'm actually kind of thrilled. It's a volunteer position. It's a non-paid position but the way I look at it is, I've already been involved in a lot of ways. We're already doing a lot of leg work. We're puttin' boots on the ground. We've got members putting out signs. We've got members putting out literature. I'm not trying to build a platform to become a politician in the future. I'm just

I just want to overall have (my children) be able to see everything. I don't want them to have iPads and an iPhone and they never know about the work that made them. I don't want them to think that Daddy just gives them all this stuff. I want them to know where it starts and what you need to do to achieve goals, and to appreciate it once you reach those goals. So, I want them to value life. **I want them to value the common worker, the work that goes into the average day, whether it be in a restaurant or any type of facility with labor.**

trying to gain more work for my membership here. That's my ultimate thing here.

We have been working with a lot of politicians in the last year. Today is the election for city council and we have been working with the candidate that is really looking to help put his community back to work. We fall under his ward, and he's looked at our apprenticeship stuff, he likes the idea of the union helping the community, training and certifying and putting people back to work, hiring locally instead of bringing in out of state companies. I've learned some stuff and I just feel like, "You know what? This is the avenue that we need to take." I figure this is one small step I can take. If it's gonna help my membership, then I will do it, even though it's a voluntary position. Even though it's a non-paying position, I still wanna do it to help the membership. The democratic party is very enthusiastic. They kind of received me and I have a lot of supporters. I think being that I come from a labor background. Hispanics did make a difference in this past presidential election. So, I think it's a wake up for our community to say, "Hey, you can make a difference." Then, if I can do this for a few people in

Oklahoma City, then I'm doing my part.

I am not worried. My family's very supportive. My wife understands the labor movement. She's all for it. She knows that I've gotta keep it moving, so when she can't come along with the girls, they're very supportive. When they can come, when they're not doing any church activities, then the whole family comes along and we turn it into a family function. I did that for a purpose. I want to educate my young girls on; "These are the grassroots. This is what you gotta do if you ever want to be involved in politics when you grow up, when you get an education. This is where it's at. It's with the people. We want to make sure you reach out to your community and explain to them who you are, what your goals are, and people will help get you elected."

I believe once you learn it, even though in the future whether they may or may not want to be in political positions, at least I want them to understand the process, and know where to start and that they are part of the process.

Me and my wife are putting out flyers, we're putting out yard signs and next month they will be in even years. My daughters are ten, twelve, and fourteen so I need to get them educated on the process. Maybe it will be their passion in the future. It may not, but I don't want them to be ignorant to the process. I just want to teach them not to forget where they came from. We do come from just an average working American family, and I just want them to know the value of the average person. We are the average person. This is what we do and I just want to overall have them be able to see everything. I don't want them to have iPads and an iPhone and they never know about the work that made them. I don't want them to think that Daddy just gives them all this stuff. I want them to know where it starts and what you need to do to achieve goals, and to appreciate it once you reach those goals. So, I want them to value life. I want them to value the common worker, the work that goes into the average day, whether it be in a restaurant or any type of facility with labor. If they want to pursue something else, a white collar job, great, by all means, let's do it, but I don't want them to forget their roots. I want them to know where we come from and who we are.

I think overall I can become part of a bigger picture. As of right now, I'm just trying to focus on my area and wake up the people who are in my immediate circle, in my community. I was ignorant to a lot of stuff till about a year and a half ago and now I understand the problems that affect me and what it is to be a part of the problem. That's the message I want to send. That's why I'm getting involved. That we all are treated equally, that we all have a chance in life; not only the rich but we, the average person, needs a little hand every now and then. It's everybody's work together for the ultimate goal, the American Dream. I have to say I am living the American Dream. I have a great family, a great job, I live in a great community. I work with a lot of good people who are always fighting for the average Joe. I'm an average Joe and I will always be the average Joe, but if I can voice my opinion to protect the average Joe, I will do that.

We are the guy next door, the lady that lives down the street, *the single mother that's working her butt off. A lot of people don't realize that. They say, "The union: the big bosses." The big bosses are not the guys that sit behind the desk. The people who are in the field, physically working, are the people we work for, so they are the union.*

Charles Hawkeye Dixon
Retired Coal Miner, Matewan, West Virginia, McCarr, Kentucky
United Mine Workers of America

I live on Blackberry Creek, where the Hatfields and the McCoys used to be. In fact, you could throw a rock from where I live and hit the little replica building they made at the sight of the election fight on Blackberry. McCoy stabbed Hatfield and the Hatfield died and they hung or shot the McCoy. So, they did a little replica of the election house and I live within 300 yards of it. I've lived on this creek my whole life. I'm 60 years old.

I'm a strong union man and Democrat. I got that mostly from my grandmother. She was a real strong Democrat and also a staunch supporter of the union. She was raised during the Hoover days, and was turned off big time by the Republicans. They about starved her to death. I spent a lot of time with my grandmother. She taught me a whole lot about hardships endured by the coal miners back then. She was a young girl during the Matewan massacre. She passed away about five years ago. She would tell me about her and the coal miners, about her home, about her house. They had a lard bucket for a dinner bucket. Most of them would have their clothes tied on 'em, with no suspenders. They really had it tough. They made their clothes out of sacs that they carried feed in. I learned a lot from her.

I graduated high school in 1970 and in 1971 I went into the coal mine myself, got married at an early age. The first seven years I worked in a coal mine was in thirty inch coal, but it was a union mine. I learned pretty quickly that these union miners, they took up for each other. The older miners took you under their wings. You didn't have that at the non-union mines. Union mines had everybody looking out for each other. You had safer mines that way.

After about a year or so I learned how to run a roof bolter. My job was to make the top safe for everybody. Thirty inch seam. You had thirty inches. It'd be like crawling under a coffee table and then working all day. What was over top though was a mountain. I worked in drift mines. They drilled into the mountain. They didn't drill down, they drilled in. The mountain might be a quarter of a mile high. We'd go into it and walk miles back into the mountain.

You had little plates, about eight inch squares, you had a hole at the center of it, then you had a bolt that was thirty inches long. That bolt would go up through the center, up through the hole, and you would put that plate up against the top and tighten it up. It would keep the top from falling in on you. If it fell there weren't no outrunning it because it weren't six inches from you. They outta outlaw those kinds of jobs. You could just imagine yourself, going to work, crawling under something thirty inches, just sittin' there all day. And then you had mud, water, rats. Still, I had to. I was married with a son, you know. That's what we all done. So it wasn't like I was an exception. I done what everybody else done. It was a way of life in East Kentucky, West Virginia, and it was a hell of a lot better than what it had been for those miners before me.

I got laid off after seven years. That was in Mingo county, West Virginia. That's where that mine was at. Working for National Mine, which was a union mine, and then I came back on Blackberry. I live right on the border. Anyway, I got laid off and got me a job at Blackberry Creek in forty-eight inches of coal and I thought I'd hit the lottery. You can't imagine working in thirty-inch coal and then getting a job in forty-eight inch coal. To most people, they wouldn't see the difference. It makes a world of difference. I felt like I'd been let out of jail 'cause I got about eighteen more inches of height to work in. I learned how to run every piece of equipment they had. The more equipment you know how to run, the more jobs you could bid for. It helped to keep your job if you did more things. I tried to learn all I could.

You spend more time with your co-workers than you do your family. You get real close to each other. You look out for each other. [The mine] was owned by Massey. Massey was the operator where those thirty guys got killed by that explosion. It was a non-union mine. Thirty of them got blown up and I worked for that same guy, same company. It's probably about a two-hour drive away, but that same company owned both mines. Union mines are safer, a lot safer. The men wouldn't put up with working unsafe. The men wouldn't put up with bosses trying to make them take shortcuts. At non-union mines, they could take shortcuts, take chances on getting hurt or killed. Production is number one. That's basically what led to the big strike in 1984. I worked for this here mine - Massey Mine - on Blackberry Creek, about six or seven years, and we came out on strike. I was local union president and the men trusted me and it meant a lot to me, and we came out on strike cause they was trying to weed out all the good strong union men and we came out on strike and they fired me for strike violence, and so I wrote a letter to the international board, and then I went to work for the international union. Then I went from the international board to becoming an organizer and I worked for the union for about twenty more years. I retired in 2005.

When I worked for the union, I organized and I negotiated a lot of contracts.

I probably sat in more living rooms with coal miners in the last twenty years than anyone in our organization, talking to coal miners and their wives, trying to convince them about the union. We were successful in some of those operations and we were not in others. In my honest opinion, the biggest hindrance is the National Labor Relations Board that's supposed to protect worker's rights. My experience with them is that they are just a hindrance to organizing. I'll give you an example. If you go in to organize a mine, first thing the company's going to do is try to find out who your staunchest supporters are and they're going to fire 'em. They'll fire 'em for whatever reason; a good reason, a bad reason, or no reason at all. Well, you, as a union rep., the only thing you can do to protect that person is file a complaint with the National Labor Relations Board. When you do that, you're looking at sometimes years before they'll actually issue a complaint and get a judge that can help that person get back to work. Well, by the time you get to the end of that process, that mine, is done being worked out. And, the same thing with negotiations. Even if you're successful with organizing a mine, win the election, and are bargaining with the mine, they don't really have to agree to anything. They could just sit there and bargain in bad faith, every day, and the only thing you can do is file an unfair labor practice with the National Labor Relations Board, and hope that they'll make them bargain in good faith. The only thing the NLRB's gonna do is issue a complaint and there you go again, through some bullshit process. It could be six, seven, or eight years before a judge will actually make them do anything, and down here in Eastern Kentucky, West Virginia, these mines don't have lives that long. So, what I'm trying to tell you is that the labor board has a

United Mine Workers America

Delegate

K B. Dixon of Local Union 6082

Delegate K.B.Dixon of UMWA Local Union 6082 attended the UMWA International Convention in Columbus, Ohio in the year 1940. The Convention was Chaired by the Great JOHN L. LEWIS, President of the United Mine Workers of America.

The Below Document is the ORIGINAL RECEIPT where Delegate K.B.Dixon was reimbursed for his TRAIN FARE from McCarr, Kentucky to Columbus, Ohio where he attended the Union's Convention in 1940.

This receipt was found on May 9, 2001 some Sixty Years Later at the UMWA District 17 Headquarters in Charleston, WV by Charles Hawkeye Dixon a International Representative for the United Mine Workers of America and PROUD GRANDSON OF

K. B. DIXON of Local Union 6082

process, by the time you step on the tail of a dinosaur, eight years later it wiggles its ear, well these mines down here, they don't have but a five or six year life span.

Everybody lives close together. Whenever they see this mine that's trying to go union and people get fired and the union wasn't able to get their jobs back, then it's harder for you to organize the next mine. Then again I don't wanna really blame the National Labor Relations Board for all because they, to a large extent, are just enforcing the law. In this country, most people think, and coal miners do too, that if it's wrong, then it's illegal. Well, that's not true. It could be dead wrong, but still legal.

It's a real hard thing. When you go and talk to people, you get to know them personally. They become real close friends of yours, and it takes a toll on you after a while when you see those friends of yours being fired and you do all you can to protect them and you do all you can to get their jobs back, but some folk crack, and it takes a toll on you after a while. And it really makes you aggravated with government agencies and everything else. The laws are a joke. The coal companies are as staunchly opposed to their employees joining a union today as they have ever been. They will use whatever tactics. They'll bring in these security guards. They'll bring in union-busting law firms. They'll use whatever tactics they can to keep their employees from going union. They'll spend tremendous amounts of money. They know that, even though conditions may be better in the coal mines today than they were fifty years ago, they know that in a non-union mine, that they can require their employees to cut corners in order to try and increase production. They know that they don't have to put up with any grumblings. They know that the inspectors, the mining law enforcement, is a lot more lax at non-union mines than at union mines. That's been proven, time and time again. They know that when they go into a union mine that if they don't make the company fix unsafe conditions, that the union miner will report 'em to their bosses. So, union mines are a lot safer. But, the coal companies know that if they keep their mine non-union, the inspectors are a lot more lenient on 'em. There's a big advantage to that company to remain non-union. They can operate with more ease when it comes to having to comply with the law.

Most people in the coalfield communities are supportive of the union, whether or not they are union. They'll tell you that. I'd go in, I'd sit down in the living room. I'd talk to the miner, sometimes to the wife, answer their questions and explain to them how the union could make things better. Mostly you'd find this 20-25 year old boy, married, maybe a kid or two, having a pick-up truck out in the yard, having a double-wide. Life's pretty good, you know. And, you're getting along pretty good. This individual weren't opposed to the union-they'd tell you real quickly that their daddy might have been a union miner, or an uncle or brother. They know the union was the best thing. They know the union would be better for them, but they was thoroughly convinced by their employer that the union was for somebody else's mine and not for their mine. They were thoroughly convinced that their employer would shut their mine down if they joined the union. They were living paycheck to paycheck, making payments on that new pick-up truck and that double-wide. They just didn't wanna take a chance at rockin' no boat. It was hard to get a majority of 'em to sign an authorization card whereby the union could petition for an election. That job was their livelihood. That job was the glue

A PICTURE of My GReAT GRANDMA, MY GRANDMA, THE TWIN SISTERS, MY DAD in THE ROCKER AND MY UNCLE CHARLES THE BABY

Thirty-inch seam. You had thirty inches. **It'd be like crawling under a coffee table and then working all day.** *What was over top though was a mountain. I worked in drift mines. They drilled into the mountain. They didn't drill down; they drilled in. The mountain might be a quarter of a mile high. We'd go into it and walk miles back into the mountain.*

that held their families together. And the company knows that. They would use that job to threaten them when joining a union; to work unsafe, to cut corners, take chances, to try and increase production. They do it today at these non-union mines as much as they ever did years ago. They might be a bit more tactful, but they still do it. That's why you still see miners getting killed. Those thirty guys who got killed up there, there was a whole lot of unsafe mining practices that led to that mine being blowed up, and those unsafe mining practices were initiated and condoned by the coal company. They wanted production. Production was number one to Massey.

I never experienced anybody getting killed at the mines I worked at. For the most part, our mines were safe. We made 'em safe. We insisted that they be safe. I worked in two of the most productive mines in Southern West Virginia, Eastern Kentucky. Union mines are extremely productive, if you have good men, and we had good men. I've seen some men with some serious injuries, but I've never seen any fatalities. We've had miners killed that lived in our

community. It affects everybody. But, you see it as part of coal mining; it's a dangerous job. There's going to be fatalities and there's hardly any coal-mining family in East Kentucky and Southern West Virginia that's been exempted from having a member of their family killed. We've all experienced it. My grandfather got killed. My grandpa was a local union president and he got killed with a roof fall. My dad almost got killed a couple of times. He got his arm crippled. My brother got disabled with back injuries. I was fortunate. I didn't work but fourteen years. I went to work for the union. If you work in the coal industry, even if you survive it, you're gonna get black lung. My dad does.

I retired in 2005. I had a heart attack in 2003 and the union had an early retirement. All the employees who had twenty years are provided with a retirement package. I asked for it and President Roberts - a good friend of mine - allowed me to retire along with the others. I still stay active. I'm financial secretary of my local union in Matewan. We've got a $300,000 local union hall. I helped build it. We've got about 1200 members. We participate in the Matewan Massacre, which they put on twice a year. We have picnics, events like that.

I do a lot of four wheelin'. And I still go and help the union at rallies. I still do a whole lot of trying to help my brothers get a pension. I still go out and make house calls whenever we start a drive somewhere. I maintain a close relationship with all of my buddies in the union. I retired but I didn't quit. When you work with people, they become your family. I'm still close with my union buddies. I'm a pretty good gabber and I enjoy it too. I like to help. I'm lucky to have them. I took a lot of pride in my buddies and co-workers trusting me. And I done my best to earn it. And it means a lot to me.

Success is how well you're thought of by people in your community and the people that touch you. It's just how people feel about you. It's your reputation. If you're a man of your word. If you try to make life better for your neighbors and your friends, people will appreciate you and have respect for you. If you've got respect and appreciation from the people that you've been raised up with, then you're successful. The CEO of Massey, he was born and bred right here in my area. He's got millions of dollars. I don't have probably one thousandth of the money that he's got, but I tell you what I do have that he'll never have and that's respect and appreciation from the people I live with. And that makes me a hell of a lot richer.

It was hard to get a picture of me. I was either drinkin' moonshine, fightin' roosters or bar hoppin'. We tried to avoid the cameras! Living here in East Kentucky, Southern West Virginia, it wasn't all hard work. If I had to do it all over, I wouldn't change nothin'. If I had another life to live, I'd give anything to live it the same way I did this one. Sure would. With the same people.

I'll tell you one other thing before we go. My grandpa, he got killed in the coal mine, but two or three years before he did, he got on a train in Matewan, West Virginia and he went to a UMWA International convention in Columbus, Ohio. I was telling the secretary treasurer about my grandpa up in Charleston, West Virginia and we found, in his records, where my grandpa was reimbursed $11.52 for his train ticket plus his meal, and he showed where my grandpa had signed his name on the receipt where he was reimbursed. And, that's the only thing I ever had of my grandpa. My grandpa got killed before I was born. I framed my grandpa's receipt, his signature on it, and gave it to my dad. He was local president. My grandpa was too. He was a strong union man too. He got killed on a Sunday. Him and his neighbor was cleaning up a roof fall, so the men could come out Monday and work. Support for the roof fell while they were cleaning it up, and he got killed by the part that was left hanging. He was respected. We're good people.

So, what I'm trying to tell you is that the labor board has a process, **by the time you step on the tail of a dinosaur, eight years later it wiggles its ear,** *well these mines down here, they don't have but a five or six year life span.*

March 9, 1992
Best wishes to my friends
"Hawkeye" and Nancy Dixon

—Carroll Hubbard
Member of
Congress
Kentucky

81

Dr. Charles Gattone

Professor of Sociology, Gainesville, Florida
American Federation of Teachers/National Education Association
United Faculty of Florida, (AFT/NEA, UFF)

I'm a dad, a husband, a professor. I'm also a musician. I like to think of myself as pretty laid back. I enjoy just hanging out with people, talking to them, listening to them, learning from them about different things.

I think one of the things that is really fundamentally human…something that makes us human is that we're social creatures, you know, in the sense that we basically need interaction. We need to interact with other people, and so because of that I feel it's important to place an emphasis on the human side of everyday life. What I think has been happening in our contemporary society is that institutions -organizations such as business, government, schools - tend to depersonalize human life, so really, the most important thing is to focus on the human side of things, because, after all, the goal is that everyone be able to live a full life. To me, that's the core of what I value. What I think is happening is that many people are denied the ability to live a full life because they are so constrained by the daily requirements of civilization. You know, having to sit in traffic for an hour to and from work, and when they get to work, they sit in a cubical. Even in those settings people find a way to be social, to make their lives more human, which is great. One of the issues is the tendency of institutions to well, manipulate is a strong word, but manipulate people into working for the goals of the institution as opposed to the goals of humanity, which are not always overlapping. Sometimes they're overlapping, but not always, and what can happen is human goals are very different from the goals of institutions. So I value love. It's kind of corny, but it's what I value. It's really important, because if you're trying to make a decision, should I do this or should I do that, I feel like, well, do you care about people? Do you care about living a full life? Helping them to live a full life? That's a love of humanity, and so, to me, that's an important guiding principle.

My work is I'm a professor. I teach sociology. Sociology, by the way, is the study of groups. Group dynamics; how they relate to one another. I tend to focus on sociological theory, which is thinking about how to do sociology, how to think about groups of people and society in general. So theory is very critical sometimes. Part of my work involves calling into question some of the traditional ways of thinking about groups of people and working to develop alternative ways of thinking about them and understanding them. One main goal of sociology is to try to understand why people do what they do. So theory basically involves thinking about how this is done and to look at how some of the sociologists in the past, for instance, may have thought they were developing a deeper understanding of human beings but were actually missing a lot of it because of their preconceptions and things like that. So for me one of the more interesting things about sociology is questioning conventional ways of thinking and looking for hidden biases or hidden assumptions that are misguided, and trying to address those and be conscious of those as a way to deepen the understanding of our own lives and of the lives of those around us.

I also do work in culture. Culture is very similar to what I've described before. It's basically beliefs, traditions, practices—things that people do in their daily lives. Groups of people in one region of the world in one time period have a set culture, and people in other parts of the world in other time periods can be vastly different from one another in these ways. And also people within the same region could have different overlapping subcultures. To me that's very interesting because it shows how people develop their world-views and how these world-views are sustained from one generation to the next socially, and also how they're transformed. How is it that you can have a set of beliefs endure generation after generation and then they change? What happened? How did they change?

Earlier I mentioned how institutional goals can often be at odds with human goals, and I feel that that's often the case in academia. After all, leaders of universities need to address very practical concerns. Many of them come from backgrounds in academia, but some of them come from a background that is more oriented toward practical concerns, let's say business, or in the case of our president at the University of Florida, who is a former dentist, many of them do what they perceive to be best for the institution. My feeling is that institutional goals are often fundamentally at odds with human goals. As a professor I have a responsibility to try to focus on furthering human goals, and by that I mean helping people develop a deeper understanding of their own lives and of the lives around them. How does the union relate to this? It seems to me that what unions can do is provide a stronger voice for professors, for the people who are actually doing the work of the university.

Professors are involved in two major tasks. One is research. As a professor you are involved in basically developing new knowledge, which serves as a foundation for everything else. So that's really important. One of the concerns of professors throughout the history of academia has been to somehow ensure that they have the freedom to pursue these goals in an open and uninhibited manner. In particular, the primary goal of being a professor is to think critically about existing beliefs and to try to find possible ways these ideas can be improved upon. And so what that means is to have an open mind and having the freedom to be able to study things that are perhaps a bit uncomfortable, perhaps a bit against the interests of the institutions, academia, business, and government. What a union does in an academic setting is it helps to give professors a bit more strength in being able to facilitate those more human goals.

The second task is in the classroom, teaching. Obviously this is a crucial component of a professor's responsibility. Part of what that involves is taking the knowledge that is already out there in journals and books and through discussions and through experience helping to bring those to the classroom, working with students to help them develop their understanding of the world around them. Again, as a goal of developing a deeper understanding so they can live a full life and help others live a full life. A key component of this however is the interaction. It's important to have an interactive dimension to this, which means as a professor I don't come in there and say, "I'm just going to talk and you're going to listen…just tell you the truth about the way things are." What I do is try to understand where students are in terms of their orientation and learn from them, and also contribute what I have to contribute. So, I see education as both helping to enlighten students but also learning from students. There's an interaction there that's crucial. I don't pretend to have all the answers. I think I can contribute to a discussion about life, and I like it when students also contribute, and then together we have this interaction and ultimately it's really exciting, it's really fun, and I live for that. It's one of my favorite things about my job.

Recently what has been happening, ac-

It's ironic, but that's the way it is. **If you devote at least part of your life to focusing on making it a better world and helping people, ironically, you actually benefit.** *Whereas, if you just think, "I'm looking out for number one, just going to help myself. I don't care about the rest of the world," studies show that people who take that approach are not as happy, not as fulfilled.*

tually you can say it's been happening since the 1950's in the U.S., is academic institutions have developed connections with other institutions in society. That's where the resources are for academia. We often get money from government and business, so you can understand why the president of universities and the deans and provosts pay careful attention to what the goals are of those institutions that we have associations with, and they are inclined to try to find ways that academia can help those other institutions. That's where they're coming from. Often times they'll create incentives and disincentives to gently nudge, or even more than that, to push faculty members in the direction of helping those institutions. That's why I feel that a union is crucial in academia, because what it does is it gives faculty members a stronger voice. It enables them to push back in a sense and say, "Yes, I know you want me to do that, but what I think is important is this." And I'm coming from a more human dimension as opposed to an institutional dimension.

Let me give you an example. In keeping with their interest in satisfying the goals of institutions, recently the administration of the University of Florida laid off several faculty members, or attempted to lay them off, and the faculty members who received notices were in those positions that they deemed to be not as valuable. Now, how do you decide if a position is valuable or not? They're coming from the point of view of, "How does this help institutions? How does this help government? How does this help business?" So, for instance, the foreign language department was one of the targets, and also philosophy was a target, and art, and English. These are targets in general in contemporary academia. Why? Because they aren't as immediately helpful in enabling those institutions to accomplish their goals.

You can, of course, make the argument that they are ultimately very helpful in the sense that they help to build an enlightened population which can then, if it's a democracy, to the extent that our society's dem-

ocratic, those enlightened people can then participate in selecting leaders who are wise and who can make wise decisions, ideally. But, many institutional leaders don't see it that way, obviously. The point is that the union recognized the value of these professors from the professors' point of view. They're valuable because they contribute to human goals and contribute to the development of new ideas, the development of mutual understanding. Foreign languages are not only about language; they're about culture, learning about other people. So the union, through arbitration, was able to say these layoffs were not in line with the contract. We have a contractual agreement. The arbitrator said, "You're right. It's not legal for them to lay these people off. They need to be reinstated." And so sure enough, they were reinstated. That's just one of many examples.

The main message I would say is that you can't do it by yourself. I'll say it again. You can't do it by yourself. What I mean by that is, I've spoken to many faculty members in academia and many people from various occupations. They usually have very clear ideas about what they want to accomplish in their work, and often times those goals are very worthwhile and I agree with them. The one time where people can be a little misguided, though, is they can take an individualist approach to this. They can say, "The main thing is that I do what I'm supposed to be doing and that I work toward my goals." That's the attitude, I see and I think that reflects a sort of general misunderstanding of the way the world works. The fact of the matter is that if you want to get to that point where you can have your own voice, and have it be influential in a work setting, it needs to be collective, working together with people collectively. It's kind of corny to say but it is true: "Strength in numbers." I've learned from experience that unions really work. When people work together, they can really accomplish great things.

I probably do eventually want to retire, but I don't really look at my job as something that I'm doing because I have to do it. I mean, if I arrange my career in terms of money…you know…I need a job because I need a paycheck because I need or want these material things and I want whatever money can buy me? That's a different thing, because then you look forward to retirement because your primary reason for doing the work is for the money, and so obviously you want it to end at some point, hopefully. For me I feel like I thrive on those kinds of discussions where we're sitting around in a circle and we're talking about social issues and students are coming up with ideas that are valuable and I'm coming up with ideas and we're debating them, and in the course of doing that, we're learning. I also feel that as you get older, it's important to keep using your mind, to keep challenging yourself. That's part of what makes life fulfilling to me.

Contrary to what one might believe just based on the surface, life is not fulfilling when you have all the earthly pleasures just handed to you on a silver platter. You could wake up in the morning, not work at all, just have food come to you, but if you reflect on that, we know that's not what happiness is all about. Even studies have shown people are more fulfilled when they're doing things, when they're actively involved, when they're challenging themselves, and in particular when they're challenging themselves in ways that are directed toward helping others, as opposed to simply helping themselves. It's ironic, but that's the way it is. If you devote at least part of your life to focusing on making it a better world and helping people, ironically, you actually benefit. Whereas, if you just think, "I'm looking out for number one, just going to help myself. I don't care about the rest of the world," studies show that people who take that approach are not as happy, not as fulfilled. So no, I'll probably hang in there and continue to work for a long time.

For me the challenge of my work is writing. I find writing very difficult, but I'm very glad when I'm done and have a finished product. So I really have to push myself to get that done. And of course, teaching for me comes naturally and I love it. I still get a little anxious before class, and that leads me to be perhaps a bit over-prepared, but I really love it. I look forward to continue doing it for many years.

One of the problems in today's society is that people are out of touch with what they really feel and what they really need. We've all been socialized, trained to act in certain ways, and I think that that training can actually lead us away from our inner desires and goals. I think that these inner goals are fundamentally good, but we need to nurture them. It's similar to Freud's Civilization and Its Discontents. Basically he was saying that civilization tends to steer us in one direction when we as individuals want to go in other directions. So success means learning how to be in touch with our inner selves and then being able to act on those feelings in positive ways to help give ourselves a full life and also others a full life and not get caught up in doing things that we've been taught are the right things to do, even though our gut feeling does not tell us that. Our gut feeling can sometimes be far superior to the kinds of expectations and goals that emerge as a result of institutional pressures. So success is being able to act on those and being in touch with those in a constructive way.

...and what can happen is human goals are very different from the goals of institutions. So I value love. *It's kind of corny, but it's what I value. It's really important, because if you're trying to make a decision, should I do this or should I do that, I feel like, well, do you care about people? Do you care about living a full life? Helping them to live a full life? That's a love of humanity, and so, to me, that's an important guiding principle.*

Joe Gattone
Pianist, Chicago, Illinois
American Federation of Musicians

Number one is I am a family man. I love my wife and kids. It sounds corny but that's how it is. I'm a classical pianist. I like playing: playing shows and playing jazz, orchestral....I like playing anything. I like the strength in my chords, playing notes that have a little friction, like dissonance to them, without being phony about it.

I like new ideas and friends, other musicians, who know what they're doing. And, usually they are as interested as I am. I like to socialize with them. You know, it's kind of fun. Sometimes, when I was in college, I would be taking a school break or lunch with two or three other guys, talking about something we just learned in class.

So, we'd come out of the classroom and have lunch, still discussing music and parts of music and musicians and what they are capable of doing, that kind of thing. Some musicians, they put a lot of trouble on their shoulders, but you really don't have to be that complicated.

(His wife interrupts with a question and, as she walks away he says, "There she goes; She's really beautiful, you know…")

I don't really think of what I do as working for money. Basically, people work to bring money home. I had big ideas. I thought about conducting, or being a soloist or something. I wanted to improve myself as much as I could and through different experiences that I could get. I was part of a big band in high school. I got a master's degree and all that. I was playing classical primarily. When you work with other guys, you're learning while they're learning too, that kind of thing. Then it became sort of like, play what gets paid, which was kind of interesting, if you don't mind being subject to follow the leader. The band leader would make a call...you know, play this, play that, and you're expected to know all those tunes,

I feel I've been successful. *One reason is because I've had different experiences, you know, like conducting and playing in a couple of these shows, and for singers, stuff like that. I'm proud of that. I feel like I've been successful, but it's hard sometimes. Not everything falls into place the way you'd like, but, I'm lucky with what we have. God has helped me. God has been helping me all the way.*

so, you know, it takes a lot of time to learn all those tunes.

Unions help maintain high standards, with contracts, for example, and stability. Instead of us working under the whim of whoever hires you, you have some protection. You can retire at a certain age, and as soon as you do, you receive a pension. I joined in 1947. Mr. Patrillo was the president of the union, the musician's union. I went from high school right into the college experience and I had to join the union for work. At that point you had to. The agents just hired union people. In order to have a standard salary, you had to be a member. Our union has developed into a pretty good union. The guys who are the leaders are good, and you don't mind working for and working with them. They're fair, honest. The contracts are fair.

You know, friends are also really important. They can really take you to where you want to go. They will help you get to

a higher point, with new experiences and challenges. Basically, I was really happy with the friends I had and the jobs I got, as I said before. Most friends will help each other. I'm obviously thinking of my friend Joe Vito. He was active in the union. He helped a lot of musicians, the way he helped me. He was a top musician. He was very fair to everyone. He was a great pianist with a great sense of humor.

When you're with people who are trying to help you, you can't tell if they're trying to help you or they're trying to get your job. That's the thing. But Joe was really fair to everyone. I wish I could say something more clear about how great he was, compared to anyone. He's like, just a wonderful man and helped a lot of young guys and a lot of older ones too. He was a great musician, with so many different experiences. He would give up certain jobs to me, for example. I think Joe helped me get to wherever I got. There were so few guys who were on the same level as him. Basically, I got to be where I am from Joe. He handed jobs to me throughout my entire career. For instance, I worked at the Blue Max for 10 years, and I got that job through him. It paid really well and it was interesting, you know.

To me it seems like yesterday. It feels pretty good to have done what I did. I feel pretty good about my life. I had a lot of people help me, I learned to be a leader and had a lot of experiences with music. There were some wonderful musicians along the way. I feel good to have played all these things; shows and all. The musicians you meet that help you, you don't realize but it goes both ways. I feel I've been successful. One reason is because I've had different experiences, you know, like conducting and playing in a couple of these shows, and for singers, stuff like that. I'm proud of that. I feel like I've been successful, but it's hard sometimes. Not everything falls into place the way you'd like, but, I'm lucky with what we have. God has helped me. God has been helping me all the way.

In 2005 the members of the Chicago Federation of Musicians awarded Joe Gattone the Dal Segno Honor. Following is their summary of his accomplishments and contributions:

His background is in the classical field with a Bachelor's degree from Chicago Musical College and a Master's degree from DePaul University. He has been the musical director for several shows including the production of Tintypes at the Apollo Theatre Center in Chicago. He has been musical director at the Mill Run Children"s Theatre for 12 years and at the Blue Max Night Club for the Hyatt Regency O'Hare for 10 years. Mr. Gattone has also performed with the Chicago Civic Orchestra as well as the Ravinia Festival Orchestra.

In 2002 his hands were filmed and dubbed into a TV sequence of "West Wing" titled "The Long Goodbye". He played the Gershwin Prelude #1 and also Bach's Aria (theme) from "The Goldberg Variations".

Kathryn Stasiowski Gottlieb

High School French Teacher, Eldred, New York
New York State United Teachers/National Education Association/
American Federation of Teachers (NYSUT/NEA/AFT)

My self-description is definite life-long learner… honestly I hate using that expression because in the educational field it's really overused, but it really does describe my approach to things. I'm just in awe of how many things there are to learn and know and be amazed by and that's also part of what drives me as a teacher. I also want to be able to pass that on to my students. That kind of approach, that kind of "Wow" thing, and I know this is weird but you can get that same "Wow" from conjugating verbs as you can get from discovering herbs in a forest and I'm just out to convince my students of that. (Laughs) Hey listen, over the years, I have seen the twinkle in the eyes of some students who look at that verb chart and go, "You know, you might have something here".

I'm normally very physically active. I'm interested in people in general. I try to be very positive. I'm definitely a big-picture person - that's the way I function, just to understand things. And, not a disclaimer but an explainer, and not in an effort to be preachy, but who I am is so tied up in what I believe so, my position as a believer in Jesus Christ just winds its way through everything I do. That's going to come up again and again. It's about foundation.

My paid work is I am a teacher of secondary level foreign language. I work in a small, rural district in a 7-12 building. I teach

French almost exclusively but I have taught Spanish also to 8th through 12th graders. That's my contract work. As a teacher, I want to open the world of learning to kids, not just to get them to have those "Wow" moments, but also to give them some tools and perspective that enable them to find out who they are, to discover what paths are theirs to become confident in themselves as part of the world and again, going back to the whole picture thing, in every way that I can, I try to address my students as people and be there for them, not just academically but in every other way that's appropriate for the situation.

I think the work I do is exciting because of the potential of relationships and the possibility of those "eureka" moments. It is very challenging most of the time because of the multifaceted ways that a teacher has to think in and be available and be proficient to deal with students effectively, but that difficulty is to me at least a healthy challenge. It's just downright fun some days. I always tell the kids, really, every day, if we don't laugh at least once about something, then we really haven't done our job for the day. And it can be at my bad outfit or whatever. And, my work is very interesting to me. I don't know if that's too banal, but it really is.

Well, see, officially [being in a union] is not obligatory. Usually the way it's put to you, you'd be hard pressed to come up with

To me it relates to our dysfunctional, topsy-turvy norm that we settle for in our culture about who's valuable for what they do. **So a union is a chance for some sort of moderation and reminder or a call for sanity…**

any reasonable ideas about why you would not join. So it's almost a decision that's made for you and I think most people come into it, especially if you're coming in just out of college, a young, first year teacher, you have no idea what the union is but all the older people look at you and smile and say "This is a good idea…We'll be there for you" and you just become a union member. I think in our situation mathematically, our union provides benefits, that's who they're negotiated through and everything, so your cost versus what you get for your dues, you'd have to be a complete moron not to. Should I say that more nicely?

I didn't have any union experience before. I didn't grow up in a family that had people that worked in union situations, so my pre-knowledge was pretty minimal, you know, probably through social studies class. So I just did it because of all the benefits. But since I was in it, I thought, OK, "What are all the daily workings of the union and what does it mean to be supporting this?" You just kind of mature into an understanding of that, but you have to inform yourself and get involved, too. You know, later on, I could've said that, "This is bogus" but in my opinion it's not.

The union is about respecting me as a worker and when I say that I mean a worker who's a person, you know, that sort of social justice concept, and the set-up of the union is designed to ensure that I'm honored and respected as a worker in as much as can be fairly done and have an appropriate relative value to the world around me. One of the things I was thinking about that unions do…To me it relates to our dysfunctional, topsy-turvy norm that we settle for in our culture about who's valuable for what they do. So a union is a chance for some sort of moderation and reminder or a call for sanity that, you know the people who get things done, from every sort of manual job to teachers and people who do mental health service jobs or whatever, remind people, that this stuff has value worth protecting as opposed to, and I don't mean to be passing judgment, to me this is a mathematical craziness, to actors, actresses, professional football players, professional wrestlers, reality show people, mostly in the entertainment industry, where we place a value on what those people "do " that are so astronomically not connected to human potential and worth that it makes me crazy. I think without unions, you would never have people fighting for people who do regular stuff and you would never have anybody who attempts to put a value on the work that people do. We see so many different value systems in our culture. It's confusing to us as adults, it's way confusing to kids and the messages that stand for what your possibilities are. I think unions offer a place of sanity or pride and a reminder that, "Hey, this is another perspective that is equally as valid as your, "I'm skinny and beautiful and kiss well on the screen" perspective. It's just something that we need to keep in balance as a functional society.

Sometimes as fruitless as it is, the unions offer that political forum which, though I'm fairly apolitical but, I also understand that in the set up that we find ourselves, this American society, that politics is a way of being heard, sometimes, and getting things done, inserting yourself in the process, and it's definitely a means of doing that for people who would remain voiceless. And for people like me, I support the arm that does all the political stuff and while I may not agree with everyone's politics, I do understand that, take politics out and the cake doesn't get baked so you just have to deal with it as a reality. Politics isn't my gift so I trust that somebody else is competent and informed and really into it. It's worth it to me to pay them and stand behind them to do that part and then to use what I think are my gifts in other ways that are more appropriate.

In my ideal, brilliant paradigm, you would have people who bring the team together, that inspire, that encourage…In my workplace, people don't consistently do that, so we have a situation where there's a lot of inner contention and, especially because it's a school setting where autonomy is very highly valued so, when your leadership is weak, people cling even more tightly to their autonomous spaces so I think in

our case the union has offered at least the possibility for unity, to get back together and have that mindset that we are working together; We must work together so here's a forum that's set up. We don't have to recreate the wheel. Let's try to make it work. I see in some instances, that definitely offsets our other issues, which should be unified, but which unfortunately aren't. I think whatever your union's tenets are give your group common ground, depending on what happens. Recently we had unresolved contract negotiations so you've already got that foundation of people drawing together. I'm not saying everyone agrees to what everyone else is saying. It gives you a point to keep coming back to and say, "OK we're all in this together." While maintaining individuality, we still have common goals. If we didn't have a union, the fractures would be how we're setting the tone every day. The union gently reminds people. Any union is about the faces and the personalities that go with it so ideally your lead people have a tone of working together, mutual respect, progress. We have different personalities in our union. There are definitely the go-to people for "O.K. Let's have a kinder, gentler opinion now" and everybody kind of knows that so we work from intense to less intense, and we get things done like contract disputes…all that kind of stuff. What we accomplish as a union makes me think about my constant amazement about ideas. If you just think of people as these amorphous blobs of ideas, don't you get it? The resource is amazing! Just throw something out there and let their minds go to work.

This past year is an example of an amazing kind of support that you just don't find everywhere, unionized or not. Our union has always voted to provide a sick bank as something that represents our values and our respect for each other and our sense that life and work are inseparable. I was able to have a job and a paycheck for a whole year without working. Half the year was my own accumulated sick days and the rest came from the sick bank. [I had] a health issue. It was undiagnosed Lyme Disease with additional co infections that I had been fighting for a number of years with declining health but I kind of just kept plugging on until a point in June of 2010 when it became physically impossible to plug on and it wasn't until five months after that that I finally had a diagnosis. Not knowing what the audience knows about Lyme Disease; the longer you have it, the longer it takes to get rid of it, so I've been fighting that whole thing and have been learning a lot about the disease, the medical system, all that kind of stuff all at once and I'm finally to the point where I'm somewhat functional again and continuing to get better.

That was a gift you know, again, that something that our union has repeatedly voted to pursue for our members and obviously the personal effects of that are overwhelming. I can see from a non-unionized viewpoint that really could cause a lot of griping. And there's something kind of weird about someone not doing their job and being paid for it but I think it speaks more loudly to an understanding and respect for people as people/workers, not just workers or beings that have to play by rules so that everything is fair for everybody all the time, that this acknowledges this is how life works and if we can do something to assuage the sometimes ill effects of your circumstances then we commit to doing that. This is the stand the union has made and that's very cool.

I just would really want to be independently wealthy like right now. Not because I want the money; there are so many things on my bucket list. There are so many things I want to do, experience, learn about, that I feel like probably 60 or 70 years isn't enough. And, if I have to be bothered with going to work every day, then that's going to be a drag. No, obviously, in my more realistic outlook, yes I want to retire someday. Do you want the list that everybody gives? I would travel, read books, garden, see my family, learn how to knit, like all those things, skills that I had never become profi-

It's just downright fun some days. I always tell the kids, really, every day,
If we don't laugh at least once about something,
then we really haven't done our job for the day.

cient at, people I have never visited enough. I think I would just sell my house and have a little cabin where I could just call a home base and then just be going around in the world, you know, building houses for Habitat for Humanity, and then going and learning how to cook in Italy and then, whatever. I mean those could be my plans. If God says, "You know Kath, I really just want you to, I don't know, become a tree trimmer in your post-retirement years," then I'd be happy to do that also.

Obviously you can figure out from my prior comments that I'm not a card holding member of the consumer society. So, material success has very little meaning for me. Yes, I'm feeling very blessed and I appreciate that aspect of what you might call success that I can pay my bills and buy unnecessaries. It's not my goal - I was going to lie - Clearly it is one of everyone's goals to be paying ones' bills. I think success more has to do with me, knowing that I am living out my beliefs, which include being faithful first and foremost to God as the center of my life, with the "love one-another principle" as the totally main functional aspect of society, and our relationship with the Creator so, as long as I feel like I'm keeping those goals in front of me, that what I do supports people whether it's in my family, in my school, in my community, that people are just the main thing. If I can be helpful, if I can play my role in any given situation, whatever that is given the moment, then I'm doing O.K

Bob Guilfoyle

Hard Rock Miner

International Representative, Deputy Director of Organizing,
Western Region, Shepherd, Montana
United Mine Workers

I guess I would describe myself as a working class union man. I'm proud of that fact. My heritage is Irish American, and I don't have to get into the history of the Irish people in this country, but we came here primarily as laborers. We constructed a good part of this country, along with people of other ethnic backgrounds. We were able to pull ourselves up by our bootstraps, so to speak, by becoming involved in politics and in union organizing. We were able to stick together. With mutual associations, we were able to raise our standard of living and become part of the American fabric.

I was born February 2, 1954, the son of a union plumber. I grew up eating at the union table. I was born and raised outside Chicago. Before I was a miner, I worked as a member of the Laborers International Union of North America/Construction Laborers. I left Chicago with my wife and three young children in June of 1980. I've lived in Montana since. I'm 58 years old. We went to West Montana and built a place up on a mountain and raised our kids there for about 13 years before we relocated to the Billings area. I was employed by the American Smelting and Refining Company's mine, an underground copper and silver mine. I became employed at that mine when it was still in the development phase.

When I moved to Montana I was 26. I always liked the outdoors; ever since I was a little kid I read books about Montana, the Rocky Mountain West. I watched guys that worked in the trades when I was growing up as a kid. The guys that I worked with back there always had this dream of retiring and moving up to Wisconsin or Minnesota or the north woods, someplace where they could live out in the woods and hunt and fish their days away. Most of them never made it. They died before retirement age or as they were retired. I don't have to tell you about guys that worked in the pipe covering trades that ate asbestos all their lives. Most died in their late forties, early fifties. I knew a lot of those guys. They never had the opportunity to retire. So, it made sense to me as a young man, to move from the big city and try to make a living somewhere I thought I would like to live. That's what prompted me to move to Montana.

I would like to retire someday. Organizing is not a 9 to 5 job - it's not something that you leave at work. There's a tremendous amount of responsibility to make the organization grow. You realize full well that your salary comes from people paid by members of my union who are working in low coal 36 inch coal seams,

crawling around 3 miles under a mountain on kneepads, working in an explosive atmosphere that could blow up and kill them anytime. That said, union mines are much safer than non-union mines, but it's still a very dangerous occupation. I understand full well where my wages and benefits come from. And, at the same time, the responsibility of trying to make the organization grow, is one that my union has entrusted me with, and it's a wonderful way to work, if you can give working people some hope. I also don't have to tell you that the majority of the time that you're out there battling, trying to bring justice to workers, you usually take a pretty good woopin' in the end. The wins are wonderful, particularly when you can bring workers together and watch them develop to where they lose their fear and stand up to the boss and they're able to get their first contract. Those are the great rewards in this job. But, when you see good people fired…

I have gotten good people fired by asking them to step up for the union. I tell them that they have a protected right to a union, and if their employer is violating that right, or discriminates against them in any way because of standing up for that right, that the employer is violating that right. But I cannot guarantee that their employer will not discriminate against them, up to and including discharge. We will do everything that we lawfully can to protect that individual and protect their right to organize. We have to prove that they were discharged and discriminated against because of their union activity.

When somebody does get discharged - let's say he's the only breadwinner in the house - and their spouse calls you up on the phone and you could hear their kids crying in the background because they just got fired, they don't have a job anymore, because they were standing up for the union - it can really take its toll.

Not that I'm complaining. I've got a daughter that was a pediatric oncology nurse. She had to get out of that field because it took a toll on her. She was doing bone marrow transplants for children who had various forms of cancer. Unfortunately, 90% of the kids that she helped succumb to the disease. It took a horrible toll on her. The toll that organizing takes on someone, of course, isn't as great as working as a pediatric oncology nurse, but it's a tremendous responsibility. To quit rambling and answer the question: yes, I would like to retire someday.

In my retirement, I see myself as just sticking around the house. I've been a motel bum for the most part for the last 22 years as a staff rep. I've lived on the road for extended periods away from my family, including times when my kids were still at home. They're all married, and I have grandchildren that I'd like to spend my time with, but I spend an awful amount of time on the road. The area that I'm responsible for is Western Canada and the U.S., which includes Alaska, Yukon Territory, NW Territories, BC, and all the southern mining States. It's a huge area. If you're going to go out and try to help workers organize, you're gone for months at a time. My idea of retirement is sticking around home and enjoying our place here. I'd like to get out and hunt and fish, tour around the mountains and go see the grandkids. Spend time with my grandkids and help them; maybe sit in the boat with Grandpa or take a walk through the hills and just enjoy what God gave us here in Montana. That's my idea of retirement.

I have four children, four girls. My

...if you had a complaint against something, you didn't have anyone to go to. You were just told you were a whining crybaby and that you ought to just shut up. If you had a health and safety complaint about something in the mine that could smash you into a greasy set of coveralls, you were told that **if you don't like it you could just pack your dinner bucket and go home.**

oldest daughter has her Masters in Special Education. She works for the school district in Great Falls, Montana. She and her husband have one child. My second daughter was the pediatric oncology nurse. She lives down in Green River, Wyoming. Her husband is an underground trona miner. She does home health work now. They have two children. My third daughter lives in Homer, Alaska.

She and her husband have one child. I've got a daughter that lives south of Mazola, she and her husband have two children.

I was only employed as a miner for nine and a half years. The way I got into union organizing is I went to work at a non-union mine in 1981. I went to work as an underground miner there. I was very glad to get the job, but I'd always worked

construction as a union laborer prior to moving to Montana. When I moved to Northwest Montana, I couldn't find a job cleaning urinals. Jobs were tough. There are not many people in Northwest Montana and there's kind of a reason for that. It's a beautiful, wonderful place. It's pristine, you could bend down and drink out of creeks without worrying about getting poisoned. Beautiful country but a tough place to make

a living, and I found that out in a hurry. I worked for a little while in a sawmill. I did some exploration core drilling; so, when I applied to this mine and got the job, I was happy to have received the employment.

I found out that working non-union, an employer can make a lot of promises that they don't actually have any intention of keeping. Of course we were told straight up that the company didn't want anything to do with a union and that they were a union free operation, and in order to keep it a union free operation, they were going to keep its employees wage and benefit package competitive with what the union side of the industry was doing. But of course, as time would roll over for a year, you'd expect a cost-of-living increase and a raise. The company would have some sort of excuse as to why they couldn't do that just then. Or, if you had a complaint against something, you didn't have anyone to go to. You were just told you were a whining crybaby and that you ought to just shut up. If you had a health and safety complaint about something in the mine that could smash you into a greasy set of coveralls, you were told that if you don't like it you could just pack your dinner bucket and go home.

Having worked in unions before, I knew things could be quite different. I suppose one of the galvanizing issues in that particular mine that got myself and some of the other guys there interested in trying to organize a union, was the ventilation and air conditions in the underground mines. They ran diesel equipment in the underground there, and I don't know if you've ever been caught behind a city bus on an open street in a traffic jam with that exhaust making you sick, but, if so, you can imagine what it's like to work in confined spaces underground with diesel-powered equipment. We were actually appalled that, in the United States of America, workers could be subjected to working under those sorts of conditions. In the 1980s in America you could work in an underground mine with diesel-powered equipment and have to breathe that exhaust in. It literally turns your tongue and the roof of your mouth black. When you'd cough, the mucus would look a lot like licorice. We were told by our employer that it wouldn't hurt you, and you'll cough it right up, and

any of the stuff you breathe in would leave your system in about eight hours.

Well, there was a fellow there who worked at the mine named Jerry Hoover who used to be a criminal investigator for some agency in the state of Montana. Once he found out he was being lied to like that, he started doing some research and he found out that there were countries in the world like Japan, that found that the inhalation of diesel particles and exhaust were so harmful for you that they refused to allow diesel equipment to be running on some of their open streets. We started coming across other studies showing that the inhalation of diesel particles and exhaust were not only carcinogenic, but also affect organs of the body and your heart and arteries and so on. We made a good-faith effort to present this evidence that we had found to the mine management. Management refused to talk to us. It was at that time that we realized we needed some help, so we turned to the United Mine Workers of America.

The Mine Workers sent some safety specialists out to talk to us. They got us in touch with the National Institute of Occupational Safety and Health. They came out and conducted a health-hazard evaluation at the mine, and at the same time they helped us try to organize the mine under the UMW banner. Of course our employer made all kinds of promises that he never intended to keep if workers made the union go away. We got beat in a representational election. Right after we lost that election the employer realized that we weren't going to stand by. They had a year until the workers would smarten up and have another election. So they wanted to increase employee turnover as much as possible. They cut wages $2.10 an hour straight across the board. This was at a time when we'd already been several years without any sort of raise. It caused a huge exit of workers and they hired a bunch of new miners. Still, about a year later, we had another representational election and we won by a good margin. Then we had to get a contract out of a vengeful employer, with what was mostly a new-hire workforce. Fact was, the guys weren't really making a living from the type of work they were doing, so we found ourselves at the bargaining table with 46% employee turnover.

The company served its bargain and broke it's promises. They actually said that they didn't think the United Mine Workers represented the majority of the work force anymore because they turned over almost 50% of the mine. So they forced us to petition the NLRB to come in and conduct another representation election. We lost by six votes in a 314-person operation.

In the meantime, I was elected president of the local union. It didn't look like there'd be any time in the near future when we'd be able to win a representational election there. I was actually going to quit the place myself and go up to Alaska to work. It was about that time, in 1990, that I took a position as an organizer with the United Mine Workers.

The mine I was working at shut down in 1992 because of depressed metal prices. Copper and silver prices went way low, so they shut the mine down rather than continue to operate it and not get as much money as they could have in the future, when metal prices went back up for the ore. They shut the mine down for three or four years and then, when metal prices went back up, it re-opened. It is a non-union mine to this day. I wish it was a success story for you, but it was nothing but six years of heartbreak.

We refer to ourselves as hard-rock miners. Hard-rock mining is underground metal mining, whether it be gold, lead,

zinc, copper, silver. Typically, those metals are found in quartz deposits, and Quartz is one of the hardest rocks. It's a very hard material to mine and, so doing, we were turned into hard-rock miners. It's all drilling and blasting and loading. You go in with pneumatic air drills and you drill blast holes into the rock, load them up with dynamite, light your fuses and blow up the rock, breaking the rock. You break it with dynamite and then you go in and load up all the broken rock with loading machines and then transport it out of the mine. Then you run it through a reduction mill on the outside where it's further reduced and then sent to a smelter where it's refined. You use metal bars to scale down any loose material so it doesn't fall on you and kill you. Then you go in and load up all that broken rock and ore with loading machines and put them in to haul trucks that take them out of that section of mine.

In order to shore the mine up to prevent it from caving in on you, you'd have to support the rock structure above you. The most typical way is to put what's called "roof bolts" into the rock structure above you. You drill up into the top of the mine and you put mechanical bolts with plates on them that hold the rock together so that you can work underneath that portion of the newly exposed rock without it falling in on you, hopefully. You keep recycling that process: drill, blast, go in and bar it down and wet it down to keep the dust out and look for any unexploded blast holes. That's when you go in and bar it down and wet it down. The ore is loaded up and then you go in and bolt it up, you support it, and then you just do it over again.

You keep following that particular vein of ore, and that's hard-rock mining. In Troy, it's kind of hard to describe, we were about a mile into the mountain from where we went in the surface adit. An adit is a mining term for a tunnel. We went uphill into the mountain. It was about a mile from the portal up the service adit until we'd actually start getting to ore-bearing. There was ventilation added further up on the mountain. I would have to draw you a diagram to explain how far into the mountain we were. Depending on where you were in the mine, if there was an emergency, you'd have to walk a mile or more. We were transported into the mine in trucks: rubber-tired, diesel-powered vehicles. We had smaller, farm-type tractors that we would use for transportation in and out of the mine. We wouldn't have to walk in to go to work, but if there was some sort of emergency, you'd have to walk or run out.

There had been people hurt and, thank God, we never had any fatalities when I was working there. We did have one brother that died of a heart attack. There was speculation that he may have been electrocuted, but we don't know that for sure. We had some near fatalities. We had some tremendous ground falls where the roof would collapse and, luckily, no one happened to be in that section. Some of those roof collapses were measured in acres of ground. God Almighty had his hand on the mountain. We were very lucky that nobody was killed.

I've done several different things in my life. When I was young I worked in construction. I worked in gas stations when I was a kid. Once I was old enough to get a Laborer's card in my pocket, I went to work as a construction laborer. I was also in the Marine Corps. When I moved to Montana I found out how tough it could be to make a living. I worked saw-mill work, I did coal drilling; but then I got a job in the mine. Mining was primarily a male occupation; we didn't have any females working in the underground as miners when I worked

there. We did have a female who worked on the surface in the crusher and in the milling department in the shop. Working underground, it was the closest bunch of guys that I had ever worked with or felt good around since I had been in the Marine Corps. It could be a dangerous occupation, but you've got somebody that's looking out for you. You were trusting the guys you were working with and you felt good about it. There's a lot of camaraderie there. I suppose that being a miner made me feel most proud of my occupation. The type of people I was working with, even though it was a non-union mine.

We didn't strike there because the turnover was high and we had a bunch of new hires coming in, a lot of kids just off the farm and didn't know much about unions. But the solidarity that we saw, and the money and the support that poured in from every UMWA local union from across the United States and Canada, flabbergasted us at the kind of support and help that was available to us. Growing up in a union household and having been a union member before, I had taken it for granted, because it wasn't until I worked in a non-union mine that I found out what it was really like to work without any protection. So that was a very valuable lesson for me.

I was very humbled when the Mine Workers offered me a position. You know, it's tough for me to talk about myself, but I was very humbled that the shock troops of the labor movement would actually ask me to go on board and work for them and try to help grow their organization. I'm still humbled by it. I'm very humbled by it. So, that is something, I guess, that I learned, if that goes to answer your question. I don't know if it does or doesn't, but that's a very valuable lesson that I learned before I became a staffer and since I've been a staffer in this working position.

I guess, success, in my view, is being able to live your life without compromise. Whether you win, lose or it's a draw in some sort of confrontation that you may have, as long as you didn't compromise your principles, and you go to your grave having never compromised, I guess you can consider it a success, in my view. It was probably the way I was raised or it was instilled in me by my folks, or maybe it was when I was a kid. I went to Catholic school and we had these Franciscan nuns from Poland that, you know, would hang a whippin' on you in a heartbeat if you were compromising - if you were doing something they didn't think was right.

Maybe the way I grew up, too. There was no compromise. It was a disciplined household. Maybe things are different this day 'n age, but I knew then when I was a kid that if I got a whippin' I had it comin'. I deserved it. Later on in life I think there's a realization—I don't know if everybody has this realization—I guess maybe I can frame it this way: a lot of times I try to tell folks that we're trying to organize, that I don't know whether or not you're a religious person or if you believe in God or if you believe that there's a Heaven, that's none of my business, but sometimes the only way that I can get any sleep at night is to think that these greedy bastards that have sold themselves out for greed and for personal gain, the ones that are stickin' it to this country and stickin' it to America's workers, that even though they should be rotting in prison somewhere, you know, they've got the law skewed now so that these guys are never going to go to prison. But one day, one day, they're going to have to stand before the Man. If you believe that way, that's the way I believe, and when they go before the Man, it's my belief that justice will be served. So,

they compromise. They sold themselves out to greed or whatever it was that made them compromise. So, I would term success as never having compromised and standing your ground and taking your lumps and a lot of it's good and a lot of it maybe 'aint. There might not be a material reward, but you got the satisfaction of knowing that you never caved, you never bowed, you never gave in, you didn't compromise.

So, I would term success as never having compromised and standing your ground and taking your lumps and a lot of it's good and a lot of it maybe 'aint. There might not be a material reward, but you got the satisfaction of knowing that **you never caved, you never bowed, you never gave in, you didn't compromise.**

Courtney Hairston

Licensed Parts Handler, Flint, Michigan
United Auto Workers

I would describe myself as an outgoing person, a caring person. I try to take people's feelings into consideration in everything that I do. I'm a person that really doesn't like to get into other people's business but if I have to be in their business, I'm very caring about their feelings. That's just how I am. I'm kind of a loner, at first. I'm not really "out there" like that but I've learned, with the union, that I have to be like that for some things, like if I want to get my point across, or if I'm trying to help someone, I have to be upfront. That's how I am.

I am twenty-five years old. Before I started working, I was a football player and wanted to work on computers and everything. I never thought that I would be a shop worker. I guess that's what life throws you…unexpected things. I've been working at GM now for six years and I never thought that I would be doing that. And now, it's different than when I was younger. I see things differently. I guess it's because of the things that I've been through, with the union and the things that I see at work.

It's kind of different now, being around different people and different things.

Growing up, you don't see a lot of things. My grandfather was middle class and he was a shop worker for forty years so, you know, I always thought that you go to work and everything is given to you. I never heard the background. Like, I'm a tier two employee at General Motors now, so I make half of what the traditional workers make. And, I always thought that, when my granddad went to work he made all that money because it was just given to him, but being there and understanding that those workers, they didn't always make what they made, and they fought for it. It's just that, if you've seen more things, when you're there, you're living what they lived. You know what I mean? And that's one thing that I got involved with: the union. I'm very into politics. I watch the debates; I watch everything. I thought that everything was given. My generation especially - you know I'm twenty-five - I just feel like we're spoiled and we don't fight for anything. I'm always hollering at my cousins, everyone; I'll

stand up and holler at them that we need to get involved, you know, like in the Occupy Wall Street Movement. It's a lot of things. I wish I had a voice. One of my dreams is I wish I had a big enough voice. Like a platform so I could say everything that I want to say and I could get a lot of people's attention. I don't have that so, that's why my involvement with the union is really big. It's really something for me to express how I feel. It gets people's attention. I did some organizing with them, with the U.A.W. I got an opportunity to go to the Nissan plant. I got to see people, my age, they're making less than I make; you know I make around $18 an hour. I met a guy. He's been working for Nissan for about the same amount of time as me, and he's only making like $9 an hour. I listen to him. He tells me the story about how he's treated, how he's this and how he's that and I'm like, wow. If I had been in his shoes and worked in his job for

that amount of years and been treated like that, or am I spoiled and I'm in the UAW and I don't know my union has been there for me and I don't know how that feels. So, that's why I say we are spoiled sometimes. I really try to get involved like that. I feel for those workers and I feel for a lot of things and I just feel like, our generation, we don't…We just want everything given to us; everything has to be given to us. We're not willing to fight for anything like, you know, the sit-down strike, how they sat down and fought for things. Right now, our generation, we're not ready to fight for something and I'm really passionate about that. You know, nothing should be given to you. At football, nothing was given to me. I worked my butt off. So, I don't feel like… Nothing should be given to us.

The reason I ended up in the plant was because I had a football injury, a really bad football injury to my knee. And then,

I wish I had a voice. *One of my dreams is I wish I had a big enough voice. Like a platform so I could say everything that I want to say and I could get a lot of people's attention. I don't have that so,* **that's why my involvement with the union is really big.** *It's really something for me to express how I feel.*

it was supposed to be a summer job, you know. The summer of '06, I was hired into Delphi as a temporary employee and it was supposed to be for the summer; we were told that we would never get hired. That's what we thought. We come in here, nineteen years old, coming into a plant; we didn't know what a union was or anything like that. So, when I was at school, it was just a temporary thing and I stayed there, because I was getting more money than I had ever made in my life. So, I mean, I never thought I would do that, but I stayed because you make that money. It's hard to walk away from, being nineteen and you're a poor college kid and you're like, "Man, I've never seen this type of money before." You work eighty hours a week and I was doing sixteen-hour days and you know, my check was…more than anything I had ever seen in my life. So, I stayed. I continued my education at a junior college, but I stayed. Cause, I knew I couldn't play football anymore. That was my decision, to stay. The decision was just monetary. It wasn't anything as far as the union…I just tried to make as much as I could because I always thought it was a temporary job, for the

summer. And then toward July, because my hiring date was July 19th, 2006, we were told we had another four or five months, because by January we're going to be done, so I'm like, "Wow, O.K. I gotta make all the money I can, because it's going to end soon." And in November of 2006, the union came in, there were contract talks, and they hired us in as permanent employees. So, like, "Wow, O.K." We got bonuses and things like that and…I've been there ever since.

I work on the receiving dock and I unload trucks. And what we do, the CCA division, is a division of General Motors that I work for, we service dealerships. So, anytime you take your car, your GM car, to a GM dealership, the parts that they need to service your car, those parts come from my warehouse. What I do, I take the parts off the truck and I take them to an area to be processed and put into a box, put a label on it, then, we print out dealership packs to different cities around the country and then, when the person gets done processing the part, I pick the part back up and I put it on the shipping dock to be shipped to different dealerships across the country. It could be from a headlight to a door panel to an emblem on your car. We do different engines. That's basically what I do, is service dealerships throughout the country. I get to see different parts of cars that I'd never thought I would see. Like, I didn't know that a Cadillac had an icebox in it. It's important that we get the parts out because that's our main goal - to satisfy our customers. Our customers are the people that need their car fixed. So, we always paint a scenario at work: If you car's broken, you need this part. You need to get this part out. You don't want to upset that customer because they might not buy GM products anymore if they had to wait a long time to get their car fixed. Ever since GM came out of bankruptcy, it's about customer quality and parts quality - nothing else matters. Timing…make sure it's there in two days, make sure it's shipped, make sure it gets to the customer. They've really changed their strategy. Before 2009, it was more about the numbers, how many parts we got out of the plant. And now it's more kind of a customer-oriented goal.

There are two plants in Flint. My plant has all tier two employees which are entry-level employees, and we make $18 or $19 an hour, about half of what [the other plant] makes, but we do the same job. They do have some 2007 hires that make the higher wage, that were hired in after us, but the people in my plant came from Delphi and GM brought us in at our tier two wage, instead of bringing us up to the regular wage. So, that's starting to be a problem at the plant now because, you know, I mean, we're doing the same job as people over there. It's not fair that they get to make all that money and we don't. I love what I do but I do think that, it's kind of wrong to have people doing the same job and at two different wages. As far as my job, I love it. I mean…it's not hard. You can't get along with everybody that you work with but you

115

know, for the most part, I don't have any problem. I'm a third shift employee, so it's not a bad job at all. I go in from eleven at night to seven a.m. Then I take care of my daughter, I get my son off to school, so it's easier if I'm home with her. She'll be two in December. I don't believe in my child being in day care; she can't tell me what they're doing. Her mom gets off work around five-thirty, six o'clock, so, I'll take a nap. On a good day, I'll get five hours. You gotta sacrifice some things, you know, when you have small kids. You do a lot of sacrifice. And I have other obligations. Things like, I'm a trustee of the Executive Board of my union, and we had a mandatory meeting for elected officials last weekend and I didn't go to bed...I got home at seven, I got my son to school, and I got her up, took her to my mom and dad's, the meeting was at ten, we got out of the meeting at three thirty and I didn't sleep that day; I think it was Wednesday night, I stayed up. A lot of sacrifices that you're going along with, but

that's OK, I sleep. Most of my sleeping is done on the weekends.

I was nineteen when I had [my son]. And that's another thing; he was being born on September 14, and I got hired in July. So, I always remember how many years I got. I've been there for six years and it doesn't seem like it. After you promise you're only going to be there half a year, you're there six years. It's kind of a blessing that we even have these jobs. The economics...There's nothing in Flint. I know I'm complaining about the pay but, you live in a city where it used to be thousands of auto workers, now it's not as near as what it used to be. They're tearing down plants and, you gotta be grateful for what you have. And I do feel like if the union didn't step in and make GM promise some jobs here, then they'd probably all be gone by now. Our crime rate is up...A guy that I grew up with got killed Saturday night. I didn't really get the story yet. Saturday I was busy with my family. Like I say, I'm a person that tends to stay away

So, that was one of my goals; to make it out of there alive, *because a lot of people didn't. A lot of people do not make it outta the hood in Flint, alive. At my age, there's been hundreds of people that got killed. I'm very open about that. That's an accomplishment in itself. I got it all from (my granddad) though, because he worked. He went and did what he did for forty years. My grandfather. That was my guy; that was my right hand man.*

from that, you know, because so many have been killed over the last couple of years. I could name people that got killed that I've known, or been around in my childhood. The crime is ridiculous. Everyday. I don't even go out. If I go out at night, it's to go to work. We stay on the outside of Flint now. I'm not scared, because I grew up around it, on the north side of Flint, which is probably the roughest side of Flint. I'm not scared of it but I didn't want my kids around it. The stuff that I've seen, I didn't want them to see. You know, I've seen people sell drugs. I've seen people shoot somebody. I've seen that type of stuff. That's just a lifestyle that you were around growing up.

My grandma and my grandpa raised me. He worked at Truck and Bus, which is another GM plant. He was always working crazy hours, and my grannie, as I got older, she got older and she would say, "Be safe" but you know, there was only so many things that she could keep you from. And if you're in the streets, you're gonna see it. So, I've seen it. I've seen drug transactions. I've seen a kilo of cocaine. I've seen it. And, I'm just glad I didn't go down that road like some of my friends did, because they're painful.

My granddad, he was my role model. His work ethic was, "Go to work everyday." He never missed his work. He never complained about it. I know it had to be hard, working forty years in a plant. That lifestyle, I just never really wanted it. My friends, they had money. They had cars with rims, pockets full of money, and I was like... No. I didn't want that. My example was home; you have to go to work everyday. He didn't miss work for anything. I don't even remember a time when my grandpa was home for a holiday. He played a big role in my life, you know. And, he was the type of person, he was like, union first. If your car wasn't union made, American made, you

couldn't park it in his driveway. He would ask you to move it out his driveway. I can remember his shop union brothers and sisters would come over, after work. They would have talks, and this and that. I just didn't go down that (other) road. I just didn't. That's one thing. I wasn't forced not to go. You know, as a matter of fact, one of my best friends growing up; we had dirt bikes together, we did a lot of things together, and as we got older and went through high school, we went two separate ways. He got shot at. He robbed a comic book store. He was in jail for five years. I never went that way. I always said, "I don't want to go to jail; I don't want nobody telling me when to get up and when I gotta do this." That's not for me. So, that was one of my goals; to make it out of there alive, because a lot of people didn't. A lot of people do not make it outta the hood in Flint, alive. At my age, there's been hundreds of people that got killed. I'm very open about that. That's an accomplishment in itself. I got it all from [my granddad] though, because he worked. He went and did what he did for forty years. My grandfather, that was my guy; that was my right hand man. He was a quiet person and didn't scream. He told you what you needed to hear. It may not have been what you wanted to hear. He was from down South, Papa. I called him Papa. He came up here from Memphis, Tennessee right out of high school to work in the plant. When he died, that was probably the closest person to me. I had the roughest time when he died, because, he was like my father figure, you know. My dad's around but I grew up with him. He died in '08. I was working in Delphi. I was at a crossroads. He was sick and I was at Delphi and we had to sign papers to go to GM. It was a hard decision: Are you going to stay at Delphi or go to GM? I asked him about it and, of course, he, you know, he gave me the whole history about Delphi and how Delphi was. "You need to be under GM." He died with me at GM. He knew. He advocated for me not to go back to college, and to stay there. He always said, "You'll be alright. The union will make you alright. You can't play football anymore so you need to stay there and make some money. Don't be crazy and give up that job." Because that's all they knew. GM took care of them for years. When GM left, it shocked everybody. I mean, that's what everybody depended on around here.

I wished he could've seen me with my union. Because I wasn't involved with the union like I am now. He didn't get a chance to see that but he'd be proud of the things that I'm doing now because, like I say, he was very big on the union thing, very big. I always asked him, "Why don't you let people [park] who don't drive a big 3 car?" He might let you slide on a Chrysler or Ford, he might, but it was really GM. If they parked it in his driveway, he would come outside, he would say, "Would you please move your car?" He didn't care who it was. I always asked him why. He was like, "You'll understand." These days we want a BMW, we want everything foreign. I've been wanting that even when I was working. I wanted that stuff. I never understood why he did that stuff but say, "Union first" and have a union sticker on his car. You know, "I drive only American made things."

That's the thing. My kids are going to know. I'm not going to keep them in the blind about why I'm doing anything. They have to learn it all. My granddad wanted me to learn the hard way, "You gotta bump your head a couple of times to actually learn stuff." I think as parents, we need to teach kids why we do certain things. My kids are going to know why Daddy only buys GM cars, because not only does it help us as a family, that's American made things. I probably sound like a union person now because we appreciate this stuff, but a lot of foreign cars are made American, but they just don't treat their workers fair. And I have a problem with that.

I know one major thing that's on my list before I, you know, die, is...I really want to finish my degree. I'm right there and I need just to go because, GM, they'll pay for it. That's one major goal: to finish my degree. I do want to own a business. I do have a goal to own a business. I'm into various things like stock markets. I watch CNBC and I invest my money and there's just so many things. It's hard to really see it, though. Because, you don't really know if you're gonna be here one day or what's going to happen. It's not certain, especially with the things that's going on. You know, it's hard to be a twenty-five year old right now. Nothing is set in stone. We could walk in tomorrow and our jobs could be gone. A lot of older people at work say, "You guys gotta do something different; go back to school, get out of this plant 'cause it's not gonna be here..." You listen to that stuff and, "O.K. Are they right? Are they wrong?" You know, I don't mind...I could work there for thirty years. I really could. I could retire from there, even though I don't have a pension, that's why I have to invest now.

Another goal would be, to live to see seventy, eighty years old. I would love to see that - to see grandkids, great-grandkids. I don't think about retiring or things like that.

I would love to help the union grow as much as I can. That is one of the things that I strive for now. To tell everybody that you can have things if you fight for them. To tell them, "Step up and fight for them. Things are not given to you!" I wish everybody knew that and would fight for some things, even if it's really not about your union or your job, but if you really want something, just don't sit back and think it's gonna be given to you. I wish I could spread that, especially to my generation. You have to work, work, work for things: fight, fight, fight, for things. So, you know, I'm gonna be a big advocate for that. For union things and stuff like that and hopefully, in the next years, we have a better economy, we have different things that people in past generations had because, you know, I mean, right now it's just up in the air. Till we take control of it and do what we need to do, it's just gonna stay the same.

I can remember the first day I walked into Delphi. I can remember everything about it and, six years later, I'm still there. Two kids later and you really can't stop working there now. You have to take care of your kids. Hopefully, I can put them through college, just like my granddad did for me. He provided. The union gave him an opportunity to provide for his family like that. I just want that for my family. I just want to be a middle class family. I want my kids to be able to go to college and not to have to worry about debt or anything like that.

Success for me? My success is defined as my achievements that I have. You want this in your life and if you attain it then that's your success. So, I feel like my success in my life would be if I can achieve all these things. I'll know when I'm successful. It's hard to explain; it's far, far down the road. Being so young, and my goals are so big. I want to do this, do that. When I achieve what I set out to do, then I'll be successful.

Being twenty-five, you go from being a kid that's in this box that really doesn't see everything. You just have life and you're not worried about anything. You know, you're a college kid one day: you're worry-free, you're partying, you're studying. You're not worried about anything. Being in a life-style with kids - Boom! The box opens up and you see the world and how it operates and how unfair it is and how everything goes, and you get mad at things. This going this way and that's not right, and my world did a 360 in like a year, couple months, a summer. 360. I didn't know all the things like I thought I did. I didn't get involved in things. Until you see what happens, what goes on, what's happening around you. I mean, you're either gonna sit there and just let it happen or you're gonna change it. So, I've decided to change it. That's why I got involved with the union, because you can't just sit there and expect things to change. You have to do something about it.

I was a kid. I was playing on top of the world and then thrown into the fire. I didn't know the world was like this. It's just a different place, man. The world is really scary, once you get in it, and you're living it and you're doing it. The world is scary because you don't have your parameters like you used to; you have to go outside of that. You can't call Mommy for this. When you get in the world, it's real. It ain't no do-over. People really need to know that.

Until you see what happens, what goes on, what's happening around you. I mean, you're either gonna sit there and just let it happen or you're gonna change it. So, I've decided to change it. That's why I got involved with the union, because **you can't just sit there and expect things to change.** *You have to do something about it.*

Jeni Hankins & Billy Kemp

Appalachian Folk Singers, Nashville, Tennessee
American Federation of Musicians, Local 1000

Photo by Kim Sherman

Jeni:

We're very excitable people. That's how we came up with 'Fans of Life' because sometimes we even get too excited over things. I think it's a huge part of our personality, and it's probably why we ended up being a duo and being a couple, because we recognize this in each other. We get excited when we return from a tour because the person at the grocery store remembered us. We really feel like it's an essential part of who we are and it's very sustaining in our work, because I think when you tour, it's a stamina kind of thing. It can be tiring, you're doing a lot of traveling. You're trying to balance practicing, you're trying to eat right because you can't get ill, because you've had this gig booked for a year and you can't just call in sick. So, when there's a lot of pressure in what we're doing, I think the fact that we get so excited over seeing people return to our concerts, or the fact that we get excited over going to a state park and seeing manatees, which we just did, things like that. We get excited over seeing lots of little things every day.

Billy:

Another thing to add to what Jeni was just saying; sometimes we actually think about people - meaning we try to consciously extend kindness to people, because life is not easy. Extending a little bit of kindness to everyone that you meet can really make a difference in their lives, and yours too.

Jeni:

I think that we feel that it's sort of an active practice that we make and so, although we are composers and songwriters and musicians and, you know - I'm a quilter and Billy is an avid practitioner of yoga - we have these things that we do that make up

our day-to-day activities. There's a sense in which we are always trying to do them with this philosophy of kindness behind them and include people that we meet in what we're doing.

Billy:

Empathy is really important to us also.

Jeni:

I think that comes in our songwriting, because a lot of the songs that we write encourage our audiences to consider stories of another person, and so we have people come up to us after a concert and say, "Oh I've never really thought about it that way before," or, "My life doesn't feel that difficult after hearing that story." So, we feel like, "Oh Wow! This is great, because this person has experienced empathy." That usually means that they're going to go through the world in a kinder way.

Jeni:

We were both outsiders when we were growing up. I moved around my whole life growing up as a kid and I had to make new friends every couple of years in school. My parents weren't in the military or anything. They were actually just really young when they had me. They were 17. They went to college and then started new jobs. It meant that I had to start over and over again while I was growing up and I think that that gave me....I really needed kindness from others, and acceptance when I would show up at a new school every couple of years, and I think that that experience showed me how important that was.

I was also a bit of an outsider in the sense that I was always into the arts, so I was always a little bit different, and dressed a little differently than the other kids at school. I learned to find a way to be accepted, and

> *When I listen to you teach a lesson, he's always saying,* **"There are no wrong notes!"** *And I think they interpret that as a great kindness because they're always told there are a lot of wrong notes and they're hitting them!*

so it was kind of an experience of wanting people to be kind to me, and so I found the best way to actually receive kindness was to give kindness first, and it usually worked out. It really goes both ways.

Billy:

I grew up in Baltimore and I stayed there for many years, so I had a lot of friends, but unfortunately a lot of my friends would end up in trouble, and I was always just outside of that picture. In West Baltimore, there were groups of people - they weren't gangs, just collections of people - and I would kind of step just outside of that and observe. I actually thought at one point I was going to be a probation officer because I thought maybe this would be a way to help my friends. And so, I think, maybe because of my parents, I was always concerned about others and trying to help others. So, that speaks about the idea of having empathy, and kindness, but artistically, both of my parents had an influence. My father is a singer and my mother played piano, so there was always music in the house. I would sit at the piano with my mother from an early age, like from the age of five, and she would be playing something by Bach or Mozart or something. She could read and play music like that, not professionally but as an enthusiast, and I would just sit there and add my 2 cents worth and my mother would say, "Billy, how did you know how to do that?" I don't feel like I've ever been afraid of music. When I approach music, anything can go and anything can happen.

Jeni:

And I think that that has always helped you in being a teacher, because Billy has been a teacher of music almost his whole life, and from a very early age he was showing people how to play, and then did that in a professional capacity at the University of Maryland. Because he's never been afraid of music, you always try to encourage people not to be afraid. When I listen to you teach a lesson, he's always saying, "There are no wrong notes!" And I think they interpret that as a great kindness because they're always told there are a lot of wrong notes and they're hitting them! For me, too, as far as my musical history, my dad was always playing music for me and a lot of it was political. And there was a sense in which my dad promoted respect for others and for their stories through

Photo by Gordon Whitted

playing the music on his guitar, and with his harmonica, that spoke about peoples' struggles, so I appreciate that from my dad. He had me on that music from a very early age.

On the 28th of February was the 7th anniversary of when we met. And only a few months after we met, we started playing music together as a duo. About 5 months after that, we realized we were a couple and that we wanted to play music together for as long as we possibly could. So, we started working on songs together: writing songs together, arranging songs, and recording. Now, we're a touring duo and we travel about 10 months of the year, playing in concerts in all different kinds of venues: libraries, festivals, house concerts, regular clubs, folk series...

Billy:

In the short sense we call it Appalachian Folk Music. Jeni grew up with a coal mining community and she heard that music there and through her parents. I grew up in Baltimore and on the West Side of Baltimore, there was a community called Ellicott City. It had 5 mills, and in the 1950's and 60's, when big coal days were coming to an end, a lot of the people from Appalachia came to Baltimore for work, and so I was really fortunate because, in Ellicott City, there were Appalachian families, meaning people who had come from Appalachia, and I knew their children because I went to school with them, and on the weekends I would go over to Ellicott city and listen to the banjos and the fiddles there, and so I was introduced to the music early, in like 10th and 9th grade.

Jeni:

When Billy says I grew up in the coal mining community of Jewell Ridge, Virginia, what happened was my parents were so young, they would send me to my grandmother's every summer to Virginia, with my sister, and that's where I sort of absorbed all of that music: dancing and gospel singing. There was one particular woman at my grandmother's church, her name is Virginia Lowe, and her singing probably influenced me more than anyone.

I think Billy and I put our two heritages together. When we met, we started to hear this music within each other and when we sang together, there were these harmonies, these awesome harmonies that occurred that really - harmony is a really tricky thing - and I think we realized that when we sing together, there is something really special about the harmonies we could create.

Billy:

Jeni is the primary lyricist and then I'm the primary music person, but Jeni also writes music and occasionally I also write lyrics. So, when we're working on new songs, it's really exciting, really fun. I think about Hoagy Carmichael, the composer. He called himself a tunesmith, and he just knew when the tune was right for him. And sometimes I feel that way. It's not right away. I call it fast thinking. Sometimes the melody can come really fast, but then you have to tweak it and work on it, and that's really exciting for me, to try to find the song in a place that I think it's ready.

Jeni:

Sometimes, like for instance, we have a song called, "We Ain't Got Time for Trouble Blues," and that was a situation where Billy woke up and he had this melody in his head. And then he had a couple of words, a couple of lyrics. And, we just literally got up - we didn't even eat breakfast. We went to the piano, and we just literally started writing, because we thought, this is our chance, you know. We're going to lose this song if we don't work on it right now, no matter what we had planned that day. A lot of times, it is an unexpected thing. We don't make a lot of appointments to sit and write songs together.

Billy:
It sounds like a good idea though...

Jeni:
We're in an interesting situation right now where we've been commissioned to write a song for a long time fan and we're finding that quite difficult because it's based on a historical event and her family, and how to approach that is quite tricky. So, that's a good challenge for us. We've definitely written songs based on historical events before, but that's a unique challenge that we have ahead of us.

Jeni:
We're part of the American Federation of Musicians and we are in a pretty unique local. Most of the locals are pretty geographically centered in the AF of M. Like New York is Local 802. We're part of Local 1000, which is the traveling musicians' union, and you don't have to be connected to a specific geographical area. We tend to have a lot of members who, like us, tour a lot of the year, and who don't primarily work in the city in which they live. We rarely actually play in Nashville. So, rather than joining our local here, which is a really active and wonderful local - we've spent time with the folks who kind of run the local here in Nashville - we decided to be part of the traveling musicians' union. It describes more what we do.

Billy:
One thing that's unique with Local 1000: If you travel all the time, it's hard for us to have a contract with every single venue in every single geographic area. One thing that Local 1000 offers is if you are an LLC, you can have a collective bargaining agreement with the Local, and then you can make pension contributions, and that's the real important benefit for Jeni and me, because we're independent and so we have to think about our future ourselves. Local 1000 gives us that opportunity to make that pension contribution, for every job that we play.

Jeni:
It's great for folks who are self-employed and not necessarily able to contribute to social security. It's just a different option for us. It's been great to actually establish our own business in a way and helps us be more organized. So, we feel grateful for that. I think also there's a feeling, being part of the local, that we can go to one of our brothers or sisters to ask advice about a business move or some aspect of business that we're not quite sure about, or about any kind of booking or touring, without feeling competitive, because it's a really competitive industry, and the fact that you're part of the union, you feel more like you can approach another union member to ask them a question. That opportunity to talk to somebody in a really open and kind way really means a lot.

Billy:
What you're bringing up is that it really offers a strong sense of community. It's hard for people who travel all the time. Our neighbors are in Gainesville, Florida, they're in Los Angeles, California; they're in Toronto, Ontario. We don't see them all

the time, we see them maybe once a year, but the union, Local 1000, offers a sense of community because we get to see the other members whenever we want, and also when there are gatherings of the local, we get to meet them there.

Jeni:

Touring can be really tiring at times and it's a lot of miles. We're going all the way out to California and back this spring and we usually go to England once a year. We go to Canada. You know, really long distances. Neither of us has any notion of retiring whatsoever. I think we'll always do what we do. We're thinking if we have a pension, we'll be able to make a tour a little less frequently and spend more time composing and working on song writing and working on pet projects that we have. The touring is how we create an income and how we support ourselves, so we have to keep out there on the road and stay in touch with our fans, and that kind of thing. I think we're thinking in the future, we might have the ability, with our pension, to be able to spend a little more time at home working on unusual projects that we have. I'm a fourth generation quilter so I have a lot of interest in textiles and sewing, and I actually spend a lot of time doing that in the car when we're going on tours, sewing away! Those are the things that we'd like to do that are a little outside and we've been looking at a way to combine sewing and music, using quilts as inspiration for composition and things like that. And those are projects that we don't have necessarily enough time to address, given our schedule.

Billy:

Thinking about retirement makes me think of a few other artists. Like, there's a composer named Elliot Carter who now is 103 and still composing, still celebrated, lives in NYC, just had a major group of his works performed there. And Philip Glass just turned 75 and is still writing music for film and for the stage and doing recordings. Willie Nelson was once asked, "Are you ever going to retire?" and he said, "What am I going to retire from? All I do is play music and golf." It's true, I think, for me. I don't feel like I'll ever stop composing or writing music or playing music, and Jeni is certainly never going to stop writing or singing. It's just something that you do, like breathing almost.

What Jeni was saying about the touring though, we really have to be very conscious about health and how we interact with people, our eating habits; when you travel

It's hard for people who travel all the time. Our neighbors are in Gainesville, Florida, they're in Los Angeles, California; they're in Toronto, Ontario. We don't see them all the time, we see them maybe once a year, **but the union, Local 1000, offers a sense of community…**

that much, you're coming into contact with so many people, your immune system has to be really strong, and so the thing that we might retire from, maybe when we're like 90, would be playing concerts all over the world. Maybe not; some people say that 75 is the new 55. The union, as far as retirement goes, looks at time more traditionally. Meaning, we're paying into this pension fund and then we will start to collect retirement at 65, like most people do.

There are different sizes of success. Like, for example, we had a really nice bowl of oatmeal this morning, and that was a success. There are little successes,

like, some days when I'm doing individual practicing, when I'm practicing scales on one of my instruments, I can make a little break-through with my fingering or something - that's a little success. When I say little, it's little at the moment but it can be major as far as something that happens later in a performance. We just came back from a tour in Florida and the concerts were highly successful. The reason is, we had these audiences of 100, 200 people, totally captivated by the story and the music. That was a major success in my mind. That's performance success. And then there are practicing successes and recording successes. When you make a record, when they come up with something really great, a lot of times they'll say, "I got lucky" and it's true. There's something that's elusive about recording, because if there were some sort of formula, then everybody would be doing it. Those kinds of successes, recording successes, getting something that you can release, that has some kind of magic. That is major for me. We can go down to the Kroger grocery store and see our friend, Wade, who is the deli person, and have a great conversation with him, and you just walk away feeling good about that, you know.

Jeni:

I think when Billy's talking about Florida, for instance, there was this one day where we were challenged to do something we had never done before. The librarian asked us to play a concert for 200 4th and 5th graders from the elementary school down the street, and the kids walked from the elementary school up to the library, and it was 10:00 in the morning. We had to get up at 6:45 in order to get there and set up all of our sound. We were really tired…

Billy:

We usually get up at the crack of 9…

Jeni:

Yeah, crack of 9. It was like we were heading for the airport in my mind, by getting up at 6:45. And so, we've played concerts for students before but on rare occasions, and a lot of times they are high school age, so here were some 4th and 5th graders and we - by the end of playing for these kids - and they were singing with us and clapping with us and they were asking questions and they were smiling and they were running up after the concert, and they wanted a pick and they wanted the harmonica to play a

train sound again and - we were so elated! It was just an unexpected gift, and we had peanut butter and jelly sandwiches, and then we played for 200 adults where I would say the average age of the person was probably 65 or 70 years old, completely at the other end of the spectrum, and at the end of the concert they're off their seats and they're clapping and you know, we're getting this standing ovation and we don't even know what to think!

We can't even believe that that's how we're spending our day! What a blessing that was! What luck! However you want to interpret it, it was just an amazing day; to start out with this bundle of nerves and feeling really uncertain of our ability to communicate to these children, and to end the day feeling that we not only really touched them and received from them tremendous kindness, but then be able to play for these people on the complete other end of the age spectrum.

I think, for us, there are always these things out there in our mind, like, "Oh wouldn't it be wonderful to win Best Oscar for Original Song?" Or something like that. But I think we realize that for us, these successes, just like that beautiful day in Florida, will stick with us forever. We have dreams, I suppose, of playing this festival or getting to play in Holland or things like that, but when you have a brilliant day like that, I don't think anything can compare to that, hardly.

Another thing that was really important and special to us was that we were able to take part with another union. We ended up meeting President Cecil Roberts from the United Mine Workers of America, and we played at the unveiling of a memorial that a woman had raised for her husband and other miners who died at a non-union mine in Cumberland, Kentucky. We met him because he gave a speech and we were asked to play music at the event, and when he heard our music, he invited us to come play at his inauguration in Virginia that same year. Then, that summer, he asked us to play at the UMWA convention in Las Vegas. And I think, for us, that was such a tremendous honor. That's one of those - we call it a "Kairos day." Chronos is the time that just happens every single day, every single minute, but Kairos is a moment that's extra special, and, getting to be with the coal miners and with that union, which has struggled constantly with getting new members, and watching people in horrible accidents in non-union mines, and the frustration that they must feel - the solidarity that they have - It was just amazing to get to be part of a union like that for a few days each time. That was a day where we felt like, "Wow! What an amazing success this has been, that our music brought us here."

Billy:

There are everyday successes and there are these special days successes. Jeni and I think the simple answer to the question, "What is success?" [is] when we've made a good connection with a listening audience and made what we feel is great music during our performance. Not that we wouldn't like to walk across the Grammy stage or the Oscar stage. That would be fun, too. That would be a kind of success.

There are different sizes of success. Like, for example, we had a really nice bowl of oatmeal this morning, and that was a success.

Wadya "Woody" Hassan

Licensed Practical Nurse, New York City

1199 Service Employees International Union (SEIU)

I wear a turban so people, when they see me, have a preconceived idea of what I am and who I am. I'm a nurse, so when I was working in a nursing home, when I came in there, people looked at me kind of strange 'cause they don't usually see nurses wear turbans or anything like that, but once they got to know me - they got that stereotype out of their head - they loved me. I was the best nurse; they were always calling on me. They needed me.

Our country is built with stereotypes and if you don't come out of your box to get to know people and to voyage out and to go to other places, you only know of the stereotypes that they put in your head. We have Indians, we have Africans, we have Japanese people: all the people of the stereotypes that we grew up with a long time ago. Once you meet these people, those stereotypes fall apart. They're just working people, trying to survive and build a family, trying to have that way. They want a house, they want their kids to have a good education. They want them to have a job. And that's all people are looking for. They want to live in a nice neighborhood, where everybody can get along. That's all people are looking for.

I was a single mother raising 5 kids by myself and I put myself through school and then I had to be a role model for my kids. I'm just passionate about my work as a nurse. I work with the physically and mentally challenged.

Back in 1989, eleven of us that were all pregnant at the same time, one of our girlfriends, her child came out to be physically handicapped. And that really affected all of us because you know, you just take it for granted that when you have a baby, everything's going to be alright, and so then I started doing research and I went into a field where people can't help themselves. When you're physically and mentally handicapped, you have to have someone who's going to be an advocate for you with the doctors and other things, so I like the job that I'm doing. I feel that I'm doing something.

I work for a non-profit agency that has around 9 residents for mentally and physically challenged individuals. My house has 6 individuals that are in need of care. They're in wheelchairs and are non-verbal and I coordinate medication, I coordinate doctors' visits, annuals and quarterlies. If they have a state audit, I have to get that together - coordinate stuff with other nurses and supervisors.

My typical day is: I come in, I have to make sure they're taking their medication, that they're going to the doctor. If they have any kind of problem that will make them more disabled, like one consumer, I have to make sure she doesn't get pressure sores. She weighs only 35 pounds. She's 63 years old. I have to make sure that she gets the proper nutrition and everything. So, I have to coordinate with the nutritionist, the physical therapist, the doctors, because she's really, really, small. I have to work with all the different teams to make sure they get the proper care.

If you would see her you would fall in love with her. She doesn't have one gray hair. The only thing is, she can't speak or move. She's all contracted from being like that. But she's beautiful; she laughs. She has to eat baby food because her body won't digest anything else. Otherwise, it's a beautiful experience. You know why? Because you're giving care to somebody else that wouldn't be able to care for themselves.

Well, it's about sharing and advocating for me. Being a mother, I guess I just fell into that groove and became a nurse. It

> *Our country is built with stereotypes and if you don't come out of your box to get to know people and to voyage out and to go to other places,* **you only know of the stereotypes that they put in your head.**

wasn't about the money; it's about caring. It doesn't matter what kind of individual: whether it's the elderly, young or whatever. I'm about giving care 100%. On my job, I give more than what they ask for. They can't get up and go home like me, and go out to a movie or go walk around, and do other things like we do, so I just want to give them care because you know, it's so.... It's a thin line. Any one of us could have had a child that was physically or mentally challenged. At what point do you think that you could take care of a child correctly? So, that family couldn't take care of the child or had to abandon the child, so somebody had to take care of them. Somebody had to give them love. Nobody would have thought that they would have lived to be 60-70 years old.

I'm so happy that when I go to the doctor, the doctor says, "Woody, you know what? You have given the best care: the skin is so beautiful, there's no breakout. It's hard to believe this person is 63 years old." They're only slated to live a certain amount of years. So, you're happy when someone gives you a high five for doing a good job, because, who else would care for them? You become their family.

I take care of my aunt. She's 97 years old. Nobody else wanted her and I didn't want to put her in a nursing home. As long as you could breathe, you should have the best possible life that there is. She still could

walk; she still cooks for herself. She's starting to slow down. She's real slow now. She's 97 years old! How many people live that long to laugh and talk? I love that! I don't mind giving her care. I wash her, bathe her, that's what I want to do. We have to give back to people.

Our country is built on stereotypes and that's what comes down to the union. People have a stereotype against the union because they think unions are gonna come in and do something bad. They're not going to do anything bad. Unions are there to help you…I'll say, gain your freedom. Because when you work at a job and you don't have a union, like down in the South, they could fire you at will. You could be the best worker but you could be getting old, or something like that, and they could fire you at will. Unions are just there to help you with your rights. You have a right to be treated in a fair manner and that's why a union is there: to make sure you get 100% of your rights, and you're not being stepped on. They help you if you need training or more education. Unions are there to help you better yourself.

I'm a delegate too. I'm like in the shops to make sure peoples' rights are up to par. I'm not going to say unions are there just to have arguments and fight with management. No. We have to be like a symbiotic relationship: Union workers and manage-

ment. We have to work together because we're working together to either come out with a better product or come out with better care for the person that you're taking care of, so management and the workers in the union have to get along. Like we have to be one family. Yes, we're going to have disagreements upon some things, but in the end, it's what's good for whatever the client, the individual, or whatever job you're doing.

I have a lot of workers; they're in the dark. They don't go to meetings. They don't know what the union's offering. You have to go there and get involved and find out what the union has to offer you and what you could offer the union. That's why I became a delegate. I became a union member, then I wanted to know, "What is the union really about?" "What is it doing for me?" And I became a delegate and I started going to meetings. I started going to trainings. I started meeting everyone. It's like a family that's trying to help you. It's trying to help your family. Me, I wanted to go back to school. They helped me go back to school. You have to keep up your grades and they'll reimburse your tuition. But, [there's] so much information. I didn't know how to use a computer. I have a Mac and every time I needed to do my homework, I'd ask my kids, "Can you help me?" My kids would say, "Come on now - Why did you buy a Mac if you can't use it?" I went to the union. They sent me to a computer course. I learned the basics. I learned Word, and then I learned Excel. I can use the computer now! I'm so proud of myself! I can pay my bills, I can do other things. I can do research projects. I'm very proud of myself. That's why the union's there. You have to go and find out. It's there to help you. It's not just about going out there and marching and screaming and all that stuff. It's not like that. You have to go and find out. It's like one big family that's helping you go and let you achieve your dreams. They even have a credit union. They can help you buy a house, a car.

I will retire. I don't know when. I don't really know what I'll do. Maybe I'll volunteer in a nursing home or a program for seniors where they go out and do stuff. I am a nurse so I'd give my time doing that. When you meet people, they give you stories that have a life. It just gives you energy. When you see one of those consumers or individuals that can't speak, can't move and they smile at you, and you know, you feel happy 'cause you say, "I gave you something." They're not just laying there in the bed, waiting in the mire. If they're looking for you, following you with their eyes, smiling, and they're turning their heads, you know you did something good. As I age, who knows what kind of physical, or mental condition I will be in. If it comes to the point that I need care, because I'm in a nursing home, at an assisted living facility, or just at home, I pray that it will be a union worker helping to take care of me. Union workers are trained, caring professionals. It's a family, helping families take care of their families. I am a union worker taking care of people, and I love it.

You know to me, success is not about money or anything like that, you know if you have a brand new car or a house. Success is about the quality of life that you live. I'm not a millionaire but my quality of

I'm so happy that when I go to the doctor, the doctor says, "Woody, you know what? You have given the best care: the skin is so beautiful, there's no breakout. It's hard to believe this person is 63 years old." They're only slated to live a certain amount of years. So, you're happy when someone gives you a high five for doing a good job, because, who else would care for them? **You become their family.**

life is that I have my kids, my grandkids. My children, they're alright. My last daughter, she's in college, she has a job. My other kids, they have jobs; everybody's fine. That's my quality of life. I'm not a millionaire but I don't have to be a millionaire. I have my family and I have my health. That's it. If you have your health, and you have your family…For some people, they don't have family at all.

Dr. Karen Hoover
Attending Physician, Gouverneur Health, New York City
Service Employees International Union (SEIU), Doctor's Council

I'm from Youngstown, Ohio, and I grew up in a labor city. When I grew up, steel mills were still in their heyday. My dad was a lumber contractor with the steel mills. He was very much an anti-union guy and a Republican, which was normal in a small, suburban village like where we grew up, outside of Youngstown. I was always, at the encouragement of my parents, interested in academics and went on to go to Worcester College in Ohio and then to the University of New Hampshire to finish up my studies in zoology, and then I married and went to Baltimore and enrolled in Johns Hopkins in the School of Public Health and Hygiene. I got my degree there and went to N.I.H. for a six year fellowship, during which time I was developing a carcinogen testing model. On moving there is when I decided to turn and go into medicine, which is really something I wanted to do since I was, like, five years old. That's when I went down to Grenada for a couple of years to med. school. It was the first experience I had living anywhere outside of the U.S. Although it was not my favorite place to live, I found myself missing it when I came to Washington, D.C., to complete my medical education.

I came to medicine late. I was a researcher at N.I.H. (National Institutes of Health), and I went back into medical school in 1984, and I initially went to Grenada for a couple of years because I just kind of walked in on the MCATS cold and I didn't do great and I thought, "Well, I have a PhD from Hopkins in research and should be able to do this." But I ended up in Grenada for a couple years and then I came back into the American system two years later and graduated from G.W. Medical School. Then I ended up in New York for residency. I went to Manhattan VA for my residency, followed by a fellowship at Bellevue in infectious disease and HIV, and then after that, in 1994, I began work as an attending at Gouverneur. My full-time job then was in HIV, and, since then, that has cut down to about fifty percent of my work. I do internal medicine the other fifty percent of the time.

My enthusiasm for medicine has not waned in the least. I have been sorely strained in my practice by the changes that have gone on in medicine, which are really huge and impact worker stability and morale and productivity greatly, particularly in the setting in which I work, which is in a city-run operation. So, I've found that, for me, what is most satisfying is the opportunity to go into smaller community clinics. For several years I worked on a medical van for one session a week, in a needle exchange program, and I found that to be most rewarding, and I sort of like to be outside of the formal, high-tech setting of the hospital, which is where I work most of my time. The hospital I work in is a fully outpatient, ambulatory care center, except for a nursing home, which sits on top of it.

I have a second passion, one that takes up a lot of my time, which is social justice. I, for many years, have been the chair of the social justice committee at the Unitarian Church here in Manhattan. The Unitarian Church, I'll just mention, has seven principles, many of them have to do with social justice and honoring the dignity of each individual, and that's why I was attracted to the church in the first place. I, over the years, have been involved in many different causes that we've brought to the church. And the most recent one has been on economic justice and changes that the right has moved the U.S. toward, starting with an iconic document called, "The Lewis Powell Memo."

So, anyway, it's been a year in which we

are talking about the threat of social security and the taking away of that economic stability for citizens. We had a speaker who wrote a book called Invisible Hand, about the road map to change the U.S. in a very corporate centered way and how this has impacted the citizens. Our next speaker will talk about the economic instability of our aging population.

I'll just mention one more thing along those lines. We hope to have a panel discussion, which will, hopefully, include Rick Wolf, who's a terrific economist and one of the few economists who point out the inequities of our capitalistic system. We'll be having a woman who represents the Occupy Movement, in which several folks on the committee were involved, during its heyday. And we will probably be having a labor rep. to discuss the impact of the right wing agenda on labor and the trends in unions and worker economic protection and stability.

I was completely, personally, aware of the design of the rich and poor, for example in New York City, police brutality became an issue of interest to me in the 90's. I had a friend who was verbally assaulted and then arrested by a policeman for no good reason. So, I became interested in that. I didn't really do anything until Bush came in. When Bush came in, that threw me 180 degrees and I became a news junky. I read as much as I could. I began to read "The Nation." I became more aware and self-educated, and around that time, I became interested in social justice at our church. I was raised Methodist. My dad actually was a Christian Scientist, but he had encouraged me to go to medical school, unbelievably! I remember, I joined the U.U. church actually asking about the social justice committee. So I guess I really had an interest back then. But I didn't become a member till, probably,

'96, and then I subsequently took over as chair and hung onto that for many years.

In New York Health and Hospital's Corporation, there's really no choice about being in a union. There are two groups of physicians at Gouverneur: one is paid by N.Y.U., and one is paid by New York Health and Hospital's Corporation. So, we do have nonunion physicians, but it's just by choice who employs you. The union clarifies for me the evolving relationship between H.H.C. and its physician employees, which is not necessarily a bright spot in my career, because there's a growing interest in divesting pension plans. We have not negotiated it for three years because I think they fear there will be take-backs instead of any progress in benefits or salary. So, we are operating without a contract at present.

I would like to know more about labor issues and relations. I only go to a meeting every three months as a delegate, and I find that the union is a minuscule part of most physician's lives. They're not people who would join a union. If I had had the choice of whether to join a union or not, I would have, no question, because it's so inherently unfair to have no voice in a relationship. There has to be communication between the employer and the employee. And the employee must have some leverage in their work situation - not only in their benefits, but in how patients are treated and how a facility is welcoming of patients.

My concern over the years has been that, with the draining of funds for the hospitals, through Medicare and Medicaid and city budgets, state budgets, federal budgets, there is an interest in divesting from our position of helping everyone regardless of ability to pay. Sometimes I feel there is a purposeful difficulty set up in people being able to contact their doctors, to make appointments. When the hospital

After the earthquake, the union, SEIU, found the International Medical Core to work with and it turned out to be a wonderful organization, very functional and they actually sponsored our going to Haiti. I stayed there about two and a half weeks and it was an amazing experience. I did volunteer work at a clinic in New Orleans after Katrina. That's where I really feel most alive. It's when I'm in that situation, frontier medicine. **I feel like that's really where I should be.**

renovated and underwent a huge capital project, which is still continuing, they shut down the walk-in clinic, which was the real conduit from the community to the hospital. Many of the people had no insurance. So, I feel that it is important that physicians have a voice in how patients are seen, are treated, accessibility of the patients for their physicians, the timeliness of appointments. The physicians are still, by and large, cut out from any planning. We are simply told, "this is the way it's going to be".

One interesting example is that when rooms were set up for physicians in the new building, there was no input from the physicians on how to arrange or physically set up a room. As a result, they are not nearly as functional or as comfortable as they could be if they had had a contractor who knew how to build hospitals, and how

to build outpatient facilities. More importantly, they didn't really let us into the planning phases of that. So, the frustration with our union is that they are not invited into things like that.

There is an active plan now to distance H.H.C. from the physicians and the union by setting up a third party who is managing about 2200 of H.H.C.'s physicians in the city. That is called Physician Affiliate Group of New York. It is a private group of professional physicians and not nurses, who now will engage in contract negotiations with many of the facilities. And, H.H.C. will no longer be in direct contract negotiations. The union really struggled with this. We would have meetings in which they would say, "We don't know who they are. We have no idea what this is."

One thing that concerns me is that part of the negotiations that H.H.C. wants to include is that, the metrics - how long a patient is in

> *I get my energy and my renewed enthusiasm for medicine from them.* **And, I never fail to realize that, as grumpy as I am in the morning, it is the patients that will restore my energy.** *It is the most amazing profession in that it's the only one in which people, complete strangers, will sit down in the office with you and within five or ten minutes may be revealing issues that they wouldn't tell their best friend.*

the hospital, if they go back to the hospital within a month - Some of this is coming from the Affordable Care Act, but there is a set of, like, twelve metrics that they are totally putting on the shoulders of physicians. It's really a team effort: all of these different areas of patient care. Number one, it's unfair to expect the physicians to be responsible for all this but, number two, they also have another set of metrics in which they look at patients' outcomes with individual doctors and they are going to, eventually, hold this over the heads of the doctors in deciding who stays and who goes. When you boil it down to numbers, instead of looking at patients and their individual socioeconomic issues, it's really an unjust system that is going to only grow stronger in terms of how to judge what a successful medical facility is, and it has nothing to do with sitting down and listening to the patient. It's really teaching to the test. In this case, it's teaching to how much medication you prescribe, how many tests you run.

I don't have a favorite type of work. One work compliments the other because it all involves sitting down across from a patient and listening to them. So, basically, the satisfaction that I get from my job each day is going into the clinic and sitting down with my computer and waiting for the first patient to come in and sit down and visit me. I get my energy and my renewed enthusiasm for medicine from them. And, I never fail to realize that, as grumpy as I am in the morning, it is the patients that will restore my energy. It is the most amazing profession in that it's the only one in which people, complete strangers, will sit down in the office with you and within five or ten minutes may be revealing issues that they wouldn't tell their best friend. It is a profoundly huge responsibility and one that, sometimes, we don't handle as well as we should.

Our population is by and large from the lower socio-economic status and they have a lot of baggage. As someone who worked in a private office, there is a difference between patients in higher economic standing and patients I deal with now. Their larger struggle with financial stability and social issues, that revolve around their family and friends, substance abuse, children taken away from them by child protection agencies, divorces, partners that leave, partners that infect their other partners with HIV or sexually transmitted diseases… It's a mix of factors that lead to disorganized lives in some cases, and it's sometimes hard to make significant progress in health. American medicine is all about treating the illness and not about protection and prevention as much as it should be. In our population, I would say it's even more of a challenge to encourage people and see people change in quitting cigarette smoking, substance use, abusive relationships. It's hard and it's something that comes home to you right away when you deal with this population. I don't know how I would be in their environment, but I'm sure most people have no idea what it really is like.

I find that, just from an educational point of view, very interesting just to listen to this, but also to have to figure out how to navigate through a system that is not very functional all the time. Like, at Gouverneur, we don't have a lot of access to counseling and to psychiatry. We've just gone through a period in which our patients were sent up to behavioral health and told, "Oh, we'll call you when we can see you." And, they never get a call. So, it's been a frustrating experience in some ways, and we don't really have the number of case managers or social workers to help. Probably the most important issue is helping people live

healthy lives, and helping them with their economic issues. In terms of people who are on welfare and who simply don't get very much money to live on, and in New York, which is one of the most expensive cities in the world to live in, it's a constant struggle.

We see a traditional underclass in New York, but more and more we see people who have had good salaries, who have not been able to find a job and so we're seeing more of an influx of the traditional middle class also. They have their own set of problems, too. Certainly, anxiety over not having a job is a big one, but it has become more of a mix, as has the neighborhood in which we live. Since I've been there, since '94, what was a very traditional Lower East Side neighborhood, a very vibrant Jewish population and a lot of Chinese, lots of Dominicans coming in, a very interesting mix. It has been a microcosm of what is going on in much of N.Y.C.

I went to med. school when I was thirty-five or thirty-six, so, I'm sixty-four now, and I plan to work for another five years in the system and then go into, hopefully, international health. I don't really plan on retiring, as such, if I can help it, as long as my health holds out.

Another thing that the union did for me was - I got a call from the union back three years ago - asking if I'd like to go to Haiti. I expressed interest in going on medical trips. After the earthquake, the union, S.E.I.U., found the International Medical Core to work with and it turned out to be a wonderful organization, very functional and they actually sponsored our going to Haiti. I stayed there about two and a half weeks

and it was an amazing experience. I did volunteer work at a clinic in New Orleans after Katrina. That's where I really feel most alive. It's when I'm in that situation, frontier medicine. I feel like that's really where I should be. I should just quit work now and do what I love, but I probably will put it off another few years, I guess, because I feel freedom is really important, and, I want to be financially O.K. As long as we have a pension, another five years would help. I'm counting on the fact that primary care is a very underemployed field right now and that I'll still be able to work, even at an advanced age.

Success? It's funny that you mentioned that. I was at work over the weekend and I was doing some Xeroxing and looked over at some stuff in the mailbox of the social worker. She had in there an article, from the Guardian in London, called, "The Top Five Regrets of the Dying." The first one really defines what I see as success: "I wish I had the courage to live a life true to myself and not the life others expected of me." And I would say, for me, that's success. The next one is, "I wish I wouldn't have worked so hard." I haven't come to that point yet. It may be PollyAnnish but that's how I see success, as being able to follow my heart. I went back to school with the help of my mother when I was thirty-six, and I never could have done that without her help, and I just feel as if that was really what I was destined to do. She helped financially and she was very supportive of that decision even though it seemed like such a crazy thing to go back to school when I had gotten into a research career. But, she also knew that my dad wanted me to go to medical school. I think she supported it from that perspective.

My mother just died at 100. She died, in bed, one night after her 100th birthday. We were fortunate enough that, on October 14, she turned 100 and we were fortunate enough to give her a party with all her relatives. Some of them came from California and Oregon. There are very few people who can have a family reunion before their funeral like that. She had moved up to Cleveland with my sister. I have two sisters: one is in Cleveland and is a retired physical therapist, and she still works part-time in a rehab facility, the other one is a computer tech who lived in San Diego for many years and just moved to North Carolina a few months ago. They're both largely retired. They're four and five years older than I am.

If I were to die tomorrow, I would go pretty much feeling like I had done what I had wanted to do. I mean, I don't mean to be self-satisfied. All these things need to be done and one of them is, I wish I had more time to devote to my friends. But, in general: I think that I went into medicine, I went to New York City, which was my dream, and I really don't have major regrets in that area. I guess I was raised by my dad to see a career as a vital part of life, so, that really defines me.

Success, in another way too, suggests to me being able to accrue enough funds so that I don't feel like I'm gonna be destitute. Having gone back to school, and having been in school for many years, I'm not as well off as many of my cohorts. It's part of the reason that I need to stay another five years here.

...an article, from the Guardian in London, "The Top Five Regrets of the Dying." The first one really defines what I see as success, and it's, **"I wish I had the courage to live a life true to myself and not the life others expected of me."**

Joey Hovarter

Sheet Metal Detailer, Moore, Oklahoma

Sheet Metal Workers, Local 124

I am mainly a husband and a father. I'm also an instructor for our local sheet metal school. I've been married for 16 years. I have an 18 year old, an 11 year old, and an 8 month old. That's been one of my goals in life - values. I would say I have traditionally conservative values. Christian values…that kind of covers beliefs, too. I'm kind of an introvert. I'm definitely not an extrovert, not very social. So, this is kind of difficult for me, to talk about myself.

I'm a detailer. I take the engineers' or the architects' drawings and then I detail them based on how our shop installs ductwork and sheet metal that we put in. We basically add all the fine details to the drawings. Most of the sheet metal is air conditioning ductwork. So, at your home, you have a furnace or something that delivers air to each room, and we create the ductwork that conveys the air and encapsulates it, and all of that ductwork has to be fabricated. So, we put on the drawings, [the] lengths, measurements, locations, sizes, onto all of that ductwork and how to fabricate it and into what specifications you have to fabricate it to. We basically put all that on a drawing. We give elevations of where to hang all of this ductwork and then coordinate it with all of the other various trades: plumbing systems, electrical systems, sprinkler systems, everything else you have to make room for. Basically, we lay out a road map for these guys to A) fabricate it and B) to install it - new construction, even old construction, remodeling.

Our international training has developed software that can help us do that. They post an apprentice competition every year, and since this is new, they really hadn't had any apprentices, so they opened it up for detailers, which is what I am. They had a competition that you go to for three days and I finished first out of 12 other competitors across the nation. The prize was a Harley Davidson motorcycle.

I started out by driving the truck, delivering stuff and then working in the field and helping them install it. Then I moved up to a foreman, and then I basically ran the project. From there I moved up into the office. Basically, what I'm doing now, [is] working on the computer, drafting details onto drawings. I'm still a sheet metal worker. Tomorrow I could change and go back into the field or into the shop fabricating and installing.

It's a love/hate relationship. I love the work I do. I hate the time frame they give us to do it in. It's so compressed. You know, time is money, so the time is so compressed that we get to spend on a project. We build things faster. With computers, everything's supposed to be faster. Everything's supposed to be more coordinated. I really like the things that I do, but sometimes it's very stressful as far as time is concerned. That would be the enemy - time. Basically I'm in a stage of where everybody's waiting for my drawings to actually start fabrication and then start installation. When we initially get awarded a job, I'm one of the first people that it goes to, and then I do all of my stuff in preparation to send it out to everybody else. So usually, everybody's waiting on me.

I don't know, most of the time, you're just so busy that you don't remember that you like it anymore. Do you know what I mean? I think that's probably the state I'm in right now. You're just so overwhelmed with trying to get something done, you don't really remember that you like it. But, like I said, I can always take a break. That's the nice thing about the union: I'm not stuck where I'm at. I mean, you're not locked into a company. There's all kinds of companies. Here in Oklahoma,

I think there's thirty different companies, contractors, that I could go work for. That's one thing the union's done for me. You're not really locked into working in the same place forever if you don't want to be. Once I've had that skill that I've learned, I can take that elsewhere.

The union put me to work. They have a hiring hall. They, essentially, will field the calls that come in for work. So, if I decided that I'm ready to change job duties, I'm ready to change companies, [I] turn in my notice and put my name on the list, and my name will go out to those other contractors if they want to hire me. So, really it's similar to a job hall.

All of our contractors basically sign a contract with the union, that they will use union help. And we bargain our wages so all of the sheet metal workers get the same wage. We have wages and then some fringe benefits, a health and welfare plan, and then we have a 401K and retirement. What we get paid, our total package, we put some of that back into our training fund and various things of that nature to upkeep the union. I do get some vacation, I do get paid some sick leave, and some holidays, but all of that basically is negotiated with the single contractor. It's above and beyond what they're required to pay me.

I graduated high school and then the very next week I started with a sheet metal contractor. I was a truck driver. I took all the materials that they fabricated and I drove them to the various jobs. That was in '93. I graduated and then started work that same summer. I've been a sheet metal worker ever since. I'm on my nineteenth year. My dad was a sheet metal worker. I believe he's coming up on forty years. He was a sheet metal worker before I was born. He had it in high school. You know, they had metal shop, and then he got into the union and they trained him as an apprentice and he turned out, and, so yeah, he's always had that profession.

I didn't really have any plans about what I was doing, so this was basically just a job to get me started and I just never have changed. If I was going to change, it probably would be to just another contractor. It has a lot of change involved in it. You may work on one side of the city on one building, and then on the other side of the city in a different building; you know, the same week or it may be six months apart.

Most of the guys that work at our shop are the same guys over and over. There are times we get busy and there are layoffs, so the labor pool just kind of shifts around to the different contractors. But for the most part, there's a core group. In order to create a good working environment, you've got to have a set amount of people. Then you know their personalities and what they're capable of. It's like a small community, where you know everybody.

I think my dad is proud to some extent. I think he wishes I picked a different field because you know, construction work is a hard life, until you get into an office position like I am. Then you get fat from sitting in front of the computer, and the stress is more. I think he has reservations both ways. Sometimes I think he wishes I would've gone to college and done something a little better. But, I don't really think we've talked about it that much.

The only actual hobby that I have right now is I play golf. I would like to…if I retire someday, I'd like to travel. My wife and I would like to travel in a travel trailer or an RV of some sort and just see the United States. Stay in various places and see various places. With the Harley here, I'm getting into riding motorcycles. That would be my next thing. I kind of take things, you

Our international training has developed software that can help us do that. They post an apprentice competition every year, and since this is new, they really hadn't had any apprentices, so they opened it up for detailers, which is what I am. They had a competition that you go to for three days and I finished first out of 12 other competitors across the nation. **The prize was a Harley Davidson motorcycle.**

know, one at a time until I master them and then I move on. I may not ever touch whatever that is again, but right now that's golf and the motorcycle. Most recently, I did that with computers. It got me into the detailing that I'm in. Basically, teaching myself computers and learning computers; working on them, tearing them apart and putting them back together, build 'em from scratch, all the software, stuff like that. I really haven't done anything else with that, lately.

How do you define success? I struggled with that. I don't really know that I have a good answer for that. Completion is the only thing I really come up with for success. I mean, once you feel like you've completed something, successfully, whether that be a job or just a specific thing that I've done, when you could look back and see that you've accomplished something. I don't really feel successful, I guess. That was a tough one for me. I don't really know. I thought about that one [question] more than I thought about any of the rest of them, and I still don't have a great answer for it. When you have a puzzle, when you have all the pieces in the right place, you're complete.

I don't know if you ever reach that as a person. As long as I would be able to retire and do the things I want to do, I think I'll probably feel successful. I could complete that chapter I guess. I consider success to be a longer journey. I still have a hard time with that. If you partition it up, some days just being able to come home from work is a success. You know, to be able to finish a job is a success. It really depends on how far you break it down. For me, lots of days, I would consider just being able to accomplish what I do in one day a success. So, long term or short term, I guess, it's a wide open question. I don't really look that far ahead. I don't really have a lot of goals to accomplish. Good or bad, I feel like I take on something that I want to do and I do it then, and when the next thing comes along, I jump to it, and I don't really have a set plan. I think you would probably have to have that in order to create success.

Overall, I think as long as I'm happy, I'm probably successful. I personally don't think I can put a number or a specific time or a specific thing to it. I think, you know, as long as you're happy, you're successful. I may not accomplish anything else again. But as long as I'm happy with that, it doesn't have to have a title to it. That's why I have such a hard time with it because success really doesn't apply to me. I don't feel like it's all based on what I think of it, but as what somebody else is trying to define it as.

[In the 2013 tornado], we lost our house and a few belongings but no lives. Union co-workers from Harrison Orr, or shall I say friends, helped during cleanup. One friend (Mark Stricklin, Sheet Metal Workers Local 124) along with my father-in-law, was there after the tornado as we gathered essentials. Only what we could carry in three suitcases we had in a closet, the rest we had to leave and hope it didn't rain. My direct foreman came to help early the next day, with Mark returning, as well as other family and some friends. We picked up most everything we could salvage and moved to the grandparent's garage.

Following the initial cleanup we had several union members meet at the house, and along with other volunteers we dismantled the house by hand and moved it to the curb in one day, hours in fact. When they finished, they even raked the yard of debris.

Countless members, contractors and locals donated cash money to our local, which, in turn, set up a fund and distributed the monies to our members affected. Our international also had a fund, which provided money as well. The amount was quite substantial, more than I received from any other organization and actually puts any other organization to shame. I would say about 50% of help was from family and friends, 45% union and another 5% from actual disaster organizations.

Howard at the 19th annual Screen Actors Guild Awards with Sally Field,
Photo: Amy Tierney/ SAG-AFTRA

Ken Howard

Actor

President, SAG-AFTRA, Los Angeles, California

Screen Actors Guild-

American Federation of Television and Radio Artists

(SAG-AFTRA)

When I first saw the question on how to describe myself, aside from the obvious, driver's license description of height and weight, what I am, really, is a working actor. That's my role in life. I'm a happily married man and have grown-up stepchildren from a former marriage that I spend time with and I work with a couple of causes. The Onyx and Breezy Foundation provides funding for various animal help, rescue, spay and neuter programs. I am also a chancellor of the National Kidney Foundation because I had a kidney transplant in the year 2000. I serve on the boards of the Screen Actors Guild Foundation and the Actors Fund. I think that's the way philanthropy works - you become more and more involved in the things that touch your life.

I've been a working union actor of all three unions for well over forty years and in 2008, I joined the board of the Screen Actors Guild. When I began serving on the board, actors were divided and our unions were facing off in a confrontation that could easily have left us permanently weakened. Instead, SAG and AFTRA members seized that turbulent, risky energy, and used it as a springboard to greater unity and strength through our historic merger.

As for my life away from acting, I like teaching. I taught at Harvard for three years in the late '80s, went to Kent State for a while to get the Master in Fine Arts that I never finished at Yale. I graduated out of Amherst in '66, and I went to Yale on a fellowship for a Master in Fine Arts. Yale was wonderful, but I left after two years to do a Broadway show. This past fall, I went back to Amherst and taught a class on acting. I've always liked teaching and enjoy it very much.

My personality, I'll leave that to you. I think I'm outgoing when it's required and a bit of a loner in a way, but I think that's really part of actors and artists and how we function. That's the nature of the beast. I'll give you just one anecdote that kind of says it all. About thirty years ago, my youngest stepchild, her nickname was Cricket, she was about twelve or thirteen, and she'd have a few little girlfriends over. A lot of times I'd be outside by the pool and I'd be walking up and down and running lines, and then I'd take a swim. And one of her friends

...there's such a sense of commitment to something larger than ourselves; *to an ideal. Labor's a movement, not an institution. It's a movement to protect a lot of people. I am honored to be a part of it and I have learned so much from people and I think one of my contributions is that I am the genuine article in terms of being a working actor.*

said, "Cricket, whenever we come over here, your dad's always over there talking to himself. Why is that?" And Cricket said, "No, no, no. He's not talking to himself. He's talking to other people who aren't here right now."

You spend a lot of time preparing and getting ready on your own. Sometimes, there's a difference between some very talented people who work in film and in television who are working in bits and pieces, but if you've starred on the stage and played big roles, whether they're contemporary or Shakespeare or whatever else, you sometimes wind up being a loner in terms of work. I think I'm relatively outgoing in my personal life, but a lot of my time is spent with my work. Also, I'm not part of an active working community where I go to an office or I work with the same people. You're going to different jobs and it changes. By its nature, it's kind of a loner's life in terms of how you move through it and how one lives. You have to live a little bit like a gypsy, because work changes. Even where the job is changes: Are you shooting on the West Coast? Is it on the East Coast? Is it somewhere else?

One of the things that always makes me laugh with my agents is that a job will come up, something that might even last

for a while, and I'll say, "Well, where is it?" They will say, "Oh, it's in Los Angeles." Now, that's like saying it's in New England. So, I'll say, "But where in Los Angeles?" It's the difference between being at the Sony Pictures lot or Warner Bros. studios or Universal Studios. Sometimes it even has to do with transportation or where you're going to move. It's very much a part of the work process for creative people, people who are working in that way, whether they're composers or painters, or writers, or dancers. There's a lot of private work.

(I quoted someone as having said Ken Howard is the least egotistical of anyone they've met in the acting field.)

If I agree with that, then that immediately makes me egotistical! Maybe I would rephrase it. Maybe the person should have said that they're sure that I'm not one of the most egotistical actors in the profession. That would be easy! I must tell you, when people go, "Oh, actors with their big egos!" Believe me, the business we're in, if you look around, whether it's producers, directors, writers, even costume designers, brilliant set designers, cinematographers, there are a lot of egos. There are a lot of big egos within the arts that you run into all the time. [But], I think the great majority of actors are really very much working talent. They're eager to get the job, do the best they can, and go home to their families. There are a very small percentage of people who are in the headlines.

I can't tell you the number of people who've come up to me and they're amazed that, whether it's George Clooney or Brad Pitt or whomever, they've said, "Oh I've met him. He's very nice. He's kind of down to earth and really easy to talk to." And I say, "Of course! What do you think? We're all just lunatics?" But, that's a very nice compliment. I appreciate it.

There are lots of levels to my work. You can get into the weeds. That's why I like teaching at Amherst, trying to set up the building blocks with young people. The word is overused, but it is a craft. It

is working and it's the building blocks of learning. It's a very physical, mental, emotional, spiritual thing when somebody's getting ready to do this work. And, it's not replaceable. The level of performance, the reason a performer is doing some material, whether they're singing or acting or dancing, can move us to laughter, to tears, to joy, to sorrow.

It's very special, the creative arts, and it's an honor and a joy to be part of it even with its ups and downs. The people that are members of SAG-AFTRA all have a sense of that. I've always liked the idea of the creative community being under one tent. I include our broadcaster members and recording artist members in that. I think it's a very creative field as well, for the people

photo courtesy of SAG-AFTRA

photo courtesy of SAG-AFTRA

who are writing it and delivering it. There's a reason we are drawn to it, and it has to do with human nature, what we share.

As far as a typical day, every one is different. I do brush my teeth almost always when I get up in the morning, that part is consistent, and before I go to bed at night. If, for example, I'm shooting 30 Rock, I'm in New York, staying in Soho, and a car is going to pick me up and take me to Brooklyn, and I'm going to shoot for a couple of days and then get on a plane. Out here [in Los Angeles], the demand has nothing to do with the acting. It's the driving, because sometimes it takes a couple of hours of traffic to get there. Other times, if it's a play, it's a whole other kind of work where you're only required to work for two to three hours, but then it's a live audience

and it's very, very stressful, and you don't get to have a second take and you've got to get it right the first time. It's also rather joyous because you have lots of feedback. And, of course, if you're shooting a film, you could be off who knows where, once again, living the life of a gypsy. Unless it's a very long shoot, you're usually in a hotel. The last couple of films I did, one was in Georgia, and one was in Annapolis, Maryland.

It's a strange life. Noel Coward always referred to people who don't work in show business as civilians, because there's almost no way to explain it to people. It's such a strange way to make a living. The strangest part of it, which kind of comes back to the value of unions, is that there are no guarantees - as I'm talking with you right now - in any way, that anybody will hire me ever to work again. Sometimes things are good, but sometimes they're not. Sometimes you get to choose to do things that are creatively very fulfilling and better in terms of your long-term career than what is the best buck, and other times you need to take something that pays the rent, but there are no guarantees.

There is no cushion. You can create one for yourself, become a corporation, have some protections, but that's where the union comes in, in a huge way. It's not only there for protection in terms of your health and safety on the set and with minimum wages, but with health and pension. I know because I had a kidney transplant in the year 2000. It would've been an enormous cost except it was covered because I'd earned my SAG health insurance. That's a huge part of what unions have done for people, have done for actors, and what we will continue to do.

I had a blockage that was misdiagnosed. By the time they caught up with it, the damage had been done. They performed something called a TURP, and then they said [in 1995], probably in about five years you're going to need a kidney transplant, and five years from then, sure enough, I did. A gal I've been friends with for a long time - her name's Jeannie Epper - she's part of a great family of stunt performers. I'd say she's the most famous female stunt performer there is. She's the only one who's won a [Taurus World Stunt Award] lifetime achievement award. She gave me one of her kidneys. That's certainly a humbling experience, when someone gives you a piece of themselves to keep you alive. I was very thankful for that, and all that was covered, because I had already been a working SAG member for a long time.

[Retirement] never crossed my mind. If a business is youth oriented, a lot of times, I think in an unfortunate way - it can make a difference to writers and directors, even producers, where they're looking for the younger viewpoint. I think sometimes they lose a great deal of talent. They move a little too soon. Now, the roles that I go up for, that they consider me for, are people who are my age, people in their late sixties, early seventies; I'm probably on the short list of people like this. But, that desire to work doesn't go away. There's always a role to be played.

I remember years ago, Jason Robards said something that was so funny. He had been offered the role of King Lear back in the American Repertoire Theater, and he said in that wonderful way, with that great voice of his, "Now isn't that typical. By the time you're old enough to play King Lear, there's no way you can remember all those goddamn lines." And, it's true! Isn't it? So, anyway, that doesn't stop me. So, there's no point retiring unless you don't like doing it. There are things about the business that can irritate me, but I love acting. I love the doing of it, and always have and always will.

It's a creative process and it is something that can be broken down. But, it takes a little more than that. I thought the most revealing remark I ever heard about it was from George C. Scott, who at some point was talking about acting, and he said, "Look, when acting comes naturally to people and you work on it, try to improve and all, there's work to be done, but it's not that hard to do. And, for people who can't do it, really, it's impossible." It's true, in a way. I know it's stressful, and as I get older it's takes a little longer, just the way I walk through it, learning the lines and all that. But it's something that in some ways always came naturally to me, like hitting a baseball or something.

Even though it's demanding, it's not

really as hard as it might be to, as Coward would say, to a civilian. It would be like me trying to get thrown into the midst of the stock market or something, making deals, using a whole different kind of language, and trying to explain it. I think the problem you run into, you may have somebody who's intelligent in some areas who will jump into the stock market and say, "Well, I'm smart enough," and just gets killed. And, that happens also in the world of show business. There are people who are very bright, with a great deal to offer, and they step into this area, whether it's on stage or in front of a camera, and they're really not equipped, and as audiences, we know in a minute! "Whatever that is, that isn't any good." "That's just frozen and stiff." "That's no good."

One of the great ironies with acting is, when you're really doing it right, it doesn't look like you're acting. It doesn't look like anything. With a certain ease, it just happens. And, it should look effortless. But, how to get to that? It's tedious to talk about unless you're in an acting class. Even in terms of teaching, people say, "You want to come in and teach for a weekend?" and I say, "Well, I can tell stories, but it won't be of any use." You really have to put some time into it, at least a semester or some time, several classes a week, just to get a handle on some of this. It's not that it's that mysterious; it just takes time to even talk about the nuts and bolts of it, and get people to have a sense of what it is.

I did this with my class at Amherst and it's kind of fun; If you want to get a sense of the demands, just go through Shakespeare's sonnets and pick one that you like - you know, it's only 14 lines, which means 140 syllables - and learn it. Commit it to memory, not just so you can write it out on a test, but to memory so you can speak it, on a breath or two, and just get it out there. It's beautifully written. And, it's amazing how long that takes, even for somebody who knows how to do this stuff. You have to do it again and again and again. Somebody would say, "How long did it take you to learn?" And I'd say, "I have no idea." I'd just run it through my head and I'd have it on a piece of paper, look at it, get it and do it again and again, think it through, wake up in the middle of the night … and finally, have it, like an old song.

A week later, you check, you have it even more and more and then, you've got it. It's in you and it comes out of you in a way that just flows and looks very natural. It shouldn't look like such a big deal. And the amount of time it takes, depending on the person, is remarkable. And then, what it takes to know it well enough that you can do it with a certain spontaneity. If you do that, over the course of a month, you find yourself saying, "How does he get this... the son-of-a-bitch, this is impossible! It's awful!" But, after a month or so, if you just kept doing it, going back to it over and over, you'd have it. You would say, "I know that! I got it! I got it in me...I can say it and isn't that nice!" I had my students do that and one student said to me, "I'll know this for the rest of my life." And, I said, "Yes, but you might want to revisit it every now and then. Just run it through your head again like an old song. Take it from me, it won't last forever." Although, some of the roles do last forever, particularly something like a sonnet; once you have it, you can probably have it forever. I've learned so many big, long parts of plays I could probably summon back with help, but I couldn't tell you what it was from.

I remember some big Broadway opening nights. I wasn't one of those performers that throw up ahead of time.

The level of performance, the reason a performer is doing some material, **whether they're singing or acting or dancing, can move us to laughter, to tears, to joy, to sorrow.** *It's very special, the creative arts, and it's an honor and a joy to be part of it, even with its ups and downs.*

I was pretty relaxed. But, when the show was over sometimes, I'd be feeling like I don't know if I'm going to cry or throw up. I asked a friend of mine, a psychologist, "What's that about?" "Well," he said, "It's close to when you steer your way through an impending accident that could kill you, and then you make it to the other end of it, and you sit there, and you've made it, and all the emotion flows through." And I said, "That's a good description of a Broadway opening night." If you think about it, at any moment, everything could go wrong.

Sports are like that. As you're going through moments that are high pressure and everything's riding on it, there's a certain exhilaration and also a certain calm. One of the dangers of performing is adrenaline. Adrenaline is good, but that can get in the way. You have to stay calm and breathe and manage so all that's under control. There's kind of a focus that you have when you're performing that even if a lot of emotions are coming out of you and are part of what you're doing, I think you probably wouldn't want to pause and think about, "How am I really feeling about what I'm doing right now?" It's probably not a good idea. It's probably better to just think what you're doing next. And then, think about how it felt when it's all over. Sure, you are feeling all kinds of things; the audience is seeing you feeling it, but acting is what you do,

not what you feel. The feeling follows. And in any human being, if you're trying to accomplish enough things and it's getting in the way, and you have to make a great effort, all kinds of feeling comes pouring out of you. It's very natural and spontaneous and of the moment.

I've worked with directors, and whenever they have a quick explanation, you know they don't know what they're talking about. It's just more complicated than that. It's like the golf swing. It's like somebody saying, "Just tell me in five minutes or less and show me a few things, and I can just go out and have a beautiful golf swing, or an ugly golf swing." That's the other thing; it doesn't have to be a beautiful golf swing to get the job done. That's why actors and actresses don't necessarily have to be beautiful. There has to be some beauty they're bringing to it, of emotion and thought process...I kind of like that analogy. I've got to think about that more; It's not how pretty the golf swing is or how ugly it is - it's whether it gets the job done. The description of it is complicated. That's why I said the golf swing. The golf swing itself is a rather simple affair that has to do with, you know, centrifugal and centripetal forces, and if you really can feel the swing and turn away and swing back and keep your head back. That's all it is. It's simple: You don't need a PhD for it.

When I studied with Stella Adler and Robert Lewis when I was at Yale, one thing that stuck in my mind, even before I started reading Stanislavsky, was…what prompted Stanislavsky to write these huge works, "An Actor Prepares" and "Building a Character"? He was trying to answer this one question: Why is it that there are some people on the stage who I can't take my eyes off, and others that I can? What is it about that person that holds my attention? Is it size? No, sometimes they are very small. Is it youth, beauty? No, sometimes it's a homely looking person. What is it? Is it the voice? No. What is that that just grabs our attention? You feel it when you're in an audience. You can tell from the balcony. Somebody comes on and they just hold your attention and there's something about all the work that they've done, their inner being, the kind of emotion they bring on, just step by step, a kind of command that comes from within. I guess you can call it charismatic, or whatever else it is. It's fascinating and it comes from all kinds of preparation and work. Just why does your eye go to a certain athlete out on the field or to a certain puppy in the litter? What is it about that one puppy? It's sort of complicated, almost spiritual, how that all happens.

As an actor, you're trying to breathe life into something that's coming off the page, and do it in a way that's arresting for an audience. That takes a lot of work. Some actors - and I think I'm falling into this trap - love to talk about it. Usually, I want to go home and work on it myself and then just show up at work kind of ready to go. The nicest compliments I've gotten from directors or producers or writers, not so much with stage, but with film, they'll come up and say something complimentary, and then they'll say, very quietly, "We're so glad you're not one of those 'method' actors." And, I say, "Well, actually, I am! I just do that work at home."

Most actors use a few different methods, but they better have a method, and a pretty extensive one, or, you know, they're not going to be very good actors. By the way, if you asked most really good actors or actresses what's required, they will all say to you - and they're not lying - learn your lines, don't bump into the furniture, look the other person in the eye, and be as truthful as possible. And, that's really true. I mean, that is all it is. It's just that the actual doing of that - learn your lines, don't bump into the furniture, look at the other person, tell 'em the truth - is not as simple as it sounds. But it is a simple act and it's what it is. I'm not trying to make it sound like it's rocket science or brain surgery. It really isn't. It's labor. It's a series of tasks.

I think [success] is a changing thing. It changes for people. For me, when I was young, I wanted to make a mark. I wanted to be somebody. I wanted to have recognition. And then, as you get older, you still want to do well, but you start thinking more in terms of giving back. The search becomes more and more one of looking for inner peace. And, part of inner peace as we get older is the sense of giving back to the world we're in, doing for others. It's loving for the sake of how good it makes you feel to love others, whether it's for your spouse, animals, or worldwide. I think it's not selfish exactly, but it is something that, in the doing of it, we feel better. So, I feel that way more and more, and I love acting and I like making a living, but the older I get, the more I want to do things that I know will give me a certain inner happiness, a certain kind of comfort with who I am. I mean, I appreciate the advice of agents and publicists and all that, and I need that, and that's fine. I was always pretty sure of what I needed to do and not do, but now I'm clearer on it. Some things are fulfilling and you feel good about it, others sometimes really aren't so. The notion of a successful life, I would think, is that as you get near the end of it, you think it was not all for naught, some of it was of some value to others. And of course, you know, real performers are suckers for that because they're really entertaining us. If you're doing it right, you're always giving of yourself to the part, to the audience, to the people who you're working with. There is something that's just in the nature of it.

One of the things that did happen to me once I got into this position, the president of the Screen Actors Guild, and now SAG-AFTRA, dealing with all these people [who work for the union], both members who are doing this for free, and also very hard working staff, there's such a sense of commitment to something larger than themselves: to an ideal. Labor's a movement, not an institution. It's a movement to protect a lot of people. I am honored to be a part of it and I have learned so much from people and I think one of my contributions is that I am the genuine article in terms of being a working actor. I'd done it for so long and in every venue, that that's where I was knowledgeable, that part I knew. To be able to help with something like this, to help others, the overall feeling is a marvelous one. It's one of accomplishing something and being, to a certain degree, selfless, because it has to be that way, otherwise it doesn't work, and it all kind of fits together.

Part of inner peace as we get older is the sense of giving back to the world we're in, doing for others. *It's loving for the sake of how good it makes you feel to love others, whether it's for your spouse, animals, or worldwide. I think it's not selfish exactly, but it is something that, in the doing of it, we feel better.*

"Our rescue dog Shadow who ended up rescuing me."
Photo by Daniela Scaramuzza

Julie Lusk

Flight Attendant, American Eagle, Bedford, Texas
Association of Flight Attendants
Communication Workers of America (CWA)

Tell me about Julie… Julie is type A, like many flight attendants: bossy, structured…Our job basically is the same thing over and over again. What's different is the passengers, the crew, the different folks that you come across every day. The job itself is the same. Because of the regulations, the routine is the same. I like that. I am organized, always early. You really have to be giving in this job. You're taking care of people, whether they're flying to a funeral or a wedding or a business function, you take care of them and that's your job. You get them from point A to point B. Love my friends, love my family, have a great time just being together. I'm outgoing, typical Capricorn really: methodical, organized, structured, not really a fly-by-the-seat-of-the-pants kind of girl. I will be forty-three. I have a husband and he works in another state, so we go back and forth to see each other. I moved my mom to Texas. I'm her caretaker and I'm an aunt, I'm a sister, lots of friends. Everyone lives fairly close.

I would say we're not a religious family. I mean it's not a specific; you know we're not Mormon, we're not Catholic, we're not anything, but I do believe that most people are good. I believe in integrity; if you give your word, you keep it. Honesty…you do the right thing, even if it's not the most comfortable thing for you, you do the right thing.

I had worked in banking, retail banking, for 6 years. I started when I was nineteen and worked at my local bank, and worked in a number of branches. [I] did new accounts and loans and everything. At some point it was starting to get old, being in the same office, same thing every day, same box. That was kind of wearing. So I figured, at twenty-five, it was time for a change. I didn't want to hate my job for the rest of my life. There had to be something else that I could really enjoy. And one of the girls that I worked with had interviewed and gotten a job at Continental. She said, "You know, you'd really love it. If you decide to leave banking, you should look into this."

A few months later, there was an ad in the paper and I conned one of my friends into going with me, and actually, we both got hired. She didn't take the job, but I did. It was time to move on and a good opportunity. It was a complete change. I was moving from San Diego to Dallas, alone. Didn't know anybody except the others from my class: totally new job, new way of being paid, new faces, new everything. But I think it was really good for me. I'm from San Jose, the Bay area, in California. I moved my mother out here six years ago.

I work for American Eagle. Actually, my friend that had gone to Continental still works there. So, I have seventeen years this month.

Our schedules are on a month-to-month basis. I've been with the company long enough that I'm actually what we call a line-holder, so I have a regular schedule every month that I get on. Everything's based on seniority. The kids that are on the list higher than me, maybe get the trips that I want, the schedule that I want, but it's pretty flexible, as far as days off and what time you start and finish, that kind of thing. So, we show up an hour before our first departure - I'm up a couple of hours before that - get dressed, drive to the airport, make sure I'm in full uniform. For me, that's important, to look professional. I'm a first responder, I'm a safety professional, so I want to make sure I look the part. People are looking to me in an emergency, so I make sure I'm all together.

I get to work, I sign in, I get my paperwork, check my schedule, find out

You know, twenty-five, thirty years ago, **they checked you for your girdle, you had to wear false eye lashes, you had to weigh a certain amount,** *you had to carry this, that, and the other thing, you had to carry their liquor with you, it wasn't put onto the airplane. If there was any food served, you had to carry that. You also had your tote bag with your wallet and your make-up and your suitcase and everything else. So, a lot has changed and I'm so thankful for those people that stood up and said, "Yes... You know what? We really need to have some rules."*

what cities I'm going to, what crew I'm flying with, how many passengers I have. I meet with the gate agent. We go over any special services: if there are wheelchairs or maybe minors traveling alone, anything unusual about the flight I need to know about before I get on the plane. We do the same with crews: go over weather, if there's any security issues - anything interesting. And we all hope for non-interesting days, those are the best.

We board the aircraft thirty minutes before departure. I'm following all of my Federal Air Regulations, "FAR's", as they call them, as far as baggage and safety. Then, "Hello!" and "Good Morning" and "Welcome Aboard."

There are certain things I must do before I close the aircraft door: paperwork that has to be done, certain rules that have to be followed before we close the door and get underway. And, it's all really, really spelled out, so that part I've got down, at this point, after so many years! Yes, I can say all the announcements without paying attention, which might be good, might be bad. They're all written down. Everything's

written down. I have a book of reference that I'm required to carry and that has everything I'd ever need to know in it. I'm required to keep that up to date.

Yeah, once the doors close, then the fun part starts, and that's talking to everybody and going over the safety information and answering questions, that kind of thing. The day could be anywhere from two hours on duty to almost fourteen, anywhere from one to maybe six flights a day, depending on how long they are. So, a lot of up and down, at least for a regional carrier, rather than an international carrier or a large domestic. We can actually fit in a few more legs than some of the major flyers, 'cause we take shorter trips.

I bid on my schedule. A regular schedule can be anywhere from a minimum of ten days off to, like, nineteen. Again, those are awarded by seniority. The more senior you are, the more days off you can get. I can pick up extra flying from other flight attendants or from what they call "open time" trips that are not currently covered. I can pick up extra and make extra money. I'm limited to the number of hours on duty per day, and hours per days in a row, so there are restrictions about that. I can work six days in a row, after that I must have a twenty-four hour break. So, if you time it right, like last week, I worked seven days because there was enough time in between the two trips - there was that twenty-four hour break.

I usually work more, and that's better for the bank account. Like I said, my husband works in another state so we're working for two places [in order] to live and a little extra bit helps. It's actually very common in the airline industry to commute. Regular people get up and they get in the car and drive to work. A lot of airline people get up and drive to the airport and get on a plane to go to work. So, depending on our schedules, I'll work my regular flights during the week, then I'll go to Palm Springs for a couple of days, and then I'll turn around and go back to work.

Right now, it's been like every other week that we see each other for a couple of days. But we talk every day. Well, you know, I love him dearly, but there's still the alone time that everybody needs and we call it "quality hotel time." Some people really like that, and some people don't. I mean, there are friends, flight attendants, and pilots, married, and they fly together all the time. I think, "Wow, how can you stand that?" So, it just kind of depends on your relationship. Quality Hotel Time or we have Airport Appreciation, like if I have a three to four hour break in my schedule and there's really not a lot to do except wander around the airport, we call it Airport Appreciation time.

I love my job. There's this big joke that if you've been in the airline business long enough, you can never have a real job again. Real job meaning a nine to five, Monday through Friday, in an office. It's so flexible, and, I mean there are days where I don't

go to work until 6 p.m. and I work for an hour, and I get paid for the hour and I get paid per diem. Sometimes I finish work and it's 9:00 in the morning. So, it's really, really different. That was the hardest part to get used to, coming from certainly a very structured 9-5 banking kind of world. That part's not structured; the job itself is, but as far as when you go to work, when you go to bed, when you get up, that kind of thing...It was kind of tough to get used to. It was very, very different. Sleep is still an adjustment. There are times where you get to the hotel and it's 11 in the morning and you're like, "O.K. Now what do I do? I can only watch so much television. I can only run for so long. I just ate so I don't need to do that. Now what do I do?"

Sometimes, when the night is so short, all that you have on your mind is sleep. "Get me to the hotel. I don't care about eating. Just get me to the bed." Then you have to be up in a few hours. So, that part's a little difficult physically, but you kind of get used to it. I'm pretty good at, "O.K. I have to go to sleep now" when it's time to go to sleep. It's gotten a little bit easier over the years.

We spend a lot of time in airports, and a lot of time in hotels. There are... right now American Eagle has a hundred and eighty-one destinations and I've been to most of them. Let's say the majority of them. We always find something to do. You know, there's a restaurant, there's a bar, there's a bowling alley, there's something to do everywhere we go. Some cities are better sleeping, some are good for eating or working out...It's just finding the one thing no matter where you are, middle of nowhere, you always find something good about it.

We do go to Canada, the Caribbean and Mexico. For example Mexico overnights; the cities are fantastic, they're wonderful:

a lot of historic churches and history and battlefields and that kind of thing. Right now, those are very, very short overnights, so really all you have time to do is go to the hotel and sleep and then you leave. So, a lot of people will go back, you know, like, "Hey, I wanna go back on my days off." You know, 'cause, I heard about this or I asked about this hiking trail or whatever, and they'll go back on their days off. It's almost free, depending on how many years you've been there and where you're going. International, you pay the taxes and port charges, that kind of thing. It's not totally free across the board, but it's definitely worth it. My girlfriends and I do a couple of trips a year to Mexico. We do a beach vacation. Nice girl time. It's wonderful.

I don't remember ever being afraid to fly. I always thought it was, you know, something…I can't think of anybody that I know, working, that would say they were afraid to fly. It's kind of a non-issue after a while 'cause you're going to work. It's not like, "Ooh, I get to go on an airplane and fly and go somewhere fun." It's just, that's my office; that's where I work. So, it's different when you're traveling as a working crew member than when you travel as just a person…(laughs) a real person.

Our company and our union is what they call a closed shop, so everyone must pay union dues. It's not required, however, that you're a member. So, as part of the hiring process, as part of the new hire classes, you have the union dues and you have to sign up. Like I said, you don't have to be a member but you do have to pay dues, and that comes out of your paycheck. So, it's actually kind of a function of both sides - management and the union.

The company facilitates the paying of dues. I signed up. I never worked for a union before; I didn't really, really understand what it meant. You know, I didn't have a real picture, how it works, how it feels to be involved in it and how it affects my life and job, my family. So, it was a big change; it was something new. Once you are in it, it becomes a blur. You're trying to get used to the new job, you're living somewhere new, you're moving all the time. I mean, you're constantly in motion. You're going from one place to another, to a hotel, to your house, back to the plane, so it's constant movement. Especially as a new person, a new hire, [the] union's kind of in the back of your mind. As you understand how the contract works, how the company works, how your scheduling works, how your hours work, it becomes a little more clear just how important the union is.

Like I said, as a new hire person you're still learning everything. You're learning company policies, the federal rules that you have to follow, also, all the information in your contract, which is so important. And, like I said, I have not worked at a company that had a union before. I didn't really understand it. The longer that you fly and work with the scheduling department - specifically, because that's the most contact the new hires have is with the scheduling department - "O.K. well...Can they do this to me? Can they reassign me? Am I still legal for this? What's the rule about that?" So, the more that you experience, the more knowledge that you need of your contract: what's allowed, what's not allowed.

I didn't really understand for a long time

what it takes to make the operation work. There's two sides to this: the company and the union. The company has a responsibility to their shareholders, to their passengers, to people that are buying tickets, to run an airline by the rules and on time. The other part of that is the workers. The workers have this agreement that this is how the rules are structured and you know this is what we're gonna work on, and the rules under which we will function and make the operation work. So, it's two sided, but it's really for one goal—to get people from A to B in a timely, safe manner.

Like I said, the longer that you do it, the more you realize how important having a contract is and having those rules. I work with ladies who have been in many more years than me, and it's quite eye-opening to discuss with them the things the company was allowed to do, the things that were O.K. You know, twenty-five, thirty years ago, they checked you for your girdle, you had to wear false eye lashes, you had to weigh a certain amount, you had to carry this, that, and the other thing, you had to carry their liquor with you, it wasn't put onto the airplane. If there was any food served, you had to carry that. You also had your tote bag with your wallet and your make-up and your suitcase and everything else. So, a lot has changed and I'm so thankful for those people that stood up and said, "Yes…You know what? We really need to have some rules."

Both sides need to agree and function under this set of rules, and that's the collective bargaining agreement. Things have changed a lot even since I've started. As a new hire, they would call you, scheduling would call you at 4 in the morning and say, "You need to be at the airport at 6." Now, they can call in the night before and confirm the assignment that they have and they can ask for certain trips. Things have improved over the years. I don't have to wear a girdle, thank goodness. They don't weigh me, thank goodness! The work hours have changed. When I started, this was in 1995, the package that I got from the company had the weight chart in it and we were weighed initially. I know earlier that year they were still doing weekly weigh-ins. By the time my class started, they had stopped doing that. But, they did have the weight chart. I'm 5'7", and I had to be 136 pounds or less.

For a long time, it was, "What do you look like?" Not whether you were smart or able to walk and chew gum at the same time. "Were you pretty enough for the job?" It didn't start that way for quite a few decades. In the last century, that's what it was about: big blonde hair, false eye lashes, short shorts, short skirts, you know, that kind of thing, and there really wasn't a focus on safety, you know. I think we've kind of turned the corner, moved away from that where it's...I mean they want you to look nice, but if you're not a "Barbi", it's O.K.

I had to work really hard to be at that weight for training. There was a law suit one year: a girl was a body builder, she looked amazing, she was incredibly fit, could totally do this job, but because she was over that number on the weight chart, they wouldn't hire her. You know, that's not reasonable, so the union had words with lawmakers and what not. You make it even. If you can do the job, you're competent, and you could follow the rules, why does it matter what you look like? It's funny, even on that weight chart, the older that you were, the more you could weigh - a bit of an allowance for aging. There are quite a few books out there flight attendants have written that are really eye opening: "Come Fly with Me", "Long Legs and Short Nights" by Marilyn Tritt. The girls in this book were working

for a small West Coast airline, which ended up being TSA in California. It's about how they started their job. They'd become best friends, they'd go through ups and downs together - they'd been through everything together. They would go on the same trips and that was who they'd spend time with.

I will retire from this job, hopefully American Eagle. We'll see how that goes, but, you know, I could see me doing this for the rest of my life. And that's kind of the usual. It's the first year or two that you're flying, you realize if it's for you or not, and, you'll stay forever, or you decide, "No, it's not really for me" and you move onto something else. But if you decide to stay, you stay forever. That's me. I think the only thing that we have for the future - because my husband is airlines as well - is a little place on the beach somewhere, and take my travel benefits and go hang out at the beach and go anywhere we want. Nothing big. I figure if I win the lottery, I'd still work, because that's where all my friends are. I wouldn't see anybody otherwise! I think it's the best job in the world. I can't imagine doing anything else at this point and I can't imagine not doing it. So, I'm not in a hurry to retire any time soon. I want to keep doing this. Yeah, it's the best job I've ever had.

As far as working with unions, that's been an added bonus. I kind of started out as, you know, "Hey, you want to help me out with doing blah, blah, blah? Um, O.K." And the more I learned about it and the longer I'm in it - it's been off and on for fourteen, fifteen years, in different capacities. I can't imagine not doing it now. People call me about all types of situations, all types of questions. It's nice knowing that they have someone that they can call anytime. You know, it's not just a number and a name on a bulletin board, it's someone who's there and who works and does your job every day and who understands the questions, where you're coming from, and someone you can count on.

My job right now with the union, specifically, is with hotels and our security team. People call me about everything. I think that's nice to have. I have friends with other airlines, bigger airlines, for example, and they don't know who their union people are. So, I think we have a big advantage. We make it a point to be seen and be heard and share with other flight attendants. That's important to me. They know that they can call me. If they're on an overnight and they're having problems with the hotel, they can text me and, wherever I am, I'll try and fix it. I am the M.E.C. (Master Executive Council) Hotel Chair. It's all volunteer. I'm going on a hotel trip tomorrow for the next few days and the union will help me with expenses while I'm traveling for union work.

Right now we have five bases for American Eagle: L.A., Dallas, Chicago, New York, Miami, and San Juan, and each of those has a local council. So, those folks are responsible for what goes on at that base and for all those flight attendants. Then you have the Master Executive Council, which is the president from each base and other representatives who oversee those local areas. I work with the Hotel Chairs from Dallas, from Chicago, from New York, from Miami, from San Juan and I'm…It doesn't sound right to say I'm in charge of them but, um, we work together. Each one is responsible for what happens at their base, and then I oversee that. I'm responsible for all hotel issues for the entire company. I fly a regular schedule, you know, trips and what not, about ninety hours a month, and our current minimum that we get paid for, is seventy-five, so I fly a little bit extra. I probably spend ten hours a week doing union work. I call it homework.

I don't have a whole lot of time. My friends are really important. There's a group of girls that I run and work out with. So, we've done a lot of running trips, where we'll go to Philadelphia, we've been to Boston a few times, we've been to California for races. We go for the weekend and we'll go do a 10K or half marathon or full marathon.

For me, success is having a solid relationship with my family, with my friends, taking pride in my job and the work with the union and being there for them. There's always work to be done and there's always more that I could do; it's just a matter of figuring out what it is and how I can do it, and how I can fit it in. That's a continuous process for me. I'm a work in progress, put it that way.

You really have to be giving in this job. *Your're taking care of people, whether they are flying to a funeral or a wedding or a business function, you take care of them and that's your job.*

Olivia Herrera Mendoza

Farm Worker, Prosser, Washington
United Farm Workers (UFW)
Translator: Stephanie Patricio Vallejo, Union Organizer

I'm Catholic. I'm a mother of five. I'm a worker. I work everyday to [take care of] my house. I very much like to participate in the work of the Union. I like to do that so there's progress to help all people and not just one. It is education that helps people progress. I'm from Michoacan, Mexico. I was born to farm worker parents. We grew up with that lifestyle: working very hard with our parents, until they were older, and then everyone went their own ways and formed their own families. My parents are not alive anymore but they taught me that.

The struggle began in 1987. I began working at Chateau St. Michelle in 1986. They [Chateau St. Michelle] had very many problems and that's why we fought for representation. They were firing people. There were a bunch of problems. There was a small union in the state of Washington. That was the United Farm Workers of Washington State. We found out that there was no law protecting farm workers, so we had to seek affiliation with the United Farm Workers. Then, the UFW began to represent us. We were in the struggle for eight years to get a contract for better benefits, a medical plan, and we won it. We won the fight. We were in the struggle for eight years and we won! Very many people helped us but we never quit. We never took our eyes off the prize. We're here. It's very good to work under [a union] contract. We have a pension plan. We have a medical plan. We won very much because we didn't have anything before. This contract is unlike any other in the state. It's the only one that represents farm workers. We would like it to be bigger because with there being more unionized farm workers, it helps everyone. It would help us.

I am 56 years old. I get up at four in the morning. I make lunch for me and my husband, because we work together. I cook; I make tortillas by hand everyday. We get ready for work. That's most of the year. However, during the harvest, which starts in September, two or three in the morning we wake up and prepare the same thing because there's no set hours. Sometimes it's one in the morning. It's whenever the company's ready for us to come in and do the work. The supervisors tell us at the end of the day, "Please come in at 2:00 in the morning..." It depends on the trips that the winery wants to make because they're delivered by the ton so we're picking the grapes, harvesting, and they are produced right there [on site]. It is also a winery so they are sent to the winery to be processed. So, it just depends on the orders that the company wants. They are sent by the ton but we get paid hourly. The processing is day and night, day and night. There's no schedule to come in or to leave during the harvest. But the rest of the year, we get up at 4:00 in the morning.

Right now, we are pruning and it's very heavy work that is done with pneumatic shears. There's a tractor in-between the vines with two arms, and on the arms there's five hoses. On each of those five hoses, there are shears. But through those hoses, air is pumped out. When we're cutting with the shears, there's air being pumped out so it's a little bit easier for us to cut branches. The pneumatic shears help us because they are not making us use as much force. We handle the shear but the air does most of the work. Although it is pneumatic, we're still doing a lot of repetitive work. Each plant requires 40 cuts with the shears and we're doing in eight hours more than 500 plants - each person, many, many plants. Now, I get paid a little bit. This year, during the time of the pruning, we get paid $10.40/hour. It's very hard work, getting paid very little.

During the harvest, it's different pay and a different schedule. We work during the harvest up to 80 hours a week. During that time, we get paid .50 cents more because it's in the contract. The harvest lasts from mid September and it goes all the way till late November, or sometimes to the beginning of December. It's only temporarily that we work the eighty hours but I feel fine. It's mostly women who work there. We feel fine. Of course, sometimes, we feel sleepy or we get tired but then it goes away and we feel fine. We like going to work. The majority of workers are laid off at the end of the harvest. It could start at the end of November till about the end of January, which means they are out of work for about 2 months

For me it is not too heavy, the work. Other places, there is much heavier work. Thanks to the union, we are not harassed and there's no pressure to work like machines. There's no pressure. They ask us to do the work that we can bring forth, thanks to the union. Thanks to the union, we are comfortable. About eight years ago, they laid us off [at the end of the season]. I went to work in the other farms, an apple orchard, and I was at the brink of tears where I felt like crying, because I saw how they treated other workers. It made me incredibly sad to see how they were treated.

It's just because they were a supervisor that they treated them this way. I've always felt that it is no one's right to treat someone else badly.

Once I hit 62, I'm going to retire. I'm planning with my husband to go to Mexico. He is retired and we would like to go for about five or six months and then come back. I would like to go to Mexico for a few months at a time, like from December till March and then work over there; do some work during the season there and then come back every year. I have my kids here and I would like to be with them. My husband has family in California and I have family in Texas. I would like to go visit them and then work a little bit. I would never want to be without work, but not with that much responsibility.

Someone who is successful must have ambition and must not be a conformist. They must say, "I want to do this" and go after it. We came here to work so we can live better because we weren't given those possibilities in our country. That is why we came here, because we wanted a better life. I'm not saying someone is successful if they have a lot. Whatever God gives us is good. Here, working is how one gets what they have and working is the means by which one can attain those things and those possibilities.

Being successful means to make progress. It can be in school or at work: for example, someone who becomes someone important and has a good job. Someone who can say, "I finished my schooling and studied such and such." Someone who can say, "I came to achieve this. I have my success." Meeting a goal. I feel like I've been successful. Everyone achieves success in their own ways and I think, yes, that I've been successful.

We came here to work so we can live better because we weren't given those possibilities in our country. *That is why we came here, because we wanted a better life. I'm not saying someone is successful if they have a lot. Whatever God gives us is good. Here, working is how one gets what they have and working is the means by which one can attain those things and those possibilities.*

Lynda Mobley

School Bus Driver, Retired
State Vice President,
Ohio Association of Public School Employees, Republic, Ohio
Local 4, AFSCME

First, I'm a wife and a mother. I try to stay positive. My union work helped mold me in my life. I was, like, thirty-two or something when I first started driving a bus. I was very, very lucky: I got to stay home for twelve years with my children, and I didn't have to go to work to help the family survive until prices went up. Who would've thought you'd pay two and a half to three dollars for a loaf of bread? I remember laughing when my mathematics teacher in high school told us we'd have to pay a dollar someday for a loaf of bread and we laughed! But, life goes on...

Being a school bus driver was a step for me, because it meant that I had to be away from the kids somewhat, but I absolutely loved it from day one. Our responsibilities, of course, were keeping the bus clean, most of all keeping the children safe. To this day, when I run into one of my kids - my kids I call them - in a shopping center, fifty percent of 'em will say, "Mrs. Mobley!" and come over and give me a hug. So, I mustn't have done too bad.

I took great pride in it and, actually, was a school bus driver trainer as well. But, to start with, I learned that, with children, for the first two weeks, every day, before I got on the bus, to go into the school building. We went over the rules real quick: you have to stay seated, you can't change seats, you know, yada yada yada...and if you do, if you change seats or if you bother someone, then the consequence is that, when we get to your school, we're going to go in and see the principal, and you'll have to tell the principal what you did, and she'll decide what your consequences are. One of the consequences will be - at that time you didn't have to assign seats -that you will no longer be able to sit with your friends. I'm going to put you in front, with me, for one week. If you break the rule again it will be longer and I'll call your parents.

And, every day for two weeks we talked about that. I also told them there were rewards. I'd send notes to parents about how great they were and, when they were getting off the bus give them a sucker with a wrapper, you know, and it worked wonderful! The high school kids, we found out, as long as I played whatever music was popular then, it worked absolutely wonderful! But I learned that if they knew I meant it, once they knew that I meant what I said, and I was not mean, we'd laugh and we'd sing sometimes. But once they knew what I expected, 99% of the time, we didn't have a problem. If I had to take them into the principal, then they knew that I really was not happy, 'cause all I wanted to do was keep 'em safe, and they all knew that. And, even the little stinkers, if they see me out in the community somewhere, at a shopping center, they'll say, "I am so sorry! I know I was a little stinker." I guess with kids, you can't ignore 'em; they have to know you care. And, I love kids, so, for me, it was the perfect job.

You always try to drive safe. You have to do safety checks before you can drive the bus, so you check it all over before you even get into drive. But mostly, it's just the love and care and them respecting you. If you don't have their respect, you don't have a chance. I felt like it was a dream job. I couldn't wait to get to work in the morning, just as much as I couldn't wait to get home after it was over with. But, I really loved working. I tried not to miss work anymore than it was absolutely necessary and, I don't know how else I can say it. It was the perfect job for me and I couldn't wait to get there every day. It's true. It's sappy, but it's true.

When I first moved to Bellevue, I had already worked for three years in

I keep going back to unions. I didn't have much self-value before I got so involved in driving a school bus and working. It was just, **I tried to be Beaver Cleaver's mom.** *You might be too young to know what that is, but it was a show where you wanted to please everybody. This (the union) showed me that I had more self-confidence and it made me, actually, who I am today...*

Cincinnati with a private contractor because Cincinnati doesn't have, at that time, was not unionized, the bus drivers, they were all private contractors. I worked for 3.50/hour. And, although I liked my boss, my husband got transferred and he told me I'd never make 5.00/hour as a bus driver. So, I came to Bellevue, and about six months later, I went to work driving the bus and, guess what—I started at 5.00/hour.

This school was not organized. There was favoritism. I'll say it again; I loved what I did. But, to give an example, if there was a football game, the man would get to drive every one of them. And why? Because they didn't think it was fitting for a woman to drive the bus. This was in '78 or '79. It had to be 1980 by the time we got organized. And, if you had a kid in the ski club, you got to drive the ski club trip and ski for nothing. But, they were taking work away from the drivers.

It was all favoritism, is what I'm trying to say. So, there were enough people that were unhappy so I said, "Well, let's have a meeting." And, we interviewed two different unions. One just didn't fit with us. We chose OAPSE. The first year all we did was organize, make sure we had enough members to get it [so] that they

couldn't keep us away from it. We actually had one more than we had to have. We had about one hundred members, and I think we had fifty-two, and that's all we needed. We even had a bus driver, another male; he was allowed to have hospitalization, none of the rest of us were. And he even said it wasn't fair and he joined.

So, with the first contract, we gained many things. We gained what the others had that we couldn't get. You had to work so many hours a year to get the hospitalization. You didn't have to work twelve months, because most schools are only open nine and a half. Now, what they do is, they take that nine and a half salary and stretch it out and pay us over twelve months, but it's always for that nine and a half month's work, which is great, because we didn't have to pay for hospitalization over the summer. If we had to pay any part of it, it came out of our salary and that was wonderful. It enabled other people to take it.

Another quest we had maybe fifteen years later or twenty; we managed to be able to have more than one job. Because bus drivers had no way to increase their hours, and extra trips at that time didn't help toward hospitalization or anything, many of us, myself included, took second jobs within the school system to increase their hours, and that benefitted us. It was the same union all those years, and, actually, all but two years we had the same field rep. and they still do.

This might be something you're interested in: My daughter, after twenty-two years in the Air Force, after being vice president of a company, which they had several of them, ended up moving back to Ohio and applied for the job. She's now a top field rep. for OAPSE. She was so frustrated with the things that she'd hear around about what was going on with people who didn't have a union, that I said, "You really need to go down and apply." And, I didn't tell her to do that until after I retired, 'cause I didn't want anyone saying that she got the job because she was my daughter. I am so proud I can't stand it. She has about twenty locals. That means she undertakes twenty

individual contracts a year - well, not a year, but when they expire. And, you know, does all the grievances and arbitrations and the whole schmear.

I hated politics. I didn't want to have anything to do with it, and Joe Ragola, our executive director, and most of the people that were school employees, we just - I don't know, it was just our mentality at that time I guess - he taught us how politics affect all of us in our everyday world. And we became involved, as a union, in politics, and involved in school board elections and state wide and national...It has been a wonderful learning experience for me.

I guess I can say that belonging to a union has been like having a new family. For me, it ended up being like that, especially when I empty-nested. They really felt like family. I went from organizing a local to becoming their president; stepped

up to a regional - I don't know how many counties were in it anymore, - of North Central OAPSE district, and from there, they elected me to the executive board and eventually to state vice president. And, the reason I brought that up is just to show people that they can move up the ladder when they feel they're ready. There are more things for you to do, and these are where you still keep your regular job. They're not paid for, you do it because you love it. And, you know you can help other people…End of sermon.

I know that I'm a good wife and a great mom. And how do I know that? Because my family tells me so! I was a good union member because I knew that I was successful helping union members, and we have to be a team and work as a whole. Being in a union is like being on a team, working for the betterment of all. That changed my life to where, it isn't just union when you do that kind of thing; it's in your whole life. It's because you can [that] you help people. Sometimes helping them is just sitting down and listening to them talk. I hope I'm that kind of person. I try to be.

I'm a dog lover and a horse lover. I have a dog, named Zack, and my husband has one, and they're part of our life. And I'm just happy. But, I should quit eating so much.

I keep going back to unions. I didn't have much self-value before I got so involved in driving a school bus and working. It was just, I tried to be Beaver Cleaver's mom. You might be too young to know what that is, but it was a show where you wanted to please everybody. This (the union) showed me that I had more self-confidence and it made me, actually, who I am today, and I'm very thankful that I had that opportunity, and, again, the camaraderie in a brand new local where everybody was scared

of what was going to happen. One thing that really helped is that my union, at the annual conference every other year, had all these classes that you could take. They gave you the notes in a little book, notebooks that went with it. So, they nurtured, not just me but all of our members, and we thought, "Hey, we can do this and take it back to our members and then teach our members." They taught us officer's training and secretary treasurer's training, arbitration training, especially grievance training. You know, I had to learn to do that.

Political importance was, like I said, a real eye opener and, to this day - I mean, I just got through working probably fifty hours per week on phone banks and walks and the last election - it really does help. And, it's amazing how the younger people just don't see the history and how it will benefit them. They then began putting conferences on in regions across the state with other field rep.s and stuff that taught us even more. Each time I learned more, I became more self-confident and, really sounds conceited, more proud of myself. It made me a different woman. I'm proud of who I am. And, I don't mean that to sound pompous.

This "right to work," really it's a right to not work. That's the next fight. I'm seventy-three and I'm still doing it. So, these young people can certainly do it.

I didn't want to retire. I had to retire because I held a couple jobs and one job was done away with and I would have been reduced to two hours/week and I couldn't afford to stay and not have health care. If I retired, I would have health care. Let's see, I'm seventy-three and I retired in 2006, so I was born in 1939. I'm sewing, cooking as much as I can in-between, traveling a little. That's the most fun. And, here we go again: I'm the president of the North Central

You always try to drive safe. You have to do safety checks before you can drive the bus, so you check it all over before you even get into drive. But mostly, it's just the love and care and them respecting you. **If you don't have their respect, you don't have a chance.** *I felt like it was a dream job.*

Labor Council; we cover five counties. Also, I'm the president of AFSCME 1184-146. It has about five hundred members. It's AFSCME's retiree chapter, sub-chapter, in Ohio. We cover about five counties as well. That's unpaid as well. And I'm a part-time secretary for the building trades. And just regular household stuff - you know, there's a lot of family involvement. I really think I would just pucker up and die if I didn't have a lot of contacts with people. It's just what I need. Everyone's different. For me, I don't want to hibernate.

I go vacationing for one week every summer with three people that were also bus drivers in various places - three ladies, in various places in the states. We became friends within the union. We were all on the executive board, and to this day, we still vacation together one week a year. And, that's just...so much fun. We have the rules: the first day, you can dis your husband as much as you want around the campfire that night, you can really get pissed, and that's fine, but you can't mention it after that. I think it's funny that we do that just so that nobody can just come and gripe.

Success...I think setting a goal, preparing to reach that goal, and being proud of yourself even if you don't. If you succeeded in moving on up in your life, and that doesn't necessarily mean position, then be proud and keep trying. We never quit learning. And, educate young people about the union.

What I learned from my children - one is a master's degree counselor, and one is a bachelor degree and she's a field rep, and one has a doctorate degree in nursing - and if there's one thing they have taught me in the last five years is do not focus on the past, do not focus on disagreements, stay focusing on success and continue to set your goals. And they get after me when I get off of that. I think it's important for all of us. It's just the way I live my life. I don't know how else to say it. I have a son, too, but I don't get to see him real often. Well, he lives in Cincinnati and he's got a bad back so Jim can't travel, so, we only see him a couple times a year. But the girls all live within seventy miles of here. One of them only lives eight miles away, so that's really nice. The boy is the oldest.

I wish everyone that's in a union could have the experiences that I had, because there's so much knowledge and so much power in a union. Imagine, having power over what happens to you and your members. It's really great!

I hated politics. *I didn't want to have anything to do with it, and Joe Ragola, our executive director, and most of the people that were school employees, we just, I don't know - it was just our mentality at that time I guess - he taught us how politics affect all of us in our everyday world. And we became involved, as a union, in politics, and involved in school board elections and state wide and national...It has been a wonderful learning experience for me.*

Ray Quinones
Doorman, New York City
32BJ SEIU

I am a doorman in New York, New York. I'm a hard-working man, a father to the most loveliest boy in the world, a husband. I love sports, I'm an outgoing person, I love going to the movies. And I'm a nice man.

I'm a doorman/porter. So, I stand at the door for seven hours/day. I gotta open the door, get taxis, grab people's dry cleaning, when people get home, I gotta give their dry cleaning to them, I gotta handle UPS packages. So, it's not a bad job. Then, at the end of my shift, I gotta pick up the trash on each floor and grab the bags and tie them up. It's actually not a bad job. We actually make good money. So it's really not that hard. I love doing what I do and it pays the bills.

Before, we had a contract but it wasn't as good as the union's. The union contract gives you dental insurance. It gives you options to take classes. You can actually take classes to learn how to be a super (superintendent); you can take air-conditioning classes, carpentry classes...So, it's a little bit more...I added my wife and my son on my health insurance. My wife and son are now covered. With the union benefits, we have 401K now. We do have to pay union dues but, you know, in the long run with the 401K, and with me and my wife having insurance, it benefits all of us.

And we could also depend on the union. If we get into any problems with a tenant, or management, we could always call the union to help us out with any situations that we're in. So that's another benefit of having a union. You could call them and they'll help represent us and help us out to keep our jobs. It's a big union, a lot of members. Overall, it's 95% better; we have dental, we have more options. We have 2 extra personal days. It's definitely better, especially in the long run.

With our old plan we didn't even have a 401K. We had nothing. So now we could look forward to retirement money. I wish I could retire tomorrow. But I guess we can't. We have to work. I'm only 35 so I have at least another 25 years to go.

Hopefully, when I retire - my son will be in his 20's, early 30's - hopefully I'll have grandkids and I'll just want to enjoy my kids, my grandkids and I just want to take it easy. I just want to watch them grow, I want to watch them live and I just want to enjoy myself because I worked hard all my life. And travel too. I'd like to buy an RV and just drive all over the world. That's one of my goals for the future. Travel, travel, travel.

Successful could be anything. Everybody wants to be rich. I don't want to be rich. My success is just to be happy. I just want to watch my kids grow. I would love to have more kids and at the end of the day I just want to be happy. Success is not only about what you have. It's just about being happy, being in love, and just enjoying

Everybody wants to be rich. **I don't want to be rich.** *My success is just to be happy. I just want to watch my kids grow. I would love to have more kids and at the end of the day I just want to be happy. Success is not only about what you have.*

time with your kids, have good health. I mean…I feel successful now. Just because I'm a doorman…I feel very successful; I have a house. I have a car. I have a wife. I have a son. I feel successful. I feel great! I don't want to be depressed. I don't want no stress. The more 'successful' money-wise you are, the more stress and problems you have.

Waking up, just looking at my wife, looking at my son, chasing him. It just makes you happy. There's a purpose of me being here now. When I didn't have a son, it was different. I got something to look forward to every single day of my life. And that's why I work so hard. When I retire, I can enjoy it with my son, and maybe my other sons or daughters, maybe.

> *Waking up, just looking at my wife, looking at my son, chasing him. It just makes you happy.* **There's a purpose of me being here now.** *When I didn't have a son, it was different. I got something to look forward to every single day of my life. And that's why I work so hard. When I retire, I can enjoy it with my son, and maybe my other sons or daughters, maybe.*

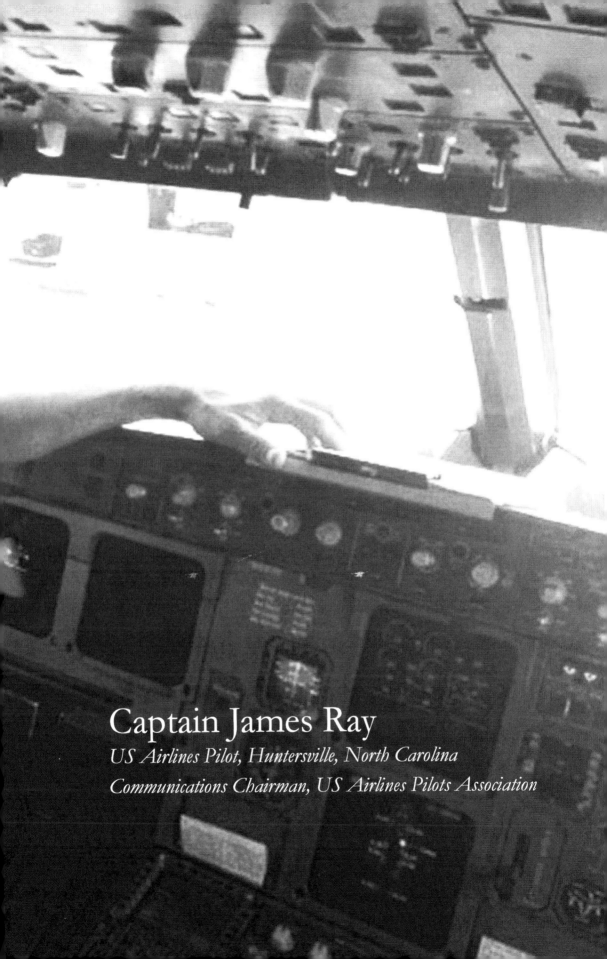

Captain James Ray
US Airlines Pilot, Huntersville, North Carolina
Communications Chairman, US Airlines Pilots Association

think the first thing that comes to mind is I'm a competitive human being, whether that is in my personal life or in my business world. I've always been competitive. Yet, I think there's a competition that we find in anything we do in life. If we're competitive, I think it makes us better. But, I'm also compassionate. I think that part of the success that we have in life has to do with seeing things through other people's eyes and walking a mile in the other person's shoes. So, while you may be competitive, you need to be compassionate and know what it feels like to be on the other side.

I think my family, and most of my co-workers, would describe me as kind. I'm very loyal. But back to the competitive side of me: I'm determined; I'm very thorough. I'm extremely disciplined with everything I do, whether it be business, whether it be my hobbies, the way I run my life, the way I run my house. That's just ingrained. It's second nature to a pilot. Everything we do is disciplined and structured. I think that's probably a good way to describe me. And, as far as relating to others, I'm a consensus builder. I'm a peacemaker. I would like people to get along, realizing that we don't always. But, I think part of my success within the union is trying to find people on different sides of the fence and draw them together so that we all work together and eventually are successful.

I think that (being disciplined) comes from the nature of my business, and that is being a pilot. Everything a pilot does is structured: we use checklists; we have flow patterns that we use in the cockpit that are memorized, making sure that every switch and every gauge we touch, with our eyes or with our hands, are all in the right location for that machine we fly. Whether it be preflight or taxi or takeoff or cruise or descent or landing or post flight, we use flows, which is a memory thing to make sure we do everything right, and then we back it up with a checklist to double check and make sure we did it right.

I have a racecar and, in my racing hobby, I have checklists, and that's something that most racers don't have. Maybe the professionals do, but in the hobbyist level, I don't notice anybody as anal as I am. Before I ever leave the garage, I have a checklist, and I check off every single item that I need to take to the track with me. I have a logbook. Aircrafts: they have logbooks, where we record the maintenance issues with the airplane. If anything goes wrong, we write it up, and maintenance works on it. I have a logbook for my racecar, and so we document every time we go to the track. Things like tire pressure, shock settings, camber adjustments, weather conditions for that day, tire conditions, pressures, etc. It's all about being prepared and being structured. I believe that makes you successful. Whether you're flying airplanes or racing cars or anything you do in life, you've got to have organizational skills.

I started flying airplanes in high school, so I've been around it all my

I know that the airline business is not unique. I know that there are other industries that push their employees too far. Without the union it wouldn't be a safe environment. **Unions have made the aviation world safer,** *and they've also helped improve the livelihood and security of my career. It's a necessary thing.*

life. I turned my hobby into a career. I would say it was not something that was within me. I think it was something that evolved through experience in aviation. My father was a pilot, so I grew up as a child going to air shows and fly-in's in light aircrafts with him, and if you asked me from the time I was three years old what I was gonna do when I grew up, the answer was I'm gonna be an airline pilot. And so I've been very fortunate in my life to always know from my youngest childhood memory that this is what I wanted to do.

I had a plan even as a child to become a pilot. I wasn't exactly sure of the route. Even in my high school yearbook, there's a page in my junior [year] that has me standing next to a Learjet and it basically talks about me flying and learning to fly in high school. I was working on my private pilot license at the time. I was standing next to what I said at that time was my favorite airplane, and I had hoped that, when I got out of college, I would fly a Learjet for a few years and then go to work for a major airline. And that's exactly what I did. After college I flew a Lear for three and a half years,

and a month before my 25th birthday I went to work for the airlines.

I had goals in high school. I had a passion, and I still to this day have a passion for flying airplanes. I'm still very fortunate that I turned my hobby and my dream into a career, and it's led me to a lot of things I never would have dreamed of. Now, so much of my life is not about the actual flying of the airplane. I got, very early in my career, involved with the pilot's union and I've been with this airline for 28 years now, and I'd say for 27 of those 28 years, I've done something for the union. So that has broadened my horizon and it's been fruitful. It's been exciting, it's been stressful, but it's all been worthwhile.

I grew up in Texas and I moved to North Carolina in 1984 when I first was hired on at the airline. I'm flying a desk more than I'm flying an airplane right now. It's not my nature, but it's the service I'm doing at this point for the pilots. But, long term, flying a desk is not what I'm interested in. I look forward to going back and being in the cockpit full time.

I'll start with the communications job. I had been, for probably ten

195

As far as being a pilot, I would say that it's enjoyable yet exhausting. It can be stressful at times. **Somebody once described my profession as months and months of sheer boredom interrupted by moments of sheer terror.** *It's kind of a funny way to stamp it.*

years, involved with media work for the union. I went to some formal training, about ten years ago, to take on the responsibility of handling the media in the Charlotte area for the national union, and that morphed into being in charge of the media for my particular airline. Then we had a change of unions a few years ago and I became the media chairman for my new union nationwide. While I started just doing local stories, now it's national stories. The first part of this job, the media portion, is what I would call external communications. Now the Communications Chairman job that I have is a full time job. Not one that I ever sought after, but one that I'm doing temporarily, just to provide a service until they find somebody else.

We had a change in leadership in the union. It's pretty much like what's going on nationally, and there was a change in the leadership of our union. The new leadership asked me if I would take on the responsibility as Communications Chairman. My first answer was, "No, thank you." They said, "Well, we'd like you to do it.

Would you consider doing it until we find a permanent replacement?" So I said, "Yeah. I'll do it until you find a permanent replacement."

I still have a life outside the airline and I do wanna go back to flying airplanes. That's what I really want to do. Ultimately, it'd be wonderful just to go fly airplanes and have days off and go spend it with my family, but that hasn't usually been the case in my career. My communications job is sending out multiple stories, reports, updates from committees daily to all the pilots; so it's a huge job, a very important job to communicate with all the pilots what's going on with the union, what's going on with the industry, on a day-to-day basis. So, it touches every committee within the airline. We are really the voice of the union, and we're the liaison between the leadership of the union and the rank and file, and we are responsible for bringing messages from the rank and file to the leadership to help them make decisions. We're also responsible for disseminating the information and the latest and greatest on what's happening from the leadership standpoint to the rank and file.

It's all-encompassing and it's a 24/7 job. So, even while I'm on my trip, I'm still doing my communications job when I'm here on my layover in my hotel. I did two television interviews here in Phoenix yesterday while I was on my layover. So, it never ends, but it's also very rewarding.

Now, the flying part...As far as being a pilot, I would say that it's enjoyable yet exhausting. It can be stressful at times. Somebody once described my profession as months and months of sheer boredom interrupted by moments of sheer terror. It's kind of a funny way to stamp it. As a pilot, you're trained for emergencies and thankfully we don't have them real often. But, when we do have them, you have to be prepared. That's part of the discipline we talked about earlier, the stick and rudder part of being a pilot. I still get a kick out of punching out of an overcast sky early in the morning with the sun coming up. I still get a challenge and satisfaction out of making a nice landing and making all of the thousands of decisions that it takes to fly on a daily basis. Keeping your passengers safe. Two or three pilots generally work together as a team, moving people safely from A to B, in an environment that is never the same twice. It's always a challenge. We always win. We always conquer that challenge. We always find a way to get people safely from A to B, but it's never the same, and that's part of the excitement about it. It's not routine. It's something different every day.

The climate is constantly changing. Weather is our biggest challenge, so you study the weather patterns, you study the winds aloft, you look for turbulence, you look at many facets of the weather to plan your flight from A to B and make it safely, number one, and comfortable for your passengers, number two, and efficient, number three. Anyway, that's the challenge I enjoy, and I still get a kick out of it, and hopefully I'll be able to do it for many years to come.

I've never been terrified in an airplane. Obviously I've had some emergencies over my career, but every time you pull the airplane out of the runway, a pilot's mentality is this: on takeoff, I'm gonna lose an engine, I know an engine is gonna fail, what am I gonna do? So the whole time I'm going down the runway I'm thinking about aborting that takeoff, and then it reaches a point on takeoff where even if an engine blows up, you're not gonna abort, you're gonna go, because you're not gonna have enough runway to stop the airplane on the runway. The airplanes that we have today will fly on one engine, so you know the airplane's gonna be able to fly. The performance may not be what it was with two, three or four engines depending on what you're flying, but the airplanes are going to fly, and so it's safer to come back around in an emergency and use the entire runway to land on. But when you reach that point on takeoff - it's called V-1 - the pilot just emphasizes the fact that he's gonna go, and that he's not gonna stop, takes his hands off the throttle, and puts both hands on the yoke. I fly an Airbus, so I take my right hand off the throttle - I put it in my lap; my left hand gets a joystick, just like computer games. You fly an Airbus with a joystick so it emphasizes the fact that, regardless of what happens, we're going. From that point on I assume that something else is gonna happen.

The entire route of a flight, we're always thinking about possibilities. What are we gonna do if this happens? What are we gonna do if that happens? Depending on the airline, every six months to a year you go through extensive training where you go through and review the systems on the airplane so you know how they work and so you have a very good, in-depth knowledge of the airplane. Then you fly a simulator for a day or two and you practice all these emergency maneuvers that, hopefully, will never happen to you in your career. Believe it or not, the jet airplanes that we fly today are super reliable, and there are pilots who will go through their career and never have an engine failure or some kind of catastrophic hydraulic failure or electrical problems. You have minor things daily, but seldom major problems. Airplanes are machines and things do go wrong with them, but usually they're minor things and we can always handle it. I've had a few emergencies in my career. Every now and then you have something a little more critical and that's what you're trained for. I won't say that's what you live for - you hope they never come - but, as a pilot, you have to be prepared for that.

Sully and Jeff are good friends of mine and I worked very closely with them through the media after that incident - the Hudson River landing. I'm also on the Accident Investigation Committee for my airline, so I'm part of the Go-Team. When we have an accident, there's a team of pilots, union members, that are scrambled to the scene. Of course, I was on a trip when that happened. I got off my trip up in Philadelphia and went straight to New York City, and my job was to work with the media. I'm the communications guy. We have experts within our field: we may have a power plants team, and we have an airframes team, we have an ATC team. We've got a bunch of teams, and we

I still get a kick out of punching out of an overcast sky early in the morning with the sun coming up. *I still get a challenge and satisfaction out of making a nice landing and making all of the thousands of decisions that it takes to fly on a daily basis.*

have the people that go out into the field and investigate the accident and look to try to find out what was wrong. In this case, "The Miracle on the Hudson," there were a lot of favorable circumstances for them to have the outcome they did. I think Sully and Jeff will be the first ones to tell you that, given the same set of circumstances, almost every pilot would have the same outcome.

The thing is, they had very little time and very little altitude. Altitude is your friend as a pilot. The airplanes fly because of the wings; they don't fly because of the engines. You can lose engines and the airplane still has a happy ending. The problem they had was they didn't have enough altitude to fly to an airport. There have been examples in the past of airplanes losing engines at high-altitude and gliding over 100 miles to an airport and landing without engines. So the thing they were missing that day was altitude and time. It was about three and a half minutes from the time they took off to the time they touched down in the Hudson. Another 2,000 feet, they could have come back to La Guardia, they could have landed at Teterboro, could have maybe made it to Newark, and we never would have even heard of Sully and Jeff. They were pilots doing their job.

At that time in the country, we really needed a good story, an honest tale. We had a lot of bad news in those days and it was uplifting. It was a good thing to happen at that time.

The Communications Chairman job is a very important position to be in at a very important time, but again, it's not what I wanna do long-term. I'm happy to do it, and I'm enjoying doing it even though it's exhausting. I'm learning a lot, and part of the journey in life is meeting new challenges. It makes you a more well-rounded, better, balanced person. I think I'll look back from this and say I'm really glad I did that. On a daily basis I don't always think that, but it's true.

The flying job; how do I feel about that? I'm very proud of my profession. You know, we ensure the safety of millions of people every day, and, as I mentioned, it's all I've ever wanted to do since I was old enough to tell people. I still look forward to going to work, and I don't know that everybody who's been in a career for 33 years can say they're still looking forward to going to work, and I do. I'm proud to wear my uniform. I'm proud of what it stands for. I hope that when I retire I make it better for the people that follow in my footsteps in this career.

When I got into this business, pilots were held up on pedestals and it was a great paying job. It had a great retirement plan. It was a really sought-after position. Between deregulation of my industry and 9/11, which took its toll on every major airline - my personal airline's been bankrupt twice since 9/11 - most airline pilots are in the same position I'm in. After 9/11 and two bankruptcies, my pay was cut in half, my benefits were whittled away, and I had to donate my pension to the Pension Benefits Guarantee Corporation, or PBGC. Basically, my airline handed the pension plan over to the government. I'll get a fraction of what I was expecting to get from that pension which was one of the greatest things about being an airline pilot.

One by one, every major airline in this country has gone broke. So, there's been a lot of things that changed my business, and I fear that there's not a lot of young people that want to become airline pilots because a bright, young person coming out of college has so many different options and it's a sacrifice. In my day, you thought the sacrifice was worth it because it paid great, had a lot of good benefits, a lot of days off and great retirement. Today, we work more hours and more days than ever before. It's really hard on the body. Somebody in their twenties, they can handle all these crazy hours that we keep, long hours all parts of the day and night all over the globe and your body never knows what time it is or what day it is. You wake up like I did this morning. I had to think for a minute where I was, and that takes a toll on your body. But it was all worth it 'cause it was just such a great career and it was great pay and great retirement. Those things aren't there anymore.

I think we bottomed out and I think our career has turned a corner. Very soon there could actually be a pilot shortage in this country, and in the world. And of course, in anything, the supply and demand rules apply. So we're already starting to see pilot salaries increasing again and retirement funds starting to come back a little bit. We'll never retrieve what we lost. You plan - in my case, 24 years before the pension was forfeited - on that retirement being there, not disappearing, so you can't make up for that. But I think we've turned a corner and, what I want to do, and I think what a lot of the people in our union want to do, is try to make this a career that young people wanna get into again. It's an important business. The safety of our passengers is important and you need a highly qualified, highly motivated, highly educated individual to do this job. I'm afraid we don't have a lot of them coming out of college. So, if we can make this job attractive again, we will hopefully attract the best and the brightest to keep this profession going and to keep our skies safe.

I grew up in the South and my grandfather would roll over in his grave if he knew I was in a union! I grew up in a very anti-union environment and grew up thinking that unions were a bad thing because of my family and the people I was around. And then I got into the profession and I realized that unions are a very necessary thing. The airline business in particular is very competitive. Management's always looking to cut costs, enhance the bottom line to gain this little tenth of a percent, a competitive advantage over the competition. My union, USAPA, U.S. Airline Pilots' Association, ensures our company doesn't cut the costs on our backs, and ensures the safety is never compromised in the interest of the bottom line. It's not just my union, but other pilots' unions. That's our goal. We can never sacrifice safety. The airlines push and they push beyond. They go too far. The thing about a union is it gives us collective strength that an individual wouldn't have. If a pilot felt like something wasn't safe and a pilot, without a union, went to the company and started demanding and insisting that they change their procedures, they might fire him. But, when the union speaks for all pilots and says, "You know what? We're putting our foot down" and they go to the airlines and say, "We're not gonna do this. You want those airplanes to fly? Then you're gonna have to change your ways and we've gotta make it safe, not only for our passengers, but for our crew members." Unions are a very necessary thing.

I wish it weren't. I know that the airline business is not unique. I know that there are other industries that push their employees too far. Without the union it wouldn't be a safe environment. Unions have made the aviation world safer, and they've also helped improve the livelihood and security of my career. It's a necessary thing.

Originally, I would have told you twenty years ago I'd like to set myself up to retire at 55 or 60, but that's not gonna be possible because of what's happened to my career financially. For pilots, they recently raised the retirement age from 60 to 65. So I foresee, hoping that my health will

provide, working until age 65 in order to be able to have the money to live the lifestyle that I hope to have for the remainder of my life. What I personally would like to do in retirement is things that I've enjoyed over my life. That's simple things, like playing golf, and going fishing, and traveling, spending time with my family, and having the time to maybe give back to others. So far, a lot of my giving back has probably been through my services to my fellow pilots.

I'd like to be able to get involved in more things to help the community, and I think as I slow down and get closer to retirement, my wife and I will become more community-minded and service-minded to give something back to others. While I feel like I've tried to better my career and that of my fellow pilots, I think perhaps something is lacking in giving back to the community. I think that would be something. Hopefully I live long enough to be able to do some of that. I don't know, whether it be working with Habitat for Humanity, whether it be working through a church, whether it may be still using my professional abilities to fly airplanes. Maybe there would be something I can do. I know there are organizations that fly children to burn centers or cancer centers and things like that. I could donate my time as a pilot to help out. I may not have a lot of money when I retire to give away, but if I could use myself to help others, I think that would be good and I think most people feel that way.

My kids and I - I've got two boys,

23 and 19 - we race. That's our hobby. By the time I get to be 65, I don't think the old man's gonna be in the racecar anymore, but if they still have a passion for it, it would still be great to be traveling and racing with them. The beautiful thing about that hobby is once a month, on average, I spend a three day weekend with my children, and so, if they still have a passion and still stay involved with that over the years, then maybe the old man can ride along and pretend he's trying to help them with what they do! Its camaraderie, it's being able to spend time with them and my wife and just unplug. That's the beautiful thing about the hobby right now: it's one of the very few opportunities I have to get away. And when I'm out there at the track, whether it's working on the car or driving the car, I don't think about anything else. Everybody needs a time to get away.

I would say for me, personally, I'm successful. I am successful if I achieve the goals I set out to achieve. If I achieve those, then generally, I've achieved happiness and gratification. Overcoming difficult challenges gives you more satisfaction. It gives me more satisfaction. I think everybody feels that way. Probably the number one thing that any parent would say is the most difficult challenges they've ever faced is raising their children. So, when your children are successful, that gives me a great sense of accomplishment. At the end of the day- and this is who I am - is that I try to please God, I try to please my family, and I try to please myself. If I can do that, then life is good. I never feel like I've done it quite good enough. I think there's only been one perfect human being to walk the face of the earth, and the rest of us are striving for perfection, and we fall short on a daily basis. And so, God, family, and myself, I've let 'em all down. But that doesn't mean that I don't try harder today. And I'll tell you this: I'm doing a better job today than I've ever done in the rest of my life, and I'm gonna continue to try that.

Roberta Reardon

Actor and Founding Co-President of SAG-AFTRA
Special Liaison for Common Sense Economics for AFL-CIO
Adjunct Professor, Murphy Institute for Labor Studies,
CUNY New York City
SAG-AFTRA

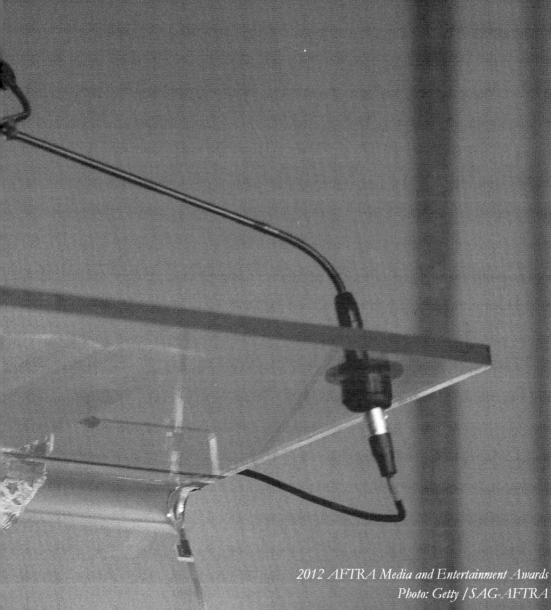

2012 AFTRA Media and Entertainment Awards
Photo: Getty / SAG-AFTRA

I have been a professional actress since my early twenties. It's how I made my living and that's obviously a very deep part of my identity. I've lived pretty much an actor's life. I started out doing some daytime dramas and then regional theater and studied acting. I started doing commercial work in New York and also worked with some experimental theater companies here. I started doing more and more commercial work, both on-camera and voice-over, which has allowed me to earn a living as an actor to this day.

I grew up in a big family in a small town in Indiana with a population of about 12,000 people. I have five brothers and I'm in the middle. My parents were not overtly political. My dad sold insurance, so as a salesperson in a small town in Indiana, wearing your politics on your sleeve was not necessarily a good idea. So, while we talked about politics at home, we were not a political family in that sense. But, my paternal grandmother who lived with us all my life, was much more political. She had worked for the state Democratic Party. She was quite outspoken, had very strong views, so I'm sure a lot of that came from her. My mother's parents were quite the opposite. They were very typical small town. So, I think my paternal grandmother had a lot of influence over me.

The town I grew up in had a men's college, Wabash College. It's still a men's college - the last one left in this country. I started acting there because they needed girls, since they wanted to do plays. So, I started acting there when I was fourteen, and I think that influenced me a lot, because I was around people who were quite different and very expressive in their opinions. This was when the whole country was starting to really foment. This was the sixties and the Civil Rights Movement was very active.

Speaking of the latter, I remember as a twelve year old, going down to Mississippi to visit an aunt and uncle, my mother's brother lived down there, and being absolutely shocked because there were "whites only" bathrooms, and segregation was alive and well. I really found it deeply shocking. I was raised in a household that was Protestant. We were Methodists and we went to church a lot. And I think as a kid, the teachings of Christianity appealed to me because it was all about equality. "Do unto others as you would have others do unto you." I really believed it, so when I began to see that the world didn't practice what it preached, it really appalled me, and, I don't know, I think part of it simply was that I was the only girl in this very male family, and I knew at a very early age that there was discrimination. There were two sets of rules: one set for me and another set for my brothers. That was the way it was and it wasn't just for me, it was my society, and I found it really appalling. It was a real time of turmoil, and it had a great impact on me. There was a part of me very early on that understood that there were values in our country that were expressed but not lived, and that meant something to me. I think my own path into it was simply that I was a girl in a male-dominated society and I was really unhappy about that.

I remember when I was a sophomore in high school, and they had elections every year for officers. I decided I would run for president of my class. I created my own party, and in my infinite wisdom I called it, "The Social Justice Party." You could imagine, anything with the word "social" attached to it automatically got "shortened" to "socialist," and that was a huge learning curve for me. Because, I thought I was naming my party after something I believed in. What I understood when it came back to me was that I had created a party that was dangerous. I might as well have called myself a communist. It was a great time of transition and I was right on the cusp of it, and I was living in a town that time forgot. A small town in Indiana was not going through any of the boiling changes that the rest of the world was, but we had television and we had rock and roll and those things really had an impact. I think in some ways, I was very much a small town girl, but in other ways I was very sensitive to the changes that were happening in society around me. I don't think I was very sophisticated about it, but I certainly was aware of it.

Nobody in my family was in a union anywhere. I remember one of my grandparents making some rather rude comment about the Reuther brothers in Detroit, and I think it was inferred at least that they were really communists. And of course, the McCarthy era happened when I was a child. So it was a very "us and them" kind of mentality.

I've always thought that I was different as a child. And, the difference started because I was a female with all these boys, and that difference extended through to my thinking. I was very sensitive to difference and how that could make you feel excluded. And I began to rebel. When I started acting, I found a place where I could express myself and be accepted. That, in fact, my imagination was useful and not dangerous. Acting was a great escape. You get to be another person. You get to use your imagination. It was really quite remarkable and very freeing, and I got to be my own person. I had always been defined by who my father was, who my brothers were, what church I went to, what school I attended—all these external definitions. I never felt that I was defined by me. With acting, I was totally me. It immediately made me feel expanded. And it gave me a sense of control that I don't think I had in my own life as a kid. I don't want to paint

There was nobody there like me. There was no one from the entertainment industry at all. There were typesetters and sheet metal workers and nurses and teachers and laborers, but no one from the entertainment business. **And I thought it was going to be just horrible,** *but within half an hour, I formed some of the best relationships with some of the strongest labor leaders I've ever known.*

a picture of me as being a miserable child. I wasn't miserable. There were many happy times in my childhood, but I was aware of differences and of wanting to find ways to express myself that didn't immediately elicit a "No" response.

I had done plays at school and I had done plays at camp and stuff, but when I was fourteen, they were doing a production of Guys and Dolls at the college and they put out a notice in the paper saying they needed talent to audition for the role and my mother encouraged me. I wasn't even going to go do it. It was one of her favorite musicals and I think she really thought I was going to go off and become one of the "Salvation Army girls," but of course, I came back and I was the "Number One Hot Box Girl!" I was one of those girls! I was in the chorus and danced. It was fun, and from there, I did a bunch of plays with them.

So, I went to college, majored in theater, and I got married when I was 19. I stayed married until I graduated from college, and then we got divorced and I came to New York and studied acting, and almost immediately got a job on a daytime drama show. I did that for a while and continued studying and then did some theater, regional theater, and I worked with theaters in New York, doing off-off Broadway. I kind of struggled for a while with questions like, "Was I really going to do this? Was I really going to stay?" I loved doing it, but I think I was also going through a lot of reevaluation of who I was. But I continued to work and started doing commercials, which actually gave me a good living for the first time in my career.

You can do a lot of theater and not make much money. It's a very precarious profession, particularly if you work out of town. You're in and out of towns and itinerant. With commercial work, it pays much better, and I fell into it and began a real career. Meanwhile, I could do theater in New York. I worked with a couple of experimental companies. I was beginning to live my life. And I had met the man who eventually became my husband (actor Walter Cline), and I was living the life of a New York actor, doing commercials and voice-overs and theater. I never was tempted to move to Los Angeles. I really love living in New York and I really love the theater and all of that, and at that time I wasn't attracted to doing film and television. Odd, but I wasn't.

I've done hundreds of on-camera commercials for everything from Campbell's Soup to American Express to Citicard to various medicines. I did a three-year campaign for Kmart in the early 90's. It was a wonderful ad campaign, and very unusual. They had basically a troupe of actors working together as a family. It was maybe a dozen of us, the regulars, and then there were other people who worked more infrequently. They called us "shopping families" and I had a husband and a child and I had two friends that I went shopping with, and they'd write these little vignettes and they were very sort of slice of life. We shot, for three years, a whole campaign of commercials. And, they were great actors. Nick Wyman, who's now the president of Actor's Equity Association, was one of the actors. There were several people who had very good careers and we all worked together and we all worked a lot. It was kind of like doing summer stock or repertoire. I'd work a week out of the month for six months a year and it was really phenomenal. It was great experience. It was wonderful training because you just worked so frequently, you had one character that you played all the time.

But then I also did a lot of other things. Eventually, as happens with this industry - usually it's an age thing - at a certain point you begin to think more about voice-over and not so much on camera because you get typed out of the business. If you look at commercials or any kind of entertainment, once a woman hits forty, you see less and less of her. The real sweet time for an actor is between ages twenty and forty, and after that, depending on your type, you'll work less and less. And, that's truer for women than men, but it's also true of men. So, I started doing voice-overs, and I've done the same kind of thing in voice-overs: a lot of major clients, a lot of industrial narration and training videos. So, it's been a very busy career that way.

In the meantime, the union work started. And it became apparent to me pretty quickly that this was something that I was good at, although I didn't start out with any aspirations to do anything other than be a board member. And, I think my second election for the American Federation of Television and Radio Artists, I ran for the local vice president and I was on the national board. I got elected to be the president of the New York local in 2003. But, before that, in 2000, we had a huge six-month strike in the commercials contracts. I was on the negotiating committee for that and also participated as a strike captain, and that was a very dramatic change for many of us in leadership, because there had been very few strikes in our industry and certainly none of them were as long as this one. It was a very difficult time. The upside was that it energized a generation of leadership and involvement because people now had something on the line. They couldn't just go about their work. The unions were on strike and it made a lot of members aware of the union in a way that they had not been before.

There were several leaders who actually stepped up during the strike, became aware that they needed to do more than just vote. So, that was good. But the strike itself was really painful. Six months on the street is a very long time. People were losing their houses, didn't know how to pay for their kid's schools. There was work in other areas because this was just the commercials contracts that we were striking, and we have several other contracts - television and film - that we can work under. But in New York, at that point, there were not very many television shows filming, other than daytime dramas, and very little film work. So, if you weren't doing commercials, you probably weren't making a living. And, it was very hard.

Coming out of that, there was this new energized sense of union and how members needed to be active in their union. At that same time, Cornell University established this program in New York called the "Union Leadership Institute at Cornell." Denis Hughes, who was the state AFL-CIO president at the time and a real visionary in this area, worked for Cornell University Institute for Labor Research and just understood that if the labor movement's going to succeed in this new era, what you need is trained leaders who understood not just how to work with their locals but how to plan, how to think about the future in terms of more than just a year down the line. I managed to get accepted into the program and actually got some scholarships and graduated in 2005. That was pretty remarkable, because I sat in a class of labor leaders from the state of New York, none of whom were in my business. The first week was up in Ithaca and there would be long, three-day weekends five

times a year. I walked in the first day in Ithaca and I thought, "What have I done?" There was nobody there like me. There was no one from the entertainment industry at all. There were typesetters and sheet metal workers and nurses and teachers and laborers, but no one from the entertainment business. And I thought it was going to be just horrible, but within half an hour, I formed some of the best relationships with some of the strongest labor leaders I've ever known. They literally took me under their wings and, I began to learn about leadership and strategy, and really the solidarity that the labor movement needs to have. It was a really remarkable experience.

These were issues that I never faced because they're just not issues I dealt with as a SAG-AFTRA labor leader. But it helped me understand comprehensive campaigns in a way that I never had before. There were a lot of classes on specific skills: finance, judiciary, organizing, how to administer a staff. In my union, I don't administer the staff. But for me, the training really answered some important questions, such as, "How can you be an effective labor leader and what does that mean?" And, "Why does it matter that you connect to labor unions outside of your own union and what kind of community relationships do you need to have?" And, "How do you build support in your community for your contract and why does that matter?" It opened my eyes to a whole world that I kind of knew existed but didn't have any experience with. And I think that's what got me deeply involved with my union.

I'm a volunteer president. I'm lucky because the kind of work I do is essentially itinerant, particularly commercials are last minute, and because I do more and more voice-over work, I have a USB microphone that plugs into my computer and I take it

> *When I started acting, I found a place where I could express myself and be accepted. That, in fact,* **my imagination was useful and not dangerous.** *Acting was a great escape. You get to be another person. You get to use your imagination. It was really quite remarkable and very freeing, and I got to be my own person.*

with me when I travel and my agent sends me auditions. I record mp3 files and send it to them and then if I get it, I go into a studio and record it. But, there's no question that my career has suffered greatly from my involvement with the union.

Entertainment unions are interesting in that, compared to other unions in this country, we have a lot of density in our industry, especially at the high end: Film and television, Broadway theater - we're unionized from stem-to-stern. Everybody is unionized for the most part: actors, stagehands, directors, writers, choreographers, musicians etc. But as you get away from the high end, that begins to thin out. And, the thing that is really changing rapidly in our world is technology, and that creates a real problem for all of us as digital technology becomes the accepted norm of production. It has changed everything we do. It used to be that in order to produce a film or television show, you had to have a big studio. You had to be in Los Angeles or New York because you were shooting film and film requires a particular kind of lighting. It requires a particular kind of

editing and it requires a lot of infrastructure. Digital technology is much more unleashed. Digital cameras are small, you can email files, you can edit digitally. You don't need big edit houses for a physical product and you can shoot in a lot of different places. And, you can shoot for a lot less money. So, the whole structure of the industry has begun to change. Beasts of the Southern Wild was a little, tiny independent film that was done totally non-union for very little money and he did not need a studio to do that production. Now, that's not to say that all productions are going to be like Beasts of the Southern Wild, but it shows you how the universe of work is changing.

When I came into the business, you couldn't wait to get your union card. It was the first thing that you wanted to do because that's where the work was. There was very little non-union work out there worth doing. That's changing, rapidly. So, we are coming under pressures that we are not used to.

When I first came to New York, before I joined any of the unions, I did some non-Equity theater and I very quickly learned the value of having a union card because they worked you for a very long time, they didn't have to pay you in a timely fashion or for rehearsal if they didn't feel like it. I had an out of town job where my housing was a very large walk-in closet, without a window. That was my bedroom, and I very quickly said this is not the life for me. I love theater but I'm not going to do it like this. So I quickly learned why the union existed.

What's fascinating about us, for the rest of the labor movement, is that SAG-AFTRA does organize freelance performers all the time. The work that I do as a commercial actor, that's job-by-job. My jobs typically take one day, so there's no shop, but we have a model that has essentially organized freelance performers for 70 years, and it's been fairly successful. The difficulty now is that the work is spreading out more and more and with digital technology, particularly in voice-over. My USB mic that I plug into my computer, lots of people have that, and because there's more casting done on the internet, the places where union actors went to get their work has changed. The ability of the union to have influence over workers has changed. I think the next ten years are going to be significant in our world if we're going to maintain our presence as the place to go to be a professional actor. I think we

have huge challenges.

Some of the things that we're struggling [with] are things labor unions as a whole are struggling with, which is a world that doesn't understand why we exist. We are no longer necessarily a destination in a career for a professional actor. I mean, if you're going to work in high-end television and film, you'll join because we have a lot of strength in there, because we control the celebrity pool and you can't make films and television without celebrities. But, when you work further down, into the rest of it, audiobooks, some kinds of music, commercials, voice-overs, narration, cable production, and it's not star-driven, then it begins to thin out, and we have to make sure that that doesn't become a non-union area of work.

That's going to be a struggle, and I think what we face there is pretty much the same struggle that many unions are facing regardless of what they do. We have locals in right-to-work states, of course, and we have members and we have production. But, a lot of the workers who live in Texas, for instance, work under our contract, get paid under our contract and don't join the union. That's a huge problem. They're freeloading, and we're going to have to find ways to pull them into the fold. So, it's my belief that

One thing that actors learn often in their lives is that we constantly reinvent ourselves. And I think that lives in a very deep part of me. **I think that I've approached my life and my understanding of myself as a path, and that's a really exciting way to look at life.**

more and more work will migrate to right-to-work states, and we have to have some way to prevail. So, the public conversation about unions affects us as well. Because if people don't understand why a union is good for them, then they won't join it, and you know, whether it's being an actor or being a bricklayer, it's the same problem.

I think one of the things we face as an entertainment union is really being able to understand the importance of our position in the labor movement. The fact that we consolidated our unions is actually a bright light for American labor. We did something very positive and we need to own that, but we can't be separate from the struggles of the labor movement. We can't be elitist, and there's a tendency to do that. "I'm not a worker, I'm an artist." Well, artists work, and that's the conversation that we must continue to have among us. The fact that we merged means that we addressed some of the changes of the future. We knew that as separate unions, we would not survive more changes in the industry and that our strength lay in being united. That's just the first step on that road.

Through all of this, I have recognized how important my relationship to other women has been. It's been a concern of mine in the labor movement in making sure there's more diversity in leadership and on committees, and recognizing how empowering other women have been for me on this journey of mine, and what an important force women are in the labor movement. I've done a lot of work with women's issues, such as pay equity. But around the issues of diversity and leadership, the importance of women's work in the labor movement is very important to me. I'm lucky because in my union, there are lots of women in leadership, unlike a lot of the rest of the labor movement. When I was president of AFTRA, my national executive director was a black woman, who for some time was the only female NED of an entertainment union. So we were kind of the odd people out in the labor picture. The women's movement was something that moved me as a teenager and it still is a very critical part of my thinking that it's really not a man's world. I think that women are more collaborative. Women assume that a group is going to do something or they work with a group to do something. Men are more singular. I just think that women have an expectation of working collaboratively.

I think a lot of my skill sets as an actor have really helped me enormously to be a labor leader because a lot of it is communication. One of the things actors do really well is they figure out characters and make things happen truthfully. We're always looking for the truth in something, and that's actually helped me a lot in being a leader, because that's kind of what I have to do leading the union. I can't just make stuff up and force people to do it. I have to really understand what the real problem is here and where is the truth here and how can we get there collectively? I don't know if that sounds a little bizarre, but I've always thought my skills as an actor helped me tremendously as a leader. Not only my communication skills, but sensitivity to people and the lives they lead and what the issues really are. That's one of the things that actors do when they act. They look at a scene and understand who they are in that scene and where's the truth and how do you portray it, honestly. So, they've kind of melded for me.

I'm sure I will retire. People do. I don't think about it as in, "This is what I'm going to do when I retire." I have been doing some teaching on and off for years, and I've been doing some consulting at Rutgers University.

I would imagine I would continue to do some of that. Maybe then I could go back and see if I could do another play. I don't know. But I don't think of retirement. I don't think about, "I'll move to Florida and go fishing." Never. I can't imagine I'd do that. I think I'd be pretty bad at that. One thing that actors learn often in their lives is that we constantly reinvent ourselves. And I think that lives in a very deep part of me. I think that I've approached my life and my understanding of myself as a path, and that's a really exciting way to look at life. My job as an actor has always been one of evolution, and I expect that my life will continue to be that way. I hope that I can continue to contribute in some way to my union and the labor community until the end.

For me, I think one of the guideposts to judge success is when I feel like I have a real understanding of where I am and where I'm going. I spent some time in my late teens and twenties being confused, really struggling and searching, not feeling comfortable, not feeling grounded. I think as I've gotten older, I've been able to feel more and more grounded and understand that this is the path I'm on and these are the things I'm trying to do. Success is part of that evolution. I very rarely feel that moment of, "Ah! I've got it!" I think the merger vote was a moment unlike any other in my life, because it was a very clear, strategic plan and it had a very clear moment of success. But, I also tell people that the merger vote was really the beginning of something. It wasn't the end of anything. It was really the beginning of now. Here's the evolution. How does that play out? How does that work?

I think success for me often is in terms of being understood. A lot of it is communication, being able to move people, to grow consensus around an issue. That is something that I take great pride in. And as for success on a personal level, I'm happy to say that I have a very successful marriage. My husband and I have a really strong relationship, and it's not like it is perfect, it's far from it, but I think we have a good, strong, working relationship that we both rely on, and that's really important. I think that I'm always surprised by the lack of permanence in life.

I think I grew up in a culture where permanence was valued and there was a kind of, "This is the way life is lived: You grow up. You get married. You die." Those are the milestones and that's it. What I've learned in my life is that those are all incredibly ephemeral. You can create those things for yourself but they're not really there. Life is all about change. And so I guess for me to be successful is for me to learn to kind of surf that change and be a part of it and not resist it. My sense of success is really centered more in my relationships. Do I have healthy relationships? Am I connected to my family and my friends? Am I being a good partner in a friendship, in a work situation, and in my marriage? Am I showing up? It's not about money. I often wish I had been more focused on money. I really unfortunately never was. It's not something that I accumulated much of, but I have very rich experiences, and so that means a lot to me. So, I guess I am successful in that I wanted to have a rich life that I could call my own, and I think I've done that, or I'm in the process of doing that. I guess I'm always looking for what's next. When I stop looking for what's next, that will be a change.

*Reardon with Ryan Seacrest backstage at the Emmy
Awards: Photo: SAG-AFTRA*

Elsy Rivas

Garment Factory Plaid Matcher, Haverhill, Massachusetts
Unite Here

How would I describe myself? I believe that I can be a really outgoing person, easy to talk to. Most of the time, when I meet someone, I'm kind of the quiet one that wants to get to know how they would react before I even try to interact. I like to help people. That's just something that I grew up with. I was born in El Salvador. I lived there until I was twelve. When I turned twelve, my father went back to my country and got my sister and me. My mother and my brother were already in this country. We moved to Chelsea, Mass, fifteen minutes outside of Boston, a big change, completely different from what I was used to seeing when I was little. Back in my country, it's not as big of a city. Moving to a city near Boston was a big transition. The reason we moved to Haverhill is because all of my family started buying houses here. I have my mom's only sister less than a mile away. I have my uncle's nearby. I have my cousins who are all much younger than me.

The language is one of the biggest issues that I had. It's been about five years struggling with it. I went through all high school with no English. And then, after that, three years later, we moved to Haverhill. It's more easy, quiet, you know, not much of a city type thing, which my parents love, but I kind of didn't like it,

because it was too quiet for me. There I did seventh grade, eighth grade and high school. I went to a technical school, and there's not too much to talk about. I didn't speak English at all. I don't even know how I did that, to tell you the truth. They used to give me these EOL classes. In there, most of the main classes, you were given a teacher that would help you. But in things like gym or art, I would have to do those all by myself. Classes like history, science and things like that, they would give me a teacher to be with me the whole time, and help me understand the class. They had to speak English only though, so I would learn. Now, academically, that was great, but trying to make friends was kind of a downfall, because it was like, "Who's that girl with a teacher right next to her? Does she need help or something like that?"

Junior year I did speak a little bit better. I was kind of getting into it, but I had a really thick accent - more than anybody else. People would make fun of me for speaking bad English. There were about ten other kids that needed the EOL teacher, but mine was the worst because I came later. But that kind of gave me a little bit of courage to learn more, and senior year I left with a bit more English and I was making my own friends. Some of them I still talk to today.

So, I was in technical school and I was

In the factory the union gives you a voice. If you don't feel like you are treated right, you go to your union representative and they'll take care of that. They'll put you and the other person together and they'll try to fix things. You and the other person are people. We don't have to be mistreated like that. And, if there wasn't a union in there, sometimes a little arguing can get overblown into, like, a crazy thing. **But it doesn't have to be like that.**

doing CAD drafting and I was learning how to work with architecture and how to draw. Drawing's an important thing for me. It's something that I learned in high school and sometimes I still do it when I'm bored, but not as much as I used to or as I should. A lot of people said that's a talent that I should do that is just going to the trash. I don't know. I can't find the time.

I love photography. If my friends are doing a party, I'm the one who takes the pictures. I love music...who doesn't? I like traveling a lot. Getting to know people from different cultures - that is my favorite thing. I am twenty-four. I love where I am now. I think everything happens for a reason. I had to go through all that to learn the language. Now, to be able to speak two languages easily, I mean, I would do it all over again in a heartbeat. Maybe I wouldn't take five years to learn the language, you know, I'd try to push myself to learn it faster, but yeah, being in this country, speaking two languages is great. Not everybody has that chance, and I do. So, I'm grateful for that.

It's a really quiet town, super quiet for my taste. I love that my family's around. And all of my friends from middle school are still around. It's alright for now. I would

like to live more in a city place, a noisy place, not like New York, but something that's not so suburban. I would love to go back to Boston.

I've been working at Southwick for about four years. I got the job because of my mother. I actually went in there to help her with the language, to translate for her, and she asked HR if they could give me a job, and they gave me an interview right then and there. My mother started just a couple of weeks before me. It's a big factory, about four hundred people. We work for Brooks Brothers; we do suits for the Army, the Navy. We do suits for professional athletes, we do suits for the Kennedy's, people like Ben Affleck wear our suits, famous people.

My job is basically to work with plaid. What I do is make sure that the lines on the welt - a welt is a little pocket that is really not a pocket, it seems like a pocket on top of the left side of a blazer, and it's at an angle - and my job is to make sure the lines are matching, going up and down, and from side to side. I also match the flap, which is the thing that goes on top of the pockets on the bottom of the blazer. In a day, if it's an easy pattern, I could easily do up to a hundred and eighty. It's a job that took me a lot to learn because it's really difficult. That's my mandatory job, but I do a lot of different things. I help around with whatever's needed. Whatever I can do, I do it.

We get paid by the piece. Technically your job is to try to make a certain amount of pieces in the time they give you. It took me so long to get to learn it. At first, they give you training and then they give you timework: they paid you whatever they hired you at, and then put you on timework. I've been working there for so many years that with my rate and the union I'm not making the same amount as what other people are making. I started at $8.25 an hour four years ago and now I'm at $11 something.

To be honest with you, the first three months I hated it. I hated it so bad because I couldn't see the lines. Because we're working in pairs, instead of me just laying them out one by one, I have to pin them in pairs so that the cutter will cut them, so it will be easier to cut them all at once, two pieces at a time. So, I have to pin them on the same spot so they can cut it. I couldn't get the lines right. It was so frustrating at first. My manager thought that I had it in me because I learned the method to do it fast, but I didn't have the speed. The biggest thing in there is that for the plaid, it can only be a certain way for you to put the fabric. You have to make sure that every line matches every single color - there's so many different kinds. By now, I know them, but at first it was frustrating. I was ready to

quit so many times. But I'm glad I didn't.

Over the years I made it, and now that I actually have it, I look back and I'm like, "Wow, I was just like a little baby crying. I could've just taken it on and just done it."

The economy's really bad. I had spent about eight months trying to find a job. That job provides you with forty hours and gives you benefits. It's a great job. I like it. I like the people that I work with, but I just think that there's something more for me out there that I'm going to go and pick up and take on.

I used to work at Target. In Target, I was a photo specialist. I worked there for a couple years. And in there when you start working, they give you this little video where it shows you why you shouldn't talk to the union and why you don't want the

union in the company and why the union's not good. They have about a ten minute video. So I didn't know better. Target was my first job, so when my mother brought me into Southwick, and I started signing the papers, she told me it was a union company. I remember asking the lady, "Do I have to be part of the union, because I don't want to pay them." And then the lady said, "Yeah. In order to be hired there, I would have to do it." And, I was just thinking in the back of my mind, "Wow. In Target they told me I can't do it and over here, there are no other options. Just do it."

So, I got the job, started working for a couple of years. Here and there, I would help other people, but not really get involved with the union. Like I said, I grew up in a Spanish family, so it's in me to help people that don't know English. My parents don't know English and they have been here as many years as I have. So, I'm always trying to help them translate papers, make them calls, go with them to places. I'm always the translator for them. So, if I see a lady up there that's in sort of the same situation that my mother would be, I go in and try to help her understand. The union representative we had at that point saw that in me, and he's the one who talked to me about getting involved. At first I was like, "No, no, no. I don't want nothing to do with it. I heard that it's bad. I don't want it." I was trying not to get involved, and he would always push me by saying, "I think you'd be good. It would be nice. Think about it." The people I worked with said, "Yeah, you should do it. You should do it." So, at the end of the day, that's how I got involved in it. Now that I'm part of a union, and I've worked in a union, I look back at the Target video and I'm like, "Wow, I really believed that."

I have been working for the union for about a year and a half. For me, the union has been such an eye-opening thing. It takes me to places that I wouldn't even picture them.

First, I started by helping people. I would just do it. Like, whoever worked around me would ask me questions; "Elsy, do you know this? Can you help me with this?" And, if I didn't know, I would go to the manager, I would ask the manager and I would go back to them. And when I got more involved, it was a little different because then people were like, say, getting in trouble, and then I would have to go get information, kind of like figure it out, what needed to be fixed or what was the worker getting in trouble for.

At first, it was just something that I was doing. After, it was something that I had to get involved in. I never thought they would do things like what they do in there. Like helping with their paperwork and helping with translations, and helping people achieve. It's an eye-opener.

I'm a steward in my company. I'm not just part of the people that I work with. I'm more involved in meetings and I have to meet with members of the company, and so I know a little bit more about it, so I hear things and I see things and sometimes I'm part of it and it's just so crazy. I never thought things would go that way. Now I'm not working for Southwick from March to June, for three months I'm in the union; I'm helping them organize. This is like eyes to a blind. It has me in places that I just never knew that people were working. In the food industry, and the struggles that they have to go through - things that they have to do in order to keep a job, to hold their household and keep their family. I'm coming from a struggling family so I kind of know that. As a little girl I didn't see that, but now that I have a better mind about it, it's just mind-blowing for some of the people that are going through it. And now that I'm part of it, it's just like; "You know what? I like this!" This is what I want to do. I want to help. I want to help these people understand. For the kids to not go through the same thing that I had to go through when I was little. I love my job.

In the factory the union gives you a voice. If you don't feel like you are treated right, you go to your union representative and they'll take care of that. They'll put you and the other person together and they'll try to fix things. You and the other person are people. We don't have to be mistreated like that. And, if there wasn't a union in there, sometimes a little arguing can get overblown into, like, a crazy thing. But it doesn't have to be like that.

In the company, it also helps for benefits, vacation time, how we work, the area we work at. There are so many things that are involved with the union: raises, how we get paid is something they are involved in. Now, I think what Target was telling me is not true at all. They were trying to cover themselves so they would not have to deal with a union because a union is more expensive. For the people, even though it's something they have to work for, it's something that, at the end of the day, it's still worth it.

School for me is not really an option. I'm technically an illegal. I have a permit to live here due to the violence in my country but I'm not allowed to like, be part of anything that has to do with the government, like I can't join the Army; that's something that I would love to do. I can't do any jobs that are in the government. I'm not an illegal per se; I have a permit to be here. I have a social, I have a license, I have a lot of things that people have, but I don't have citizenship. In order to go to college, if I don't have citizenship, I would have to pay out of my pocket to go to classes. So, financial aid is not an option for me.

From high school, after the shop that I took in there, my biggest dream was to do graphic design. That's what I wanted to do. When I started thinking about going to college, I actually looked into this college, "Institute of Art" in Cambridge (Massachusetts). The guy that I went and showed my art to was in love with it. He thought I was going to be so good in there, and you know, it was perfect for me because I could go to that school and this and that, but as soon as he started talking to me about money, it was just a downfall. That is actually one of the things I love the most. Well, you know what, if it didn't happen, it didn't happen for a reason, because if I worked my way around to go to college, I would have never been part of this and I would have never got that job in Southwick and finally get someone to get me to be part of the union. The opportunities it has given me are huge.

What is success? That would be something that you push yourself to do. I mean, it could be something like completing a goal that you want. Something like, success for me would be, you know, finally doing that one thing that I'd say that is out there for me. If I find that thing that is out there for me to do, then I'll be like, "Alright, this is what it is. This is what I want to be doing for the rest of my life. I'm happy where I am right now in my life. There's no issue with money, there's no issue with family, there's no issue with where I'm living. I love my job, I love what I'm doing." I mean, at that point, it's something that you have overcome; something that would like, stop you from getting to your goal to what would be success. For me, success is the biggest goal that you have in life. I feel like I'm in the process. I am going step by step, but yeah. I do feel like I'm moving along with it.

I love where I am now. I think everything happens for a reason. I had to go through all that to learn the language. **Now, to be able to speak two languages easily, I mean, I would do it all over again in a heartbeat.** *Maybe I wouldn't take five years to learn the language, you know, I'd try to push myself to learn it faster, but yeah, being in this country, speaking two languages is great.*

John Roeber

Boilermaker, Butte, Montana

International Brotherhood of Boilermakers Local 11

I'm self-motivated. I'm old school. I believe in coming through the ranks. When I was coming up through the ranks, you respected your peers and respected the elder members. There was a way of life back then like, if you didn't quite cut the mustard on a particular job, you were sent home. You don't see that today. That's what I mean by old school. We did things different back then. They're more pampered today then they were back then. I'll give you an example. In a boiler, you can be like 200 feet up in the air, and I remember when I was young, I was working with one of the older gentleman and he said, "Roeber. I want you to get up there and start tearing that scaffolding apart and see what you're made of." So, I had to get up there and start working at heights 200 feet in the air...versus today, where some of our young apprentices, they don't even like to get off the landing.

I'm blessed to have a family and I'm blessed to provide for them. Even though it was a challenging career because, the profession that I picked, we don't have a lot of heavy industry in the area, so I found myself on the road much of the time, trying to provide for my family. In the 80's, it was a struggle to try to survive because the middle 80's were kind of like it is right now. The work opportunities weren't as many.

Our local here in Montana is for field construction boilermakers, so we work on coal fire generators, and chemical plants and refineries. When I first started the career in Montana, which would have been 1977, I used to be able to get at least 1500 hours, for the first 10 years, in the state of Montana, which would have been a pretty good average year. But as the years went by, that was cut down so I found myself traveling a lot. I actually worked 37 states through my career, and went across South Dakota

48 times, to leave the state to try to make a living through the years. I got pretty good at traveling and not having to use a map. But that was the nature of the beast, so to speak. Work started slowing down around here. We didn't have as much work, so if you were going to be a career boilermaker, then you'd have to find work elsewhere. One good thing about our profession is the money follows the man. If I went to work in Kentucky or New York City, then all my hours toward my pension and my annuity would follow me wherever I went. I was able to accumulate hours through the years.

There would be different pay scales. Like in New York City, I worked in Astoria, Queens, six months after the World Trade Center was downed. We stayed in Parsippany, New Jersey and then drove in. We worked like 35 straight days. That kind of area, wages are a little higher because the cost of living is more. At least my money would still go into my insurance, so I was always able to keep my insurance going when I had downtime. That was one good thing about this profession -- you end up having so many hours in one particular field, as a boilermaker. I see a lot of people who had different careers, where they did this, and did that, but at the end of the day, they really didn't have anything because they had too many opportunities to make a living and they didn't really have any hours in the pension. I had all my eggs in one basket, so to speak, so I actually have a pretty good pension, as long as it's still there when the time comes. With what's going on in today's world, it's a little different, but I always believed that I have a window of opportunity to have a good retirement. So, that was always good.

But the sacrifices were pretty hard on the family. Sometimes, I'd leave in January, February, March. But I'd always try to come back for my youngest daughter's birthday on the 7th of March. Then, in spring you'd always be working. So, April, May and June, I remember one time, my middle daughter's daughter - her birthday is May 28 - she told me when she was like 18 years old that I never was home for her birthday, so I actually scheduled my work around her birthday. So that particular year, the 28th fell on Memorial Day Weekend so we took the whole weekend off and went up to Yellowstone Park. Them kind of things were the hardships on the family… not being here. But, I always tried to have a couple of months off during the summer if I could. Our business is either spring or fall for work. During the summers the boilers run because they generate electricity for air conditioning so July and August we have some time off and then I'd always leave in the fall and try to come back and go hunting somewhere around the middle of November and then I'd always take the time off at Christmas. We decorate pretty heavy for Christmas. The reason why that started is I was always gone and I always thought when I came back I would give something to the kids so, since '87 up until this point, we'd always decorate. Now, we're at the point where we have a pretty elaborate Christmas display. That started where we always wanted to give the kids memories of what we had through the sacrifices of being a boilermaker. We're pretty well known for our decorating.

I guess the biggest thing I think you got to know about me - you know I was talking about the sacrifices through the years that we did, right? There were a lot of times where I wasn't there for basketball games or baseball. We had four children. We have three daughters and we had a boy. Well, the boy, he became a boilermaker in his younger years, but anyhow, we ended up losing him here back in 2005. And, I really don't talk about it a lot but I think it's kind of the hardship part of being a boilermaker, because I've heard that a lot over through the years. It's important to know about that because…we lost the boy. He was a boilermaker, and I think it has a lot to do with the hardships and the career that I chose. The way we lost him is that he committed suicide. I think it's important that you know that so that you can understand where I come from. Part of the problem was - he always told his mom - is that his dad wasn't there for him, so that gets back to the hardship of the career. How do you justify? You can't be in two places at the same time. You go after the money and let your guard down on other things so that's how that goes, through the years. That's hindsight, I guess. If you could do it over, I probably would. It's part of my life. It's part of what happened. One thing I learned about it, life can be cruel, but life goes on. Look at what we've seen when we go through the years in

People would ask me what was I. *Well, if I told them I was a boilermaker, they wouldn't know what a boilermaker was so I would tell them I was an energy consultant because I travel all over the country trying to restore energy to the nation through working on boilers. So, they thought, "Johnny did pretty good".*

the military, when people go through that. It's like that. It's something that we have to face. You get up every day and address it. It was hard on the family but we get through it. We've been blessed with six grandkids. That's why we decorate like we do now, because of the grandkids. So, we appreciate that kind of stuff. You get blessed and life goes on. You just got to appreciate all that stuff.

We lived in Butte. I come from a family of eleven. My dad was a miner and he got up and went to work everyday and I think it was just the way we were brought up. We didn't have everything. Some families had more than others. My mom and dad did provide for us. It must have been just the way we were brought up, seeing how life wasn't the best back then but hard work paid off.

Hard work, I guess, that's what we tried to embed in our own children. So, if you get up and be productive, then things pay off, but you do have your ups and downs in life. Nobody has a crystal ball or anything so you gotta deal with what you get, right?

I was thinking about [the meaning of success] the other day. I remember our 20th high school reunion. My wife and I are high school sweethearts. That's where we got to know each other and from that point on, we're still high school sweethearts. So, we were at our 20 year reunion and that kind of question was brought up. How do you rate success? Well, the first thing people do at the reunion is ask you what you do. "What's your profession?" Because a lot of people become doctors, lawyers, things like that. People would ask me what was I. Well, if I told them I was a boilermaker, they wouldn't know what a boilermaker was so I would tell them I was an energy consultant because I travel all over the country trying to restore energy to the nation through working on boilers. So, they thought, "Johnny did pretty good" because he was an energy consultant. But after the reunion, how I measured success would be…As long as you have your health and your financial means, that's how I would measure success. Here I am 57 years old, I'm still alive. About three quarters of all the people I graduated with are dead, for one reason or another. Just being on the earth and being able to see the sun come up every day and have my health, that's how I measure success. And I still have my family.

I'm a 35 year career boilermaker. In 2006, I became the business manager for the union. I'm still doing that. It is a full-time job.

As a field construction boilermaker, I'd have to call the union hall and get a dispatch and say, "OK, so I'm going to go to Eastern Montana Colstrip." That's where our coal fire generators are. I'd get a dispatch and then I'd have to pack all my clothes in a suitcase. I'd always have to make sure that I had all my bills with me or I'd have to pay 'em. You'd have to make sure your car was mechanically capable of going 350 miles. You'd have to plan. You'd have to think about renting an apartment, so you'd have to get set up. Most of the time I'd room with somebody, that would help cut the cost. Then, you'd go there and get hired in and then you'd be working 10 hours a day, probably on the average back then was 6 days a week, and then you'd go in and tear apart certain parts of the boiler and would work on it. In our profession, you have to be a highly skilled welder. That took some skill. Basically, in my day, you'd be up there

for 8-10 weeks. If I had Sundays off, I'd drive home to try to spend time with family. In my younger days I did that.

If you ever look at a boiler, you see how high it is. Inside it, there's a boiler and there's a cavity, and that's where the firebox is. It's all open on the inside so, you go into a door up on top. You'd have to build scaffold or something like that. So, the difference between the top of the boiler and the bottom, inside the boiler cavity is open; that's where the 200 feet comes into play. A boiler actually is built so the boiler hangs off the top of it and it hangs down and the reason why is when the boiler is running and it gets hot, they actually grow almost about 2 feet, they grow down. These are big ones, where they generate electricity.

What I do now is I administrate the union hall. I make sure members are represented out on the job. I do collective bargaining when that comes up, grievances, you have to handle those, try to find them work through organizing. That's very important. Basically, I'm an elected official, who's a member. I'm a spokesman for the local.

The work I did as a boilermaker was less stressful. I could kind of come and go as I pleased. I only had to please myself. This business manager job is more stressful, especially during hard times, so it puts more stress on you. I think you age quicker. Because in good times it probably wasn't as stressful as it is in bad times, because people are having a hard time paying their dues, they have a hard time out on the job. The reality now is, the perspective of union people, a lot of people don't like union people, so you have a hard time trying to convince people that you know, we're not bad people. Actually, a lot of people think that we're union thugs or something. We recruit all the time but we don't hold anyone hostage.

If they want to, they can stay in it. If they don't, I let 'em leave. You do pay money to be a union member, but you have better benefits because of it. You have a pension, health insurance.

How I got in the union is I learned how to weld when I was younger and I started in a shop, and the window of opportunity was there for me to come out in the field and I guess it was because of the money and the benefits and making a half decent wage. When I was younger, I was lucky to get in the union and then I was able to hang in there and get hours of work. I was lucky because I've always had health insurance, an annuity and a pension because a lot of people don't have that. I feel very blessed to have been a union man through the years.

Actually, hopefully, I'm going to retire in a year or so here and what I want to do is finish all my projects that I never did get done. When our trailer burnt down, and I built our house, I tore down this big industrial building and it's been laying in my yard all that time. I was going to put it up and make my own welding shop, so I could stay home. It's one of those dreams that just got lost. We were always trying to find ways for me to stay home and make a living and raise the family and that never happened. One thing or another happened and I never put it back up. I guess you could say it's on my honey do list. And, I have a little bit of property. I want to build a summer home for the three girls, so they can have that. And buy a sailboat and teach my grandkids how to sail. That's the plan. As long as I got my health, I'm going to give it my best shot.

It was quite the investment that I made in June 2004. Brent, our son, worked on it all summer long, well into the fall. With his hard work and determination, he finally got it up and running. After that, it then sat in the back yard for a few years. When Brent died, I had decided one weekend, which was Easter of 2006, to take the grandchildren over to the cemetery, which is only two blocks away from my home. This went on for months, and the kids looked forward to going because they took turns driving. **When I look at this picture,** *it makes me realize that you need to take in every little minute and cherish it, because life is way too short.*

John Sayles

Filmmaker
Directors Guild of America, Motion Picture Editors Guild
Screen Actors Guild, Writers Guild of America, East

John Sayles on set Amigo. Photo by Mary Cybulski

I think the important thing is, **before the Screenwriter's Guild, the studio could just take the nephew of some studio head and put his name on a picture,** *or if they had a famous guy, William Faulkner, or somebody like that, they might throw his name on a picture just for the cachet of it, when it hadn't even gone through his typewriter…*

I would describe myself as somebody who is self-employed and serially employed and basically pessimistic but not cynical. Pessimism is that you often think that things don't usually turn out very well. Cynical is you're actually glad that things don't turn out well because it justifies shitty behavior. I'm a Libra. I usually see things from many different sides.

My work is multifaceted. I make a living as a screenwriter for hire, writing screenplays for other people. I also write novels on my own. They don't pay very well so I couldn't make a living doing that. Occasionally I get to make a movie that I've written myself and there I'm often an employer. I think three of the seventeen [movies] were financed by a studio. But all the others were, basically we started our own company and found the money or used the money that I make as a screenwriter, and there I'm usually the president - each movie has a different company - so I'm in some ways an employer including of myself so I end up, the company which I may have financed will pay me as writer/director/editor and actor, if I'm in it. You know, it's a combination of being self-employed, like when I'm writing a novel or writing a screenplay on spec or serially employed.

When you say you're a screenwriter, I basically have to be given a job, I have to audition for jobs, so I could have half a year or more where I don't have a job.

On our own movies, first I write the screenplay. If it never gets made, I never get paid for it. Then we budget it. I schedule it, which is usually done for free or very little money, do some location scouting, and then if it gets financed, we go into a preproduction period where you find all the locations, you hire the actors, you prepare the crew, you think about how you're going to shoot it, prepare for the shooting, and have a low budget movie that's very ambitious, which is mostly what we make. The better you plan, the more smoothly it's going to go and the more you're going to get out of your four to six weeks, although I've had as much as eight weeks to shoot a movie. So, you could just get more done and have it be better if you're never waiting around trying to figure out what to do next if you've planned it really well. Then, during the shooting, we generally shoot five or six-day weeks. What I prefer to do is, because the equipment rental is expensive, we try to keep the number of weeks down because you rent equipment by the week. If you go over two days into the next week, you have to pay for the whole week, and it's pretty much the same thing for actors. So, what you tend to do is try to end at the end of a week. So, we'll start with a five-day week and then work a six-day week and then work a five-day week. And it's all union workers on the film so the screen actors' guild and IA and a couple of the others, the Teamsters. a bunch of unions are involved and they all have their rules about overtime or working Saturdays or over a certain amount of hours. Except of course our last movie, where we shot in the Philippines, where they have no unions pretty much anywhere, including in the film business. They can work 24 hours on and 24 hours off, which we chose not to do because it's too fucking crazy. And, we basically worked people like we would've if we were in the States. And on a day like that, I basically get up at the crack of dawn because you gotta maximize your daylight for shooting, and I'll work for 10 hours directing and then maybe go to dailies afterward and then do my homework for the next day. So, the shooting periods are pretty intense. I don't like to work long days. I just don't think that well after a certain amount of hours. We try not to, whether we pay overtime or not, work that long hours. Actually, one of the few complaints we've had from crews on some of our movies is that there's not enough overtime. You know, they're used to it and the production is getting behind the eight ball, and having to pull these incredibly long days where the crew goes into golden time. And then, there's postproduction. I am the editor on my own movies and there's not the time pressure. You're not worried about whether the sun is up or down, but, because I'm self-employed, I'll work as many hours as I want. I'll try to keep my assistant down to eight hours/day, when I'm editing. The last part of it, you go through timing and the look of the picture, which is darker, redder, greener, brighter, all that stuff, and sound mix. And finally, when the movie is done, you try to find a distributor because we often don't have one. And then, when the movie opens, there's this other job which is absolutely unpaid which is to go around and do publicity for it. I average per movie, 200 to 300 interviews, so that's just part of the gig.

I've been very lucky to get to make a movie every two to three years, but I don't get a lot of offers to direct Hollywood movies. It's not like I'm turning stuff down. The fame doesn't really convert into anything like employability as a director. The last three movies that we've made we had to self-finance. Nobody's invested in one of our movies for ten years. We haven't even gotten a distributor in the last two; we had to self-distribute. The economics of that world, the independent movie world, is always pretty fragile and right now it doesn't really exist as a business. There are a handful of companies that still do it, but most of them don't give an advance when they take a movie. If they make a huge amount of money, they'll give you back some. That's really why I have to say, for a living, I'm not a director. I'm a screenwriter for other people. I'm really lucky to be able to do it. I've had what I call "real jobs", where you have to get up in the morning and go to a factory or a hospital or whatever and punch in and do the eight hours, and it's pretty alienating. You know, I was probably the Paul Bunyan of orderlies, I don't think I'll ever be as good at anything in my life as I was at being an orderly because I was big and I was strong enough to move the patients without hurting them and I was calm and wasn't squeamish about blood or death. I was willing to hang with the patients when it was time to do it. I was getting $1.10/hour and, it's not the most fun in the world.

When I get to write a screenplay, I like writing, even if I'm helping somebody else tell their story. It's frustrating and usually the movie doesn't get made, but I write stuff just for the fun of it. It's kind of like if I had been a professional athlete, I think it was Babe Ruth who said something like "You mean they're going to pay me to play baseball?" So, I'm very lucky in that way.

Right now I'm in the Screen Actor's Guild of America 'cause I occasionally act in other peoples' movies. I'm in the Writer's Guild of America East, which is the screenwriting union. I'm in the Director's Guild of America, and I'm in the Editor's Guild. I would say those are Guilds.

The Writer's Guild, basically if you're going to work for a studio and they're a signatory to one of these unions, you have to join. So, finally, my first screenwriting job, paid screenwriting job, was way back in 1978. I signed up and I think I got $10,000, which was minimum, for the screenplay and the joining fee was $3000. And that's the union that I think I most identify with. We've gone out on strike twice. Two of my novels were written during those strikes. "A Moment in the Sun" would not be done yet and certainly wouldn't be some 900 pages long if we hadn't had a nice, long strike.

You know, we've lost a little bit of ground in both strikes, but nothing compared to what we would've lost if we hadn't gone on strike. Because of the Taft-Hartley law, all the unions in the movie business are Balkanized, there's a writer's guild and a director's guild, and the editor's guild and there's the IA (International Alliance) and the Teamster's, and there's a couple other little guilds that have specialty craft people within them, and the screen actor's guild and all of our contracts come up at different times so there's no chance for a mass industry strike.

I would say the Writer's Guild is a very strange union in some ways in that there aren't many teams of writers, but what happens in feature writing, which I've done for the first part of my career anyway, the Hollywood norm is to have more than one writer on a project and at the end of the day, if the movie gets made, the studio says "OK, we say this writer and this writer are going to get credit. That's who we want to get credit." Any other writer who has worked on it then is informed by the Guild that that's the credit they're going to put on the movie and if they feel they have contributed enough to the script that they should get credit too, then it could go into adjudication. And that's one of the most important things that the Writer's Guild does. It's this adjudication because a lot of your money comes from residuals and if your name's not on the movie, you get no residuals. You don't get any percentage of the TV sale or the HBO sale or something like that. And very often, your contract says that you'll get x number of percentage points if you get credit, so you get a bonus of some sort if you get credit. I've been on movies where there were as many as fifteen writers listed and sometimes I don't feel that I contributed that much and sometimes I say "I'd like to have my name thrown into the pot. I feel like I should get credit too." I think the important thing is, before the Screenwriter's Guild, the studio could just take the nephew of some studio head and put his name on a picture, or if they had a famous guy, William Faulkner, or somebody like that, they might throw his name on a picture just for the cachet of it, when it hadn't even gone through his typewriter, barely.

Because I'm self-employed, I don't know that I'll retire. I think I will be retired. I'm older than most writers in Hollywood

We've gone out on strike twice. Two of my novels were written during those strikes. *"A Moment in the Sun" would not be done yet and certainly wouldn't be some 900 pages long if we hadn't had a nice, long strike.*

right now, and I'm only 61. It's a very youth-oriented industry, including for directors and writers. Who knows if we'll get to make another movie. Certainly I don't have any money left, having spent the last bunch of it on Amigo. No one's investing in our movie so even though I have three or four scripts written, who knows if I'll ever be able to finance one of them. I don't have an idea to write another novel. I'm still getting work as a screenwriter, mostly for cable TV. I don't want to retire because it's not a job that you have to go in and do. You can do it from anywhere. If I end up not having fun doing it, I will retire, but it's not anything I plan on doing right now.

I get to do something I like to do. That's pretty much it. With any one of our projects, the way that I do it I'm usually pretty happy, you know there're things that I don't like about the movies or that I wish were better, but I've been pretty happy with the final project, which is so rare for people who make movies. Most screenwriters, you know, some are thrilled by the movie that got made out of their screenplay, more or less thrilled about it, even my friends who are DGA directors, often the best cut of the movie, the one they would have preferred is not the one that goes on the screen, and sometimes it really is something that they almost have to consider taking their names off of because it's such a bad representation of what they wanted the movie to be or

what it could've been. So, I don't really have to do that. When we do get to make a movie, I pretty much, within the limitations of the budget and just the variables of filmmaking, make the movie that I wanted to make. So, whenever we get to make a movie, I feel like we've been successful. If we get any kind of release on it, that's another form of success. We certainly aren't making any money at the box office these days, so it's almost like the world's most expensive hobby. But yeah, if somebody gets to live the life they want to or do the work they want to, they're successful.

When we do get to make a movie, I pretty much, within the limitations of the budget and just the variables of filmmaking, make the movie that I wanted to make. **So, whenever we get to make a movie, I feel like we've been successful.** *If we get any kind of release on it, that's another form of success.*

Photo by Ric Kallaher

241

Tom Tanner

Ironworker, Local 14 President, Arlee, Montana
International Association of Bridge,
Structural, Ornamental and Reinforcing
Iron Workers, Local 14

I would describe myself as a family man. I have a wife and four kids. Me and my wife were high school sweethearts. We were both going to college and she got pregnant. She was the valedictorian of our high school class and she had a free ride to college, she had a scholarship [but] it was pretty obvious who was going to work, and it was me. I went to the Native American Ironworkers' training program. It was a pre-apprenticeship for the union and that was in Chicago, Illinois. So, I left Arlee, Montana, a town of about 1500 people, and the reservation I was born and raised on, and went to Chicago (laughs). I didn't realize there were that many people in one city, let alone the whole world. It was very - I was taken back by it - public transportation and everything that went with it. I mean it was... How people would walk by and not even notice if you were standing or sitting. Where I come from everybody knows everybody. It's a real community of people, not a city where it don't matter to them if you're red, yellow, green, blue, or any other color. They're going about their tasks and their daily order. I was impressed and I enjoyed it. It was a real eye opener for me. I went to that program for 18 weeks; when I left, my oldest daughter Megan was four months old. She and my wife, Jennifer, took me to the train station in Whitefish, Montana. They put me on a train to Chicago and I came back and went to work that summer. With the pre-apprenticeship program, they give you automatic entry into the apprenticeship program. I went to work late that summer of August and I never looked back. I've had three other kids since then: Ashley, Thomas and Brooke, and me and Jennifer have done them very well with the union.

I'm really blessed to have a woman that's as strong and independent as she is, because working iron requires an absurd amount of traveling. You're always going. It's been that way from the beginning. The amount of travel, it's incomprehensible for a lot of people. You tell people what you do, how often you're home, and they look at you and they'll say, "I can never do that." They think, "How can you be gone that much?" And they'll look at Jennifer. "How can you handle him being gone that much?" But, it's just kind of how we grew up together. It's just...you gotta go where the work is. I think as a construction worker, as an ironworker, as a union ironworker, you gotta go where the work is. As much as you'd like your work to be at home, it's all about the road. You're always going places to build different things. It takes me to the whole Northwest, from Washington to Oregon to Idaho to Montana. Yeah, I've been all over the country building bridges, dams, buildings.

The nice thing about the union jobs and union membership is that I know at the end of the day, I have a pension. In the meantime, my kids have health insurance and we've got the livable wage. The wages make us middle class Americans. We can afford to send my daughter to the prom with a nice dress. We can afford to have my boy be in wrestling and my other daughter's in softball. We can afford to make a living. It's a struggle for a lot of people because of the low wages for some jobs, but I'm able to earn a decent wage because of the skills that I've learned from the ironworkers.

I don't know that we've had it easy. I don't think that our parents had it that easy. I think people are going to have to continue to work hard for what they believe in and continue to fight for what they want to have. When people give up the fight or quit believing, then you're going to have real trouble. You're going to have two or

The world doesn't end at the reservation lines, and there's a lot more opportunities once you take that first step. **The first step off the res is kind of like the first step on the iron. It's a big step.** *You take a deep breath and you take a big step and once you find out that high beam is gonna be there, you take another step. Same thing with leaving the res; once you do, you know it's okay to keep going.*

three minimum-wage jobs just to get by, and that's where people in these next few elections and in the direction this country's going, the way they want unions out of the picture. It's definitely the wrong direction for the American middle class.

When I got into the Ironworkers, it was August of 1996. I worked primarily on bridges, dams and steel structures. Most of the work was bridges and dams. That was the mainstay of our work. It was all over the place, building different structures. I was mainly a reinforcing ironworker, which means I had a lot of rebar jobs. I just worked with the same gang - the same gang of ironworkers, we traveled around with. There might be two or three different guys from the area that would come in and out of our group, but for the most part, it was five or six of us that just went from one job to the next, or we'd pick up a couple guys from the area. Some of them would stay and others would go, and some guys would spend enough time on the road and they'd go home. And then, sometimes, work would just go flat and we'd all go home [laughs]. So it wasn't a perfect world, but we put in a lot of rebar and a lot of bridges and we put a lot of steel beams up bridges, too.

Since then I was voted a business agent in 2000. Then I was voted a representative

by the membership of Local 14 - The Ironworkers Local 14: I was voted by them to be the Montana rep., in 2000. And then, in 2006, I was elected president of the union Local 14, and that was by the entire membership of the union in Eastern Washington. That was a big day. I was very proud of that.

I was lucky to get in with the Ironworkers and I continue to work around them and continue to make friends. You know, birds of a feather flock together. A lot of the family guys pay attention to each other because they know that they've got a family at home, and you have a family at home. They're not out there sitting in the taverns, you know. All of your money goes home.

What I do now is I procure employment for members of the local. We go out to try to get any and every job that's got iron in it. We try to make sure that our contractors are getting it and that in turn gets the members to work. Everything we do is to try to get work for our members. That's our mainstay right now. That's our main goal: getting as much work for the Ironworkers Local 14 as we can, and their contractors.

Idaho is our neighbor state. Idaho is right in the middle of our local and it's a right-to-work state. There's a lot of non-

> *When we leave this earth, I don't think that anybody's gonna remember what car we drove, what house we lived in, or how much money we had in our bank account.* **When we leave this world, people are going to remember what kind of person you were,** *how you treated people, and basically, they'll remember a lot more who you were other than what you had.*

union competition that comes out of Idaho. There's a lot of smaller, non-union competition here in town, in the area, and we continue to fight that on a daily basis. But, we've approached the guys who are non-union and asked them to join the union, and for whatever reason they have - they're scared of it or they've heard too many different things about it or they just don't want to do it - they don't elect to become members. We have a membership of about 600. It covers western Montana, northern Idaho and eastern Washington.

I love the work that we do. I love the guys that we represent. The work we do and the guys we represent are probably some of the most passionate tradesmen there are, and they all really care deeply about our trade. We know that it's our future to go out and do the job right and do it on time, and if we don't do it safely, if we don't do it, we lose that. We'll lose that market and once that's gone, we'll lose our trade. We believe in quality, safety and production.

It may change from day to day, but I think, for the most part, I think you're still out there representing your union. I don't care if you're putting a bolt in the bridge or if you're sitting in an office trying to get work for your members. I think you do it out of pride. You do it out of what

you believe in and who you believe in. I think that we all believe in each other. The ironworkers believe in each other. We're a brotherhood of ironworkers: brotherhood and sisterhood. We've got a lot of female members, too, and we all believe in each other. I think that's the biggest thing to enforce. Like it or not, you're selling a product and your product is the craft. It's a craft; it's a trade. I believe that.

When we leave this earth, I don't think that anybody's gonna remember what car we drove, what house we lived in, or how much money we had in our bank account. When we leave this world, people are going to remember what kind of person you were, how you treated people, and, basically, they'll remember a lot more who you were other than what you had. I think sometimes people get that mixed up, and they think if you have the biggest house or the nicest car or the most money in your account that you've made it, and I think how we treat people, how people treat us in return is the real marker of who you are and how you seemed.

I was born and raised in Arlee, Montana, and I still live there with my wife and family. Arlee is on the reservation of the Confederated Salish and Kootenai Tribes. We're Flathead Indians. I was raised by my grandparents. My grandmother on my maternal side is a far left, far, far left activist, real compassionate. So I get my compassion from her. My grandmother on my paternal side, she's all business, she's very smart, she's got a lot of education. And, my grandfather on my father's side was a businessman. He knew a lot about making money; he knew about that. He knew that he had to do something, and at the end of the day he liked to make it worthwhile. And my dad is a hard worker - gets up early to do whatever needs to be done for the day. He's never worked by the clock. He works until it's done…All good influences on me.

I didn't even know what an ironworker was. I had no idea what an ironworker was. There was a sign on the counselor's office that said, "Do You Want to Become a Union Ironworker? Make $12 an Hour in Wages." And, at that time, $12 an hour was a pretty good wage. It had one of those little tear-off tabs on the bottom with the phone numbers to call. I called it and they said, "Fill out these applications and you can go to Chicago, and when you get done, you can go to work as a union ironworker." So, I went back to Chicago not knowing exactly what an ironworker was but knowing that I could make 12 bucks an hour, thinking that was a pretty good deal, and when I got back and found out what we did… I remember the first time they sent us up on iron, up on the steel framework on the iron in Chicago… that was a little bit terrorizing. You know, all of a sudden you're 12 feet off the ground with an eight-inch piece of iron between your legs and that's it. We were at 12 feet because it was just training, but we've been at 180 feet since. It was terrifying to take that first step across that I-beam. When have you had to do that before…coming from a small, western Montana town?

Getting started was hard. It was hard getting started. It was hard to become accepted. But once you've been accepted, once you got into the brotherhood, then it was like a family within a family. All of our wives know each other. All of the people we work with know each other. We know each other's kids. It's just a big extension of your regular family because you spend so much time with each other. When you're on the road with a guy for three months, five days out of the week you're with your partner on the road, two days out of the week you're home, everybody becomes like family. It's all in the same. You know, when we go home, we're home, but we're back with each other on Monday through Friday, and it doesn't matter if you're working in the office or working in that gang, that's your crew. And when you're working with your crew, that's your extension of your family.

The union sent you to work, and, you know, that's pretty typical in building and construction trades, and that's the Building/Trades union, as opposed to the AFL-CIO (American Federation of Labor and the Congress of Industrial Organizations). The AFL was the trade unions and the CIO was your teachers and your privatized unions, I guess. Your trade unions have always been that way. Your trade unions, whether you're a pipefitter, an operator, your union sends you to your job and dispatches you to your work, and when you get done you come back to your union hall. There are some mornings in the union hall where there are fifteen to twenty guys sitting around playing cards, and other days where everybody's working and it's just an empty union hall. We check with each other. We talk to each other. You know, we'll ask, "Where's little Joe?" "Oh he's in Wisconsin, working." "Where's Kyle Johnson?" "Oh, he's in Portland, working." Or, "How 'bout

Marvin? Anybody heard from Marvin?" "Oh, he's down in Minnesota." We keep in touch with everybody and work with each other and still keep track of each other even though we're not working with each other.

I think that's what keeps most of us in it, that sense of brotherhood. Because, it's not just the work that the ironworker does - there's three types of work that the ironworker does: the hard work, the dirty work, and the scary work. You know, you get to be 45, 50 years old, still working; you get to wonder what the hell you're doing. You get to that age, see the people you've been working around with for the last 25, 30 years and, this is your family.

At 35 years, 35,000 hours, or age 57, and you got to have two out of the three, and you're eligible to retire. Hopefully, by that time you're running the work. Hopefully, by then, you're a supervisor and you're just pointing fingers and directing traffic.

I hope to retire. I'm working for my retirement. Retirement is the goal. When I get to my 35 years I want to retire and I want to be able to go home and do what I want to do and do it when I want to do it. I don't know what I want to do. I just know that when I wake up and I decide I want to go somewhere or that I want to do something, I'll have the ability to do it because I'll have a pension. I'll have an income coming in that I've worked for 35 years. Then I can go South in the wintertime, so I don't have to sit up here in the cold, wet rain and snow, and I can take my kids or grandkids to Disneyland so they can see different parts.

I'll probably spend some of it traveling and just being comfortable; being able to retire comfortably without having to struggle…don't have to pick up a job down at Walmart because I can't make it on my pension, you know? You see a lot of old people around at different places. You know

they're supplementing their retirement because they don't seem to have enough to make it.

Along with being president of the union, I'm the Pacific Northwest District Council TERO representative. TERO stands for Tribal Employment Rights Office. So what I do is, I'm a representative for the Northwest District Council. I go to different area reservations and we offer training; we offer opportunities for people to get in the Ironworkers. We try to work on our relationships with the area governments, help secure the work on the reservation for union workers. Kind of comes back to everybody being a democrat and believing in the same thing: helping each other, giving the folks on the reservation an opportunity to get in the union. Granted, not all of them want to be ironworkers and that's just a fact, I guess. But the ones that do want to become ironworkers have the ability to come in and visit with me and fill out an application, and, when we see the opportunity, we take them in, give them a shot. The nice thing about it is, when I go out to the reservation, being a native—maybe not from their reservation, but being a native—they can see that it's possible to make it.

The biggest obstacle for kids on the res is they've got to leave the res. It is scary for them because that's their comfort zone; that's where their family is and where their extended family is; that's all they've ever known. A lot of them have never - well, they've made it to the city, but not for extended periods of time and not on their own. They made it with their family member and they went there and did what they had to do and went home, but they've never gotten up and left their family and went to a whole nother arena and come back, you know.

We're trying to do a regional training

center in central Washington so we can take the kids into an 8-week course, similar to what I went to in Chicago, but trying to make it a little more regionalized. We're looking for funding right now, but, of course, funding is hard to get. I really don't know that I would have did it had I known how big of a step it was, and it wasn't until I got there that I realized, "Wow. What did I do?" At that point it was too late to turn around and go home. You just sucked it up and made it through, but it was definitely an eye-opener…but a good one, too. At the same time, it opened my eyes. The world doesn't end at the reservation lines, and there's a lot more opportunities once you take that first step. The first step off the res is kind of like the first step on the iron. It's a big step. You take a deep breath and you take a big step and once you find out that high beam is gonna be there, you take another step. Same thing with leaving the res; once you do, you know it's okay to keep going.

Our reservation is 1.8 million acres. You can hunt, fish, go to school, and there's a post office, grocery store, etc. Easy to see you don't have to leave, but when you do, there's a bigger world out there.

I've known my wife since grade school. She's definitely the glue that keeps everything together. She's a very strong lady.

Without the union and the opportunity to be in the union I could still be right where I was, looking for a decent job. Without that opportunity to go out and make it, it would not be far-fetched for me to think that I would have never left the res. I probably would have went from day job to day job. I probably would have worked for the tribe in some capacity. I probably would have done a little ranching, a little logging, a little bit of work in the woods. I probably would have ended up working for the tribe

at a lower scale job because I wouldn't have had an education or any formal training. I would've probably been a 10 to 12 dollar an hour guy and, you know, barely making it. That's why we're going back to the res with a training program. I've gotten into the position where I can go back and give that opportunity to other kids and other people who are interested and they can have the chance to pursue it. At least give them an option. If they don't want it, we're not forcing that. We're presenting an opportunity, is what we're doing.

It isn't a home run as much as people would think it would be a home run. There are a lot of tribes and there are a lot of tribal people that have resentment for people trying to take their people off the reservation, taking their kids away from them. There are other people who see the opportunity there and really embrace it.

I define success through my kids and my wife…your family. If your kids are successful, your kids are achieving things, if you help them have the opportunity to do what they want to do, whether it's playing well at sports or, y' know, doing what they want to do. That's my goal, to give my kids the opportunity that I didn't have. When things are good at home, when things are good with the family, that's when I feel like I've had success.

Lisa Tierce

Assembly Line Auto Worker, Retired, Tuscaloosa, Alabama
United Auto Workers

I'm a mother first of all. I like helping people - I always have - and I believe that what my union work did was help people, help them secure their lives. That's what my family always said - I do for everybody else but I don't do for myself. I think of myself last. I think I became that person because my mama was a single parent, and I watched her struggle for so many years, trying to raise me, my two sisters, and my brother. I'm in the middle. I helped her all I could until we lost her two years ago. She was 77. She always told me that I always felt responsible for everybody. Why I feel like that, I don't know.

I'm a mother of two. My youngest daughter is deceased. She was 20 - an automobile accident in 1994. It's still hard. My oldest daughter will be 40 this month. She has children. I have a stepdaughter in Oklahoma and have grandchildren there. I know God helped me get through. He walked for me when I couldn't walk myself. I know that. God gets you through. He don't put more on us than what you can handle. Sometimes you think he is, but he's not going to do that. He helps you cope with it, and, like I said, when you can't walk yourself, he walks for you. He got me through the hard times.

I love having friends. I'm easy to talk

to. I like meeting new people. You know, because I'm not the only one in the world who's had a lot of bad stuff happen. There's other people a lot worse than me, and I love helping people. It doesn't matter how I'm helping; it may be cutting the grass for them. But in my union work, I like to give people the confidence that they need to realize that they don't have to be treated like robots. They are human beings. I was active in the union for 13 years, right up until I had to retire.

I had to medically retire. My upper extremities were damaged; I had problems in both shoulders, from work. It was a lot of heavy lifting. I had five surgeries on my shoulders alone: I had wrist surgery on both hands - carpal tunnel, and now I can't - it's hard for me to reach back or reach up. It would hold [but] once I would go back in there, I would have to go back into surgery.

We built the axles for Mercedes, ready to be assembled. It was a complete axel, ready to be attached to the rest of the subframe. We just built the axel itself on part of the subframe, completely assembled with breaks, everything. We started out with an empty subframe on the conveyor belt, then the next station it was automatic to just put the bushings in. And the next station, you had the housing and the differential,

> *There's other people a lot worse than me, and I love helping people. It doesn't matter how I'm helping; it may be cutting the grass for them. But in my union work, I like to give people the confidence that they need to realize that* **they don't have to be treated like robots.**

and, then, you put the CB shaft into the differential. You had to really use some force to pop it into the differential. The next station, there was a robot that torqued all that down, and then, the next station, you put in bolts. The wheels were off to the side and other people were building the wheel-ends. We had to set the breaks and break lines and everything, and then it went through an inspection before it went off the line. Then it went to the next station and it had to be hoisted, the whole axle, and then put in a crate. You had to guide it; it was very heavy. We rotated on each one of these jobs. Every two hours, we changed jobs.

To begin with, we had some hoists to lift the subframe, and we still have that. A lot of it you had to do manually for the first, I would say, five years. That's what got a lot of people. Now it's a lot better because we got our union; we looked into safety and changed some things. I started working there in 1997. The union came in 2001. I retired 2011, January the first. At first, I didn't like it [the work]. We had a lot of the supervision - they talked really bad to you if you weren't doing it fast enough. Of course, that was before we got our union. I've seen them curse people. It just

kept getting more and more where I hated going in there. They didn't do me that way. I think they knew who they could and who they couldn't do that to. But, it was bad. I just couldn't...It was all I could do was to stand there and listen to it, you know. And, I wanted to say, so bad, to the people, "Please, stand up for yourself." But then you knew if they did, they'd be out the door.

We tried to organize in 1998 and we lost that election two to one. Everybody was scared. They fired me and five other guys. They fired the guys in September. They fired me in December. They told me that they let me go because they didn't want to hurt me any more than I already was. But I knew that wasn't it. It was because I was so vocal about the union - it was when we were trying to organize. Then, the UAW came in and we went to federal court and all six of us got our jobs back. They brought me in the day that we had our second vote. That was in 2001. I was out of work for a year. We won the second election two to one. I think [we won] because people seen what exactly they could do and you had no recourse. The company kept telling all the people that they would keep this tied up in court forever, and that we would never come back. Bob King and Rob Gettlefinger helped us get our jobs back.

I had always been union. In the 70's and 80's, I worked under the Rubberworkers. I seen what unions could do for you. I'm 56 years old. The union makes a difference. The people have a voice; the supervisors just can't come out there and do anything they want to do and say anything they want to say…it's more structure. Before, they could come out there ten minutes before you were supposed to get off and say, "Sorry, you gotta work over two hours today."

Once the union came in, I loved it. From the very beginning, I had the role of steward all those years, and then the last three years I was chairperson. I still worked assembly and I did my job as a steward and I did my job as chairperson. It felt more confident. You knew you didn't have to go in there and just take anything. You're never going to please everybody, but as long as you please the majority and you know that they got some back up, some recourse, then that's a good thing. It works for me. Unions are great. I just believe in 'em. It's in my heart. It's best for the company. It's best for the people. It's a more structured environment. You have a voice in your workplace.

I didn't want to retire. Physically I couldn't [work]. The doctors told me that I couldn't. I would be right back in surgery in three months. And I had so many, five on my shoulders, I didn't think I could handle another surgery.

I love time spending with my grandchildren. I wouldn't take nothing for that. And my kids, I've got time now to spend with them. I do still help out with organizing, when they call and ask me to. I work a little part-time and sometimes I volunteer, whenever they need me. We have a pool and we spend a lot of time out there with the whole family. The kids are in school. My granddaughter, she's three, but she still goes to school. I take them to school every morning along with my niece. My niece lives with me. I take the kids to school and then after I get back, I do my housework, and that takes a while. And then, I like to work outside in my flowers. And then it's time for the kids to come home. All of them come here.

I define success by how you live your life. Set your goals and make sure you get there. It may take forever but you will get there if you're determined. Being honest. You're never gonna get anywhere if you're not honest. And, having a healthy family. I'm very much at peace. If I can continue to help people, I'm O.K. Whether that be with my children or my grandchildren, or people outside of my home.

I have to say how I raised my girls; I raised my girls always telling them, "Have compassion for people." Because, if you lose that, you have lost a great deal.

I have a great husband; he's very understanding and always has been. He's supported me and all my union activity from day one. We've been married 23 years. He's an equipment operator, getting ready to retire. We can spend some time, do things that we want to do. We like travel, both of us. We both love the beach. We'd like to drive, see different things…hopefully within the next year. He's 60. He's had a lot of health problems, heart problems, so, life's too short not to do this, to go ahead and retire. I learned that from losing our daughter.

I'm happy when I'm helping other people. If I'm not helping other people, then I'm lost, don't know what to do.

We can spend some time, do things that we want to do. We like travel, both of us. We both love the beach. We'd like to drive, see different things, hopefully within the next year. He's 60. He's had a lot of health problems, heart problems, so, **life's too short not to do this, to go ahead and retire. I learned that from losing our daughter.**

Audrey Trimiew
Oreo Cookie Packing Tech,
Richmond, Virginia
Bakery, Confectionary, Tobacco,
Grain Millers Union (BCTGM)
Local 358

I have that outside voice where I can go and someone will listen and I don't worry about if I'm in trouble or am being heard. And, the union offers a lot of things that the company does not offer, like insurance, different types of information that you need to get out there for your family. It helps you in a lot of ways. When you need counseling or you need anything... **The union is like an extra bonus ticket.**

I'm a person who loves the Lord and I'm really blessed. I'm in good health and I have to give that to the Lord. I'm outgoing, honest, giving, talkative, and I pretty much say what comes to mind. If you were talking to me and you said XYZ while we were having a conversation, like, if you didn't like someone or if you did like someone, I would pretty much say what I think about that person and, if you didn't like it, you know, that would be your problem. I'm strong-minded and confident in myself and very independent. I tried to not lean on no one but to make sure that I am able to hold up my end of myself. I really believe that you have to be strong-minded and confident in what you do and what you want. I think that in life, you know, you have a lot of choices and it's up to you to make the right choice.

I have four kids, and my kids range from age 21 to 28. I'm a single mom who raised four kids and they all finished high school. Two have finished college and I have two that have about two years to finish. I'm very proud of them. I have a lot of compliments at work, like, "I don't know how you did it," because, you know, it's hard to get two to finish, much less four. They're very strong-minded like I am and I always

tell them, "You have to have education because I don't know if I'm going to be here to take care of you or not, and you have to go on and do for yourself because that's important in life."

My mom had nine kids: five girls and four boys. She stressed in us at an early age that we each had to do for ourselves and take care of ourselves, and she worked three jobs to put us all through school and seven of us through college. The other two are working on their degrees now. So, I took what my mom had instilled in me and instilled it in my kids, which made me a successful mom. I love every day that they come to me to say, "Mom, I'm really, really proud of you. You did the right thing. You showed us the right way."

You know, they made a few mistakes down the line, and so did I, but I told them you have to learn from mistakes and move on. You can't let them beat you down in life. So, it's important to me to describe myself as being a proud mother of four and also a grandmother of two. I have one grandchild that is biological and one that is my step-grandchild, and I love them each and every day. My oldest daughter finished James Madison University and her degree was in Human Resources. My second-oldest daughter's in nursing school now as a registered nurse and she has until summer of next year and she'll be finished. My son is at Delaware State and he's in aviation and airport management. My baby girl, Natasha, just finished JMU this summer. She graduated early and she is a technical writer. She has a B.S. in technical writing and she is now working for a company in her field and she's doing very well and she's 21 years of age and I'm very, very proud of her. She's getting ready to buy her first home!

My mom is well and talking and living today and she's very important in my life. And, I thank God that I had her in my life and she instilled the right values in me. I'm 55 years old. She lives 20 minutes from me.

I've worked with Nabisco-Kraft for 18 years. I first went to mixing, and after five years I went to the packing department. I was working on each and every line: Ritz, Premium, Wheat Thins, Vanilla Wafers, and I was really falling in love with Oreo. I had a passion for Oreos. I went to the supervisor that was there at the time and said, "I want to be on the Oreo line. I want to work for you." He said, "If you want to work for me then you have to know this line inside and out." So, I told him, "I will learn the line and I will work on Oreo." So, he says to me, "Well, O.K., I'll give you a chance if you learn the line."

So I took a week and I took my breaks, my 20-minute breaks, and I came in before work and I stayed after work, on my own time with no pay, because I wanted to learn this line. I was determined to work on this line. So, the next week I went to him and I said, "Well, I know this line and I can work anywhere on this line." And he said, "I'll give you one week to prove to me that you know this line." Ever since then, I've been working on the Oreo line.

The Oreo line is very demanding, with long hours and hard work. We start off with the RSM; that's when you mix in the ingredients. I work on the back of the line. The metal detectors are the most important thing on the line because they detect the metal in the cookie and we don't want anything to get out there that may have metal in it. You check and make sure that you're doing it the right way, and it has to be done the right way because that's the most important thing. Then, you have the trays. The trays go into the loader and it loads the cookies up, and you have two machines there; you have to keep it completely loaded with trays so it won't run out, so that's a continuous job. The next thing you have is a loader. The loader is where you're checking your cookies. You're making sure the cookies are not broken, and you're continuously looking out for something that you see wrong - anything that you see wrong that is not supposed to be there.

Then you're going to the inspection area. The inspection area is where you check if the cookies are coming out of the loader properly and that they are lined up in the tray properly, and making sure each cookie is looking like it's supposed to. The next thing is the area where everything is completed and the cookies are sealed and ready to go into the boxes to be shipped out. You're watching to make sure everything is proper and the corner has Nabisco where it's supposed to be. It is our regular function every day that we have to do. Once you look at everything on that package of our cookies, then they're ready to be boxed and shipped. Then, you have, not least but last, the relief person that relieves everybody for a break. And they relieve you to go on your break and they wait for you to come back. And that relief person has to be in each and every spot to make sure that they give everybody a break.

I love my job. I'm very proud and happy to have a good job and be able to go to work every day. I don't complain because I feel like, you know, **this is a job where you go in to make someone else happy.** *If they love it, then I love it.*

All of these jobs are important and they have to be done in that order, in that way, to make sure that we are doing everything that we're supposed to do for the customer and for ourselves. Because I know that if the customer is not happy, I'm not happy.

Sometimes when I go to the grocery store, I'm looking to see who buys Oreos and who don't. And I go down the Oreo aisle and I'm looking to make sure everything is like it's supposed to be. I'm making sure our cookies, especially Oreo but any other product that we deliver, is looking good, and make sure that everything is how it's supposed to be. And I'm walking through the store to see who has Oreo cookies in their grocery cart. A couple of times I have looked up and I had this big smile on my face and the kids have big smiles on their face and I say, "Oh, you're buying Oreo cookies!" I get so happy, so excited because I'm like, "Oh my God! I'm glad! I'm glad!" And the kids, they have a big smile on their face and it really makes my day, because I'm really an Oreo person and I love them.

I love my job. I'm very proud and happy to have a good job and be able to go to work every day. I don't complain because I feel like, you know, this is a job where you go in to make someone else happy. If they love it, then I love it. I work 40 hours a week, and for most of the 18 years that I've been there, I've worked weekends or overtime. When the plant's closed, I'm home, but most of the time, when the plant's open, I'm there. And, because I had to provide for my kids, and I had to do what I needed to do in order to get them through school and to take care of them, most of my life has been towards them. And that has gotten them through college and gotten them to the point to where they are now.

I'm in a union because I feel like that's an extra voice that's needed in the workforce. I have that outside voice where I can go and someone will listen and I don't worry about if I'm in trouble or am being heard. "Does this need to be changed?" or "Does that need to be changed?" I feel that's something that's always needed in the workplace, because that could be for the good or for the bad. And, the union offers a lot of things that the company does not offer, like insurance, different types of information that you need to get out there for your family. It helps you in a lot of ways. When you need counseling or you need anything… The union is like an extra bonus ticket.

I haven't had any problems that I really had to go to the union. But I'm going to give this example: When I think that something is wrong, or something is going on, like for instance, this week, they're talking about our pension. And, Hostess owes a billion dollars to our pension fund, and they have been bankrupted and therefore people are all upset at work and they're like, "What are we going to do?" and "They're talking about cutting our pension and we may not be able to retire right now," and all of that.

So, I called the union rep. yesterday and I told him. I said, "Listen, you need to either come down here and get out on the floor and talk to people, or you need to put something in black and white to let them know that everything is OK, and that we're going to be OK, and that our pension is going to be OK, and that we don't know anything about a definite decision and we won't know until November." And I told him, "You need to get that out there and let the people know because you have people who have high blood pressure and it's very stressful, especially the people who are trying to retire at the end of this year." He told me, "I will get the word out in black and white, but I'm going out of town today,

Lift up your hand to thee

I look into your face and all that I can see
is the beautiful young black woman you've grown up to be
I know daddy's girl that you'll always be
But you have to go out and explore the world you see
I will not be there to hold your hand or guide you along the way
But just know I'm only a telephone call away

One day your name tag will read Chaday Trimiew
"A brilliant register Nurse you see

Then you will go on life to be that
Internal surgeon doctor that you always
Promise me

As you go through trials and ~~trivitation~~ tribulations
Lift up your hand to thee
And he will provide your every need!

☆ Audrey

264

but I will make sure it gets out, Audrey. I promise you." And I said, "OK, I really appreciate it."

I wish to retire. I want to get to enjoy my life. I have worked very hard to get where I am and I want to travel. I like bowling, and boating, and I like fishing and being on the water, just sitting back and relaxing; it makes you feel like you're in a whole different world. I like cooking, I like reading, I like writing, I like a little bit of poetry, and I'm hoping, someday, I could make a book and I could get my poetry out there, and I could really make a difference because that's what my love is, writing a lot of poetry.

I told my kids that I wanted them to live in a different part of the country or different states so I could take three months of the year to visit each one of them and to join my grandkids. I said, "I won't be in your way. I'll just stay there three months with you. You don't have to worry about a nursing home. You don't have to worry about anything. I'll just be there to spend three months with you and then I'll move on to the next one." And I told them, "I would love every minute of it because that's really what I want to do." If they want to live near each other, that's fine too. I was just giving them something to think about. And they tell me "Oh Mama! You tell us all the time...." And I tell them, "You know, it's just something for you to think about. Even if you live close, I still would do three months with you, and three months with this one, and that one and, you know, and move on."

I find success as knowing what you love, being happy with who you are, being able to live each and every day in good health and, you know, to me it's not about material things, because I mean, you can't take material things with you, so you need to enjoy what you have in life and be happy with what you have in life. If it's meant for you, you're going to get it, but if it's not, then don't worry about it. I tried not to worry and I say this because I'll think about it in the moment and I'll say, "Well, O.K. Audrey, you know, if it's meant for you, it's going to happen. If not, don't worry about it because something is always going to come along and take the place of whatever that is." And, I tell my kids my health is pretty good because I don't stress about a lot of things. I may think about it in that moment and I may think about it six hours from then, but then I let it go.

That's what I love about myself. It's that I don't stress. I don't have a lot of gray hair, I don't have a lot of issues. I think that is mostly being comfortable with yourself, being happy with yourself, being in love with yourself, being in love with the Lord, and being in love with everything else in life. You don't have a lot of worries. You don't need to worry because what's going to happen is going to happen anyway. We have no control of it. I am who I am. I love life itself.

Thomas Walker

Engineer Technician Fire Department, Aurora, Colorado
International Association of Firefighters
Local Chapter 1290

By describing myself I have to give my history because that's, of course, what I'm made of. My life experiences brought me to the place of where I am today. When I came on to the fire department, twenty-four years ago, I was actually kind of unemployed when I applied. I had been doing the financial services business, there was a huge letdown in the market, and I was unemployed at that point in time. The fire service was nothing I ever really pictured myself going into. So, I applied at that time.

The fire department has a process, which is different from normal jobs, which is, fill out an application and get an interview. You know there are some days you're going to be unemployed. The fire department is a process of testing, before you're put on a list. That municipality, city, or district, or whatever gives you a callback and says, "OK. You're on top of the list. We're going to offer you employment, do a background check on you." If you go through an academy where you go through training and so forth, at that point and time you're offered a job, and for about a year, you're on probation, before you're given a permanent job. So, when I came on, I was young. I had my wife and two girls. That's where I was right then. It was exciting. It was twenty-four years ago. I'm now fifty-one. My daughters were young - in elementary school. It was different. I figured, "I'll wing this until the next job comes along." Twenty-four years later, I'm still here.

I am a firefighter, but first I am a family member. My daughters are grown up now and everything. They're both college educated. My oldest daughter has her master's degree and my youngest daughter's in a master's program right now. They both live in Washington D.C. at this time.

Also, I think I'm community minded. I'm not really speaking to the geographic community, but the community as far as race and so forth. The black community in the metro area - I'm very involved there. In the fire department, we have very little representation on the job, so its been an objective of mine to try to increase those numbers on the job and to help in that community whenever I can. And, I guess as far as right now, that's the best description of myself. My personality? I always look for humor in situations. Some people say I joke too much. I think I'm a hard worker. I'm responsible; I take responsibility pretty high. I'm an honest person, for the most part. And, I think I'm a likable person, but I'm not really afraid of not being liked. If something doesn't agree with me, or if I disagree with someone in some area, I'm not shy about sharing that with them. Hopefully, we can agree to disagree. If not, I'm O.K. with not being liked anymore.

My work is a twenty-four hour a day job. We come to work for twenty-four hours: 8:00 one day and leave 8:00 the next day. It's twenty-four hours on and twenty-four hours off for three shifts, and after that you have four days in which you're off. It involves checking out the equipment and everything.

For the most part, in the fire department, we are an EMS department, which is the Emergency Medical System. Most of our care is emergency care. The fire station where I'm at right now, if we get twelve calls a day, nine of them are going to include emergency medical, maybe extrication or something like that. It's seldom that we get a fire. We work three shifts per week, if you may, every seven day rotation, and out of those few shifts we might get one or two fires. We're first and foremost firefighters, but most of our time is consumed with medical - emergency medical care.

When I go home, when I leave the station, I find that I'm still recognized as a firefighter. Everyone knows that that's what I do or knows me well enough. If they have a question that regards that, they feel free to ask me, and everything. Even when I take off the uniform, the responsibility still lies with me. Since I represent a city, in this case the city of Aurora, I still maintain certain standards. You know, I can't smoke, no heavy drinking, stay out of contact with the police and so forth...be a good, honest citizen. And I think that's some of my basic values anyway, so it's not a hard transition that I had to do.

I had to sign a contract saying I wouldn't use tobacco products. It's part of the training and so forth. If you take on a higher risk, the city, they make sure they're protecting their investment, so they make sure we're all nonsmokers. Now, when I came on the job, twenty-four years ago, that definitely was not the case. Most of the guys in the station were not just smokers but heavy smokers. I would go in the room and the smoke would be up to the ceiling because everyone had a cigarette in their hand. You don't see any smoke inside a station today.

Part of my current fire station activity includes working in four person crews. The way we respond to emergencies in the city of Aurora, Colorado - you don't plan emergencies so we don't know what's coming up - but we know the pattern of how things go. We know that you're going to have medical emergencies, therefore, we train at least to the basic EMT level in medicine. We have to have medics that ride on the vehicle and so forth. That's most of our calls. Our action is we work as a team to resolve any medical emergencies or any emergencies.

When people pick up the phone

When I came on the job, of course I thought this was temporary. **I never visualized myself running into the place that everyone was running out of.** *I'm fine with following the pack with that situation. But, as I did it - went through the training and got on the job, and noticed what I was doing - it kind of fit my life style anyway. I love to be helpful; it releases adrenaline. I can be helpful to someone else. So it automatically fit my life style.*

and dial 911, it could be something we're used to doing all the time, or something we're not used to. Like the mass shooting that happened. There was something. We get shootings in the city of Aurora. But, at a more mass level - we train for it and everything - but the places that we were trained for it, it doesn't tend to happen there. You know, the mass shooter doesn't plan like, "O.K. I read the book. I'm going to go have my mass shooting over here." We didn't really plan for the movie theater, which is the most recent one I can recall, so therefore, we had to improvise for the situation. I think we did a pretty good job. We worked with our police department, and they're in charge of certain things and we're

in charge of certain things. My current position as an engineer with the Aurora Fire Department - I drive the apparatus to the location. I'm responsible for the safety and getting there on scene and returning back to the station. Other duties would include helping in any medical situation. I have to take on individual patients myself until they arrive at the hospital, or before we transport them to the hospital.

We all have different things that shock us and take us to that emotional level. When I had young kids and I would respond on medical calls where kids were hurt, or had died, of course I remember my own young kids and everything. But, the training is repetitive. Our bodies just take over based on the training we have, and we go ahead and do what we're trained to do. As far as responding to the shock and everything, it's kind of on a delay basis. At least it is for me, on a delayed basis, that I respond to this, physically and personally. Later on, it tends to work for me.

Sometimes we use situations: we humor each other around the station about situations that might shock us. We use humor, and we have the ability - the city provides us with the ability - to talk to a psychologist about our feelings and how to deal with these feelings. On something as horrific as that…I don't know if you can prepare for something like that. It's probably post-traumatic as it comes out. It's laid into your subconscious and it's going to be there and you have to deal with it and talk it out and deal with it as it comes up. It's important to deal with that. I wasn't there that night. I happened to be off that night. But the next morning as things came up and as the investigation went on, I was involved in that part. I talked to some of the guys who were there, you know, off my apparatus that were there at the theatre, and they responded. We're used to practicing with mass casualties and so forth with the city quite often. I think the thing we can't control is what other people do. We're practicing with people who know what they're doing, and when you go into a scene, you can't really estimate what people are going to do when they're in shock. So, we look for those things and try to comfort them or correct them.

In the situation that happened at the theatre, those guys went in and no one knew where the shooter was, or if there was one or more shooters. They just went in and did the job. They could have been in harm's way and so forth. We know that when we sign on, that we're going to be in harm's way. After it's all said and done, I'm glad no one else got hurt, but we knew that when we went in. When we go in structure fires, with buildings with glass, where certain things could happen, we signed on. Your spiritual life kind of kicks in there and everything, and you hope for the best, of course. We've been reasonably successful. Traditionally, in this city, we've been reasonably successful with things.

When I came on the job, of course I thought this was temporary. I never visualized myself running into the place that everyone was running out of. I'm fine with following the pack with that situation. But, as I did it - went through the training and got on the job, and noticed what I was doing - it kind of fit my life style anyway. I love to be helpful; it releases adrenaline. I can be helpful to someone else. So it automatically fit my life style. My kids adored what I did. I kind of brought them in to do certain things and certain projects that we did throughout the years. And they just liked being really good citizens. I got friends all over the world who do the same thing I do. I got friends in Germany and Great Britain and so forth, [from] touring around the world, we all have some of the same passions - some [I met] through professional organizations.

One situation came up with a firefighter here. When I was a child, I was a military brat for a while and I lived in Germany. And the peculiar thing about that was, recently, a guy from Germany - [from] the same town I went to high school at - was visiting in the metro area and he just wanted to visit a fire station. Well, the woman who does staffing for us, she knew I knew some German and she was concerned about his ability to communicate, so she sent him to my station, and, of course, his English was really good so I didn't have to butcher the German language too much. But, he's visited a couple of times now, and I just happen to know when he rode with us that he lived in the same city where I went to high school. So, we still communicate every now and then. He sends me pictures. Now the high school where I attended was torn down, like, two years ago. He sent me pictures of that.

Other relationships have been established through international organizations that I belong to that include people from all over the world - Barbados, London… Now, through the professional organizations, a lot of times I can go to different towns, different cities, and just look up who I might be familiar with in that area, [and] visit with them every now and then.

How do I feel about the work I do? I feel good about it. It's my make-up. I feel good about it. I think it's important. A lot of times, when people think of firefighters they think all they're around for is fires, which is really not true. It's just a misconception they're having because like I said, when you dial 911 if you're having chest pain, if there's car accidents or a medical problem, you get the fire department at your door, pretty much first, and then you have your ambulance come down that we contract with, that transports you to the hospital. Along with that we do fire drills at schools and some teaching at schools, as far as fire safety, how to handle emergencies. If there's an emergency of any substantial amount in the city, you dial 911. For the most part you're gonna get either the police department or the fire department.

I joined the union… It probably had a lot to do with peer pressure when I went into the academy and so forth. Everyone was joining the union. They were our bargaining unit for our jobs, as far as we get for support. We would collectively bargain with the city for the contract that would come up every year, every two years. That was the purpose of the union. I know that in other cities where they don't have a union, where they hire at-will, employees have limited rights. When I got on the union, I stayed with the union and pretty much everything was good for years and years. I've had some difficulty with the union, especially more recently. My difficulty doesn't really come with the International: it comes with the local branch. Because, like I said earlier, I'm very active in the Black community and I'm very active in trying to recruit more from my community onto the department we serve. The community is like 18% African American, but on the Aurora Fire Department, you have probably less than 3% black. And, some say, "Well, it's not really that important." But I think it's more important now than it was before. Before, when we were just pretty much a fire department, it didn't matter when you went in: put out a fire, pull people out of harms way, out of the fire and so forth; it didn't really matter. But now, 75-80% of our calls are EMS, which is a face-to-face action. You're dealing with a very diversified population. The city of Aurora is one of the most diversified cities in the state of Colorado and that's where we work. But, yet, the department isn't very diversified, so what that means is, when we go into households when you're not familiar with that culture or that community at all, sometimes you make mistakes unintentionally because of our lack of familiarity.

The fire department of 1989 was an all male fire department. In 1989 we hired our first female on the job. Well, if we were responding to someone who had a female issue, and you have all males, your comfort level may not be the same as if there were a female member. The same happens in communities. If you have all these people who look the same and they have nothing really in common with you, your comfort level is different. Now it's even more important that we diversify our fire department.

The union is put together a little bit different, especially on the local chapter. They represent the majority. They have majority vote and majority rule. So, whenever you involve anything that involves community, and maybe even gender specific, it's mostly white males that will tend to carry, so it's mainly those needs of white males that tend to be addressed. But as far as the International, it provides good bargaining towards the city. It provides a good life. I've had a great career so far. I've been successful at being a good father and providing an education. My daughters are good, well-rounded citizens now. They're on their way to do great things and so forth. I think that was basically provided for me through the union. If they didn't have the collective bargaining efforts, I may not have stayed on the job as long. I may not have had the rights I had, without the union. So, it's a great thing… Sometimes it works

as a two edged sword for things I want to accomplish, but predominately, it's done great work for me.

Being in a union, the international association, it has things that address these issues. This history I think goes back to the Florida firefighters. I'm not sure which were in a closed shop. A closed shop when you're hired, if you're hired by this municipality, or whatever, you have to join the union, you don't have a choice. Well in Florida, back in the day, they'd join a closed shop, and they noticed when they went to different fire stations - you know this was a very segregated area - the black firefighters that were in that union and in that station, they noticed that when they went to a firehouse, they would get the worst, no matter how long they would be on the job or whatever, they would get the worst jobs. They always had to clean the toilets. They were being discriminated against and so forth. The international union said, "Well, we need to address these issues also for this community. All union members need to be treated well in the same organization."

So, they created a Human Rights area. I went to one of the conferences with the International union, as a representative from my Local, and what I found out as of lately - by lately I'm talking about the last 5-7 years - what I found out is that they gave certain tools and things on how to deal with these issues that pretty much pit one firefighter against another firefighter. I brought it back to present it to the local union board and president, and he said, "Yeah, yeah…It's not my job." He pretty much threw the stuff away. And that's what happened. When that occurred, it created a wedge between me and the local union, and it created a wedge between other people like me that were in the union, who find that a lot of their issues weren't being addressed on the local level. So, a lot of the black firefighters, they pulled out of the union. If I didn't have so much invested, I probably would've went with them. But I stayed on because I have a lot invested on the International level. Because of that, I have different savings programs and so forth. I'm involved on the International level, so I stayed in the union because of that, and we're still doing the same job, we're in the same firehouses, and I didn't want waves to continue on even though it does...

I try to manage it as much as possible. Sometimes I feel like, "Am I crazy or is there really an issue here?" Those who pulled out, they asked why I stayed and I told them my reasons. For the most part, they respect me. I haven't had much of a backlash on that side. On the other side, we have 325 members on the fire department, and when the black firefighters - a number of them pulled out of the union - I believed in why the guys did it. I didn't necessarily agree with the techniques they did, but I believed in why and it's still an issue. The issues still haven't been addressed and whether it ever will... It probably won't unless a different

administration takes place on the local union. But I notice that a lot of times I walk in the room and there's conversation going on, and I walk in the room and it quiets down and the conversation changes. As far as personal injury or personal attacks or anything, I haven't felt them, but I feel the cold shoulder kind of going on.

I think we all want to reach the level of retirement. I don't want to do this my whole life, until the last day, or anything like that. I do want to retire someday and I visualize it sometime in the next ten years, maybe even sooner. I can retire fiscally probably in about five and a half years now, but as far as me planning a retirement right now, I haven't put it in pen any time I set to retire. I'm probably more toward seven to ten years rather than the five and a half years, partly because how much I'm enjoying it, and, a couple of years back, we had self-driven retirement accounts and, due to a slug in the market, about five years ago, we lost a lot of money. In order to build up those retirement accounts, I plan to stay on a little bit longer.

I have a bucket list, perhaps, that I want to accomplish. One of things I've said that, while I've been here, I've gotten different teaching certificates and so forth because

The city of Aurora is one of the most diversified cities in the state of Colorado and that's where we work. But, yet, the department isn't very diversified, so what that means is, **when we go into households when you're not familiar with that culture or that community at all, sometimes you make mistakes** *unintentionally because of our lack of familiarity.*

I figured, after you can no longer do, then you can start teaching. Those who can no longer do, can teach. So I can offer some teaching to young firefighters at community colleges or wherever that may take place.

Also, what I want to do is kind of slow down in life and fill the bucket list maybe with more international travel. I have people I've created professional relationships with around the world. There's other parts of the world I really want to go to. I probably want to visit all the seven continents before it's all over. That's something I enjoy doing. I've taken scenic photography. There's different areas of the world I want to explore. I might take on a second career, maybe in travel or something like that, to accomplish these things.

You can define success a number of different ways. If you're a spiritual person, you might define it based on your spiritual beliefs. That's one way I might define what success is…If you're positive and a good citizen in your community or in your country, that's another way to define success.

Before I leave the job, one of my passions would be to hire my replacement. I think this is an ongoing issue that affects many parts of the country as far as recruitment, keeping communities represented on the job. I would want someone that would have at least the same passion as me. I would want to help them get on the job, in place, before I leave the job. It's just one of my personal commitments.

In the area where I work now, as far as the geographic area - the Denver metro area - it's one of the big areas for refugees coming to America. I didn't know this 'till about half a year ago, when we started running into communities that we just weren't familiar with. We should learn more about that. I know that in the Aurora Public Schools, there's, like, 89 different languages spoken, which kind of reflects the greater community of what's going on. Those are things that probably need to be addressed. It's just to make life better for everyone else around. If you make situations better than before you arrive, that's one way you can define success, I guess.

When we go into an emergency situation, if we can maintain things or make it better than the way it was when we arrived, then we succeeded. That's pretty much how I would define success. I seldom have left a scene that wasn't better off than it was before I arrived. Someone picked up the phone and dialed 911 and we responded. I think we helped out well over 90% of the time. Almost every time it was perfection. Successful means most of the time. Sometimes you run in on someone who is in the hands of death and you can't pull them out of there to save them, so you're not successful on that one. You didn't succeed. Those have existed; they do exist. But we stopped the bleeding; we stopped the hurt. Did anyone else get hurt? I think we've been successful. I think I reached a high level of success in my professional career. I feel good about it. I think I have a good life.

Acknowledgements

I would like to thank my publisher, Tim Sheard, at Hard Ball Press, for believing in the importance of this book and for making it a reality. David Bass added his calming and creative influences in the face of an overload of ideas and under the pressure of time. I am grateful to Mary Whiting for her high speed, eleventh hour editing, and words of wisdom and wonder in support of these personal stories. I owe much to Esther Cohen for long-standing, consistent encouragement and being the initial force behind the idea of first-person storytelling. Logan Jaffe widely broadened the original design ideas and the scope of the project, and Wendy Shames, Sonya Rudenstine, Stephanie Sharpe and Catherine Boswell sustained me with their unwavering friendship and constant interest in updates. My good friend Eve Kravitz saved me with her extremely insightful and sensitive transcription services.

I leaned heavily on Carrie and John Westmark's highly dependable and lightening fast responses to forever evolving questions and editing and design work for last minute samples, not to mention their everlasting love and support. Sandra Murphy Pak also helped with long hours of transcribing, but mostly I treasure her unceasingly enthusiastic and extraordinarily selfless encouragement; she is my self-elected "personal assistant".

Edith Williams, my diehard, hardworking, always accessible—even when overseas—magically creative, swift companion and co-worker throughout most of the book's creation: artist extraordinaire, friend, organizer, and most of the brains of the operation-I am forever in your debt!

Especially warm thanks to my family: my sister-in-law Kathryn Gottlieb for her enlightening interview and editing assistance, my mother-in-law, Jean Gattone, who wanted to know every detail every step along the way, my father-in-law, Joe Gattone, for his walk down memory lane, and my father, Herb Gottlieb, whose pro-union political history makes me proud to be his daughter. And to my mother, Marjorie Gross: I obviously would be nowhere without her. Thank you for serving as president of my fan club, brave and shameless cheerleader to all who would (and wouldn't) listen, infinite bragger and all embracing supporter of the whole kit and caboodle!

To my inspiriting children, Max and Angela, for their patience, their service as soundboards, and the giving of their opinions, valuable feedback and ideas, you constantly exhilarate! And to my husband, Charles Gattone, the man who makes real all of my dearest dreams, who stretches the possibility of imagination, and who believes in and loves me beyond comprehension and reason.

Finally, I feel immensely honored to have had the opportunity to interview the 34 people in this book. Tremendous thanks to Leslie Simmons, Sandi Curriero and others for putting me in touch with such wondrous human beings. The intimate sharing of their hardships and successes, their life stories and ideas, have thrilled and inspired me to no end.

44887777R00164

Made in the USA
Charleston, SC
06 August 2015